THE ANTECEDENTS OF BEING

An Analysis of the Concept *de Nihilo*
in the Philosophy of Saint Thomas Aquinas

A Study in Thomistic Metaphysics

A DISSERTATION

Submitted to the Faculty of the School of Philosophy of
The Catholic University of America in Partial
Fulfillment of the Requirements for the
Degree of Doctor of Philosophy

By

SISTER MARY CONSILIA O'BRIEN, O. P., M. A.
of the
Sisters of Saint Dominic,
Mount Saint Mary on the Hudson,
Newburgh, New York

WIPF & STOCK · Eugene, Oregon

Wipf and Stock Publishers
199 W 8th Ave, Suite 3
Eugene, OR 97401

The Antecedents of Being
An Analysis of the Concept de Nihilo in the Philosophy of Saint
Thomas Aquinas, a Study in Thomistic Metaphysics
By O'Brien, Mary Consilia
ISBN 13: 978-1-4982-9486-7
Publication date 4/18/2016
Previously published by The Catholic University of America Press, 1939

To Mary

SEAT OF WISDOM

DAUGHTER, MOTHER AND SPOUSE OF

ETERNAL UNCREATED WISDOM

THIS APPROACH TO HUMAN WISDOM

IS DEDICATED

WITH FILIAL AFFECTION

THE ANTECEDENTS OF BEING
An Analysis of the Concept *de Nihilo* in the Philosophy of Saint Thomas Aquinas

THE ANALOGICAL ANALYSIS OF BEING

An Analysis of the Concept of Nature
in the Philosophy of Saint Thomas Aquinas

PREFACE

Our day is witnessing a rapidly reviving interest in the philosophy of the Schools, with special emphasis on the philosophical system of Saint Thomas Aquinas. It is this reversion of outstanding modern thinkers to the metaphysics of the thirteenth century for guiding principles in their attempted interpretation of reality, that has prompted the problem with which this dissertation concerns itself. The modern schools of idealism and of phenomenalism have been unsatisfactory in their efforts to explain reality to the adequate satisfaction of the human mind, ordained as it is by its very nature to reality and to truth. Corrective principles must be sought; and these principles we hold may be found in that system of philosophy which rejects neither the objectivity of substance nor the actuality of phenomena. Thomistic metaphysics embraces the reality of being as well as the reality of becoming; hence its explanation includes the testimony of sense experience and meets the demands of a rational faculty ordained to grasp reality in its *raison d'être*.

The author acknowledges and herewith expresses her deep appreciation and gratitude to her Community, and especially to Reverend Mother Mary de Lourdes, O. P., Mother-Prioress General, for the opportunity to pursue courses at the Catholic University. To Doctors Charles A. Hart and John K. Ryan for reading the manuscript and for their helpful suggestions and criticisms, gratitude is also expressed. A special expression of thanks is due to the Very Reverend Ignatius Smith, O. P., Dean of the School of Philosophy, who suggested the problem and by his unfailing helpfulness has made possible the completion of the work. To all the professors under whom she has studied the author expresses her appreciation for their kindly interest. The unfailing and helpful service of the Librarians of the Catholic University is here gratefully acknowledged. To the Superiors and Librarians of the Dominican House of Studies, especially to the Very Reverend B. J. Walker, O. P., Prior, and the Reverend A. W. McLaughlin, O. P.,

Librarian, the author is deeply indebted for the use of the Dominican College Library and the courteous service rendered her by them throughout the entire course of her studies.

To all the above and to others whom she has not named but who have contributed in some way to the completion of this work, the author acknowledges her indebtedness and expresses her gratitude.

TABLE OF CONTENTS

	Page
PREFACE	VII
INTRODUCTION	1

CHAPTER ONE
Primary Concepts and Other Basic Notions 17

CHAPTER TWO
Creation: Production *ex nihilo sui et subjecti* 35

CHAPTER THREE
Generation: *Ens in Fieri* 56

CHAPTER FOUR
Substantial Change: Its Intrinsic Principles and Related Notions 78

CHAPTER FIVE
Some Non-Thomistic Interpretations of Reality 111

CHAPTER SIX
Philosophies of Flux and Thomistic Principles 177

Conclusion 188

BIBLIOGRAPHY 191

INDEX 200

INTRODUCTION

1. THE PROBLEM VIEWED

Being and non-being are infinitely separated, Saint Thomas tells us. And it is precisely somewhere between the extremes of these two notions that we must seek the antecedents of being. The immediate task of this introduction is to set the limits within which we propose to confine our discussion. Being in all its latitude is a vast field for investigation and one worthy of the many works written on the subject of metaphysics, that science which has for its object *ens qua ens*. The limits of a doctoral dissertation are necessarily restricted to the solution of a specific problem with its entanglement of implications and applications. This dissertation is no exception, and its specific problem is to determine the antecedents of being.

But being is an all-inclusive notion comprising all reality, and its implications are manifold. The notion of being seizes, tentacle-like, upon whatever is or can be, and hence a very important preliminary step must be to trace out those principles which burrow deep into the heart of our question, and discard others, though important in themselves, which do not have direct relevancy to the problem in hand. We cannot hope to follow all the possible leads which may be uncovered throughout our investigation, hence only those aspects of being and non-being shall be admitted to the inner circle of our attention which have an immediate and absolute bearing upon the question. These will be made evident in the course of our presentation.

Metaphysical being is a fascinating subject with which to deal, as it opens up whole vistas of reality not only perceptible to sense but intelligible to mind as well. Nothing that *is* escapes the all-penetrating and all-inclusive concept of being. The range extends from the almost nothing of mere undifferentiated capacity for being, to the Unique Being whose essence is existence.[1]

Ens est id quod non est nihil absolutum. Being is that which is or can be. "Nothing is opposed to the idea of being except non-being," says

---

1. Cajetan in *De Ente et Essentia*, c. 6, q. 12.

Saint Thomas.² Here we have a description of being. It is vague, of course, and a concept that, as here expressed, is least in comprehension and greatest in extension. It is not a definition, for to define being is impossible.³ Only classes can be defined, and the notion of being transcends all genera. We may describe it otherwise by saying that being is that which has a relation to existence. Anything that can be, though *de facto* may not be, is being. Anything that is not and cannot be, has no relation to existence and hence is not-being, nothing. The dichotomy is absolute. Outside of being there is nothing. What, then, are the antecedents of being, and where shall we find them? Are they discoverable in the notion of nothing? It seems not, in the light of the principle: *Ex nihilo, nihil fit*. Then perhaps they are to be found in being? But, *Ex ente non fit ens, quia jam est ens*. Are we then to conclude that being has no antecedents? Parmenides thought so.

We must go (strange notion to the uninitiated) within the notion of being itself to find therein its antecedents. This alone will break the Gordian knot of the opposing schools of Elea and Ephesus, and their separate attempted constructions of a first science. This extraction of the antecedents of being from the very notion of being involves no contradiction. There is no strain put upon the principle of identity or that of contradiction. Viewed in the light of Aristotle's doctrine of potency and act, the notion of being can be seen to yield the solution which unites in one proposition the seemingly disparate theories of Parmenides and Heraclitus. Aristotle's solution of the antinomy might be stated very simply thus: There is something real, but nevertheless a kind of non-being, which in some way is not really a non-being at all, but really *is*.³ᵇ Aristotle called it *potency*.

Plato had reached the notion, though confusedly, when confronted with the problem of explaining multiplicity.⁴ Aristotle perfected Plato's

---

2. "Nihil autem opponitur rationi entis nisi non ens." *Sum. Th.*, I, q. 25, a. 3.

3. For the nature of definition, cf. *De Ente et Essentia*, c. 1: " ... id per quod res constituitur in proprio genere vel specie est hoc quod significatur per definitionem indicatem quid est res." Cf. *Metaph.*, III, 2, 998 b 5; Coffey, *Ontology*, p. 35.

3b. Cf. *De Gen. et Corrup.*, I, 3, 317 b 15.

4. Cf. The Sophists, 241D, 257A, 259E; also *Phys. I*, 9, 191 b 35. Cited by Garrigou-Lagrange, *God, His Existence and His Nature*, II, p. 328.

concept by formulating his doctrine of act and potency, and naming potency to be that intermediary between absolute nothing and pure being. Potency, Aristotle held, is the non-being which in some way *is*. And thus he bridged the chasm between *Ex nihilo, nihil fit* and *Ex ente non fit ens*. His solution involves both of these propositions; it yields the axiom: *Relative non-being is being in potency*.[5] We have at least limited our field to the intermediate state between absolute nothing and actual being; to the non-being which in some way *is*. It is precisely there, in that medium suggested by Plato and given precision by Aristotle, that we hope to find an answer to our inquiry: What are the antecedents of being?

The concept of being when probed reveals to our minds various aspects under which we may view reality with differing degrees of clarity and fullness. Between the concept of being-in-general and the concept of Absolute Being there is a world of difference. The former is the common tie binding all reality loosely into one concept. It is least in intension, greatest in extension, common to everything and distinguished only from nothingness. This constitutes our initial concept of a thing; it is the most imperfect of all the ideas we possess, is confused, obscure, and of little cognitional value, telling us next to nothing about the essential elements of the real, though it comprises them even to the very last of their determinations. It simply ties up all reality within the periphery of one form.[6]

Different from the first vague, confused notion of being as distinct from nothing, there is the metaphysician's concept of being. This latter is a perfected cognition of the initial concept of being. It is the concept of subsisting being. However nothing has been added by way of extrinsic determination in the elaboration and attainment of this more perfect and distinct concept which is now had, for there is nothing apart from being that is not being. Therefore any additions to being

---

5. For a brief historical sketch of the thought of the earliest philosophers, cf. *Phys.*, I, *passim*, esp. 8. For being as potency, cf. *Metaph.*, IX, 1046 a - 1052 a; *ibid.*, V, 7, 1017 a 35 - b 9; St. Thomas' Commentary, *lectio* 3.

6. "Nam illud quod primo cadit in apprehensione, est ens, cujus intellectus includitur in omnibus quaecumque quis apprehendit." *Sum. Th.*, I-II, q. 94, a. 2. "Illud quod primo intellectus concipit quasi notissimum et in quod omnes conceptionem resolvit est ens." *De Verit.*, q. 1, a. 1.

must be made by way of intrinsic determinations and modes. Treating of this point, Saint Thomas says:

> That which the intellect conceives as best known and in which all other intellectual conceptions are resolved is the idea of being. All other conceptions of the intellect therefore express something which is an addition to being. But to being cannot be added any differences which are extrinsic to it, like those differences which add themselves to a genus, or accidents which add themselves to a subject, for these differences extrinsic to being would be nothing, because everything in nature whatsoever it is, is being. Being is not in a genus, as Aristotle proved in his Third Book of Metaphysics. When, therefore, we say that all conceptions express an addition to being, they do so inasmuch as they express a modality of being which is not expressed by the sole word, being.[7]

The metaphysical concept of being is not intuitive but reflex. It contains within itself every perfection and reduces finite multiplicity to unity. In its highest reaches the metaphysical concept of subsisting being is that of Subsistent Being itself, the most perfect that it is possible for us to acquire naturally. It is Pure Intellect, without imperfection, identical with Pure Being. It is being in the highest possible sense of the word, the richest and most comprehensive concept, the most restricted in extension since it is the notion which identifies the Unique, the Absolute Being.

The only link binding together under one form our weakest and poorest concept with our richest and most pregnant one, is the note of being — *id quod non est nihil absolutum*. The human mind can attain to its notion of Self-Subsistent Being *a posteriori*. It is not within the power of the created intellect naturally to know God as He is in Him-

---

7. "Illud autem quod primo intellectus concipit quasi notissimum, et in quo omnes conceptiones resolvit, est ens; ut Avicenna dicit in principio *Metaphysicae* suae (*lib.* I, *cap.* ix). Unde oportet quod omnes aliae conceptiones intellectus accipiantur ex additione ad ens. Sed enti non potest addi aliquid quasi extranea natura, per modum quod differentia additur generi, vel accidens subjecto; quia quaelibet natura essentialiter est ens; unde etiam probat Philosophus in *III Metaph.*, quod ens non potest esse genus; sed secundum hoc aliqua dicuntur addere supra ens, inquantum exprimunt ipsius modum, qui nomine ipsius entis non exprimitur." *Ibid.*

self; nevertheless this notion is included in the adequate object of our intellect. Being *per se* is the direct cause of beings and endows everything that is with reality.[8] The identification of being-in-general with the metaphysical concept is no more than mere seeming. "Something-that-is" is the only note of unity between them. Much less is there any other note of similarity between the first confused concept of being and the highest and most perfect form of the metaphysical concept, namely, Subsistent Being. They are poles apart, as we shall see subsequently.

Various analyses of the notion of being present us with the notion in its relation to existence, or to subsistence, or to metaphysical grade, or to degree of reality. It is not our purpose here to distinguish among them, but rather to present some idea of the kinds of being which mark off the interval between absolute non-being and absolute being. It will constitute, as it were, a checking-off process, by which at its conclusion we might be enabled to eliminate definitely certain grades of being and so restrict our search for the antecedents of being properly to those beings which in some way are definitely "non-beings which are."

Within the fecundity of the metaphysical concept of being there is Self-Subsistent Being Whose very essence it is to exist.[9] He is above and beyond all causation.[10] He is his own sufficient reason. Within the same metaphysical notion of being there are found spiritual beings, varying in kind, some of which are an angel, a human soul and a thought. Existential being may be distinguished therein from essential being, the former comprising all actually existing things, this book, that pen, Socrates; whereas *essential* beings are real essences which prescind from the note of existence; they are indifferent to existence or non-existence.

8. " . . . Deitas dicitur esse omnium effective, et exemplariter, non autem per essentiam." *Sum. Th.*, I, q. 3, a. 8, *ad* 1. Cf. also *Sum. Th.*, I, q. 25, aa. 1, 2, 3.

9. "Unde cum Deus sit ipsum esse subsistens, nihil de perfectione essendi potest ei deesse." *Sum. Th.*, I, q. 4, a. 2. "Deus est ipsum esse per se subsistens; ex quo oportet quod totam perfectionem essendi in se contineat." *Ibid.* "Deus non solum est sua essentia, . . . sed est suum esse." *Sum. Th.*, I, q. 3, a. 4. "(in Deo) sua essentia est suum esse." *Ibid.*

10. "In Deo autem nihil potest esse causatum, cum sit causa prima." *Ibid.*, I, q. 3, a. 6.

In thinking them, the mind merely thinks of the whatness of the thing, not of its existence. Such a notion of this kind is humanity.

Privation is a lack of being in a being, as blindness is a lack of sight in one who is capable of having it. *Possible* beings or essences are real beings of the mind. They consider the essence of a being not actually in existence; our concept not only prescinds from the note of existence, but it positively excludes it in its initial stage.[11] By a further act of the mind, we can refer the merely possible essence to existence. However, apart from the mind's notion of the essential notes, namely, the sociability of the intrinsic constitutive notes, the possibles of themselves bear a transcendental relation to existence. This consists in their referribility to existence. In this is found their reality. They never exist in the real order, hence they are ideal beings. However, they are real in the ideal order and so are distinct from logical beings which are solely the fruit of one's thoughts — notions of relationships which the mind sees between its concepts, such as the relations of genus and species and differentia, or the concepts of nothingness and privation, or the objects of universal ideas. These have no extramental reality, actual or possible. Possible beings conceivably may exist extramentally, but logical beings never. They are *entia rationis,* called beings in so far as an affirmative proposition can be formulated about them. Saint Thomas speaks of these in the first chapter of *De Ente et Essentia* wherein he discusses Aristotle's division of *ens per se* into, first, the division of the ten categories, and second, that which signifies the truth of propositions.[12] The latter are *entia rationis.*

We come finally to *potential* beings. We have, first, relative potentiality, which consists in a capacity for further determinations in an

---

11. Cf. *Sum. Th.,* I, q. 25, a. 3. Also P. de Munnynck, O. P.: "L'Idée de l'Être," *Extrait de la Revue Néo-Scolastique,* mai, août et novembre, 1929, p. 6.

12. "Sciendum est igitur quod, sicut dicit Philosophus in quinto *Metaphysice,* ens per se dicitur dupliciter: uno modo quo dividitur per decem genera, alio modo quod significat propositionum veritatem. Horum autem differentia est quod secundo modo potest dici ens omne id de quo affirmative propositio formari potest, etiam si illud in re nihil ponat; per quem modum privationes et negationes etiam entia dicuntur, dicimus enim quod affirmatio est opposita negationi, et quod cecitas est in oculo. Sed primo modo non potest dici ens nisi quod aliquid in re ponit: unde primo modo cecitas et hujusmodi non sunt entia." *De Ente et Essen.,* c. 1.

existing subject. The capacity for becoming an oak tree, which is in an acorn, is an instance of relative potentiality. This is a "non-being which in some way is." It is not an oak tree *hic et nunc*, and so *as oak tree* it is non-being. It is being, however, in so far as there is within the actual acorn the absolute determination for becoming an oak tree rather than a rhododendron. Its potentiality will be brought to actuality by the act by which the oak tree becomes existent.

Absolute potentiality is the distinctive character of *prime matter*.[13] It is not potentiality for further determinations in an already existing subject, but rather is it pure indetermination, pure potentiality for substantial being, awaiting actualization. It has more of potency than any other degree of being; it is essentially formless passivity and imperfection.[14] It is not realizable in itself, but only in conjunction with form which it limits[15] and by which in turn it is itself determined to a particular kind of being, as for instance, a man, a plant, a mineral. This lowest grade on the ladder of being is frequently referred to as the *prope nihil*.

At the fountainhead of this hierarchy of beings is the Source of all being, Who must necessarily be excluded by His very perfection from

---

13. "Non igitur potentia materiae est aliqua proprietas addita super essentiam ejus; sed materia secundum suam substantiam est potentia ad esse substantiale." *In I Phys.*, 14. "Materia enim dicitur substantia non quasi ens aliquid actu existens in se considerata, sed quasi in potentia ut sit aliquid actu haec dicitur esse hoc aliquid." *In VIII Metaph.*, 1.

14. "Cum enim materia, inquantum hujusmodi, sit in potentia, oportet quod primum principium materiale sit maxime in potentia; et ita maxime imperfectum." *Sum. Th.*, I, q. 4, a. 1. "Materia prima est maxime in potentia, et principium imperfectissimum...." *Ibid.*

15. "Sed materia dicitur quod habet esse ex eo quod sibi advenit, quia de se esse incompletum, immo nullum esse habet, ut dicit Commentator in *II De Anima*. Unde, simpliciter loquendo, forma dat esse materiae, accidens autem non dat esse subjecto, sed subjectum accidenti; ... Sicut autem omne quod est in potentia, potest dici materia, ita omne a quo habet aliquid esse, quodcumque esse sit illud, sive substantiale, sive accidentale, potest dici forma...." *De Princ. Nat.*, col. 2. (Opusc. 27, p. 480, Vives.) "Materia, quidem per formam, in quantum materia, antequam recipiat formam, est in potentia ad multas formas; sed cum recipit unam, terminatur per illam. Forma vero finitur per materiam, in quantum forma in se considerata communis est ad multa; sed per hoc quod recipitur in materia, fit forma determinate hujus rei." *Sum. Th.*, I, q. 7, a. 1.

this study of the antecedents of being, since nothing is antecedent to Him. He is the Prime Mover, the Uncaused Cause, the Ultimate Sufficient Reason for all things. His own words, "I am Who am" express His eternity. From Him, all creation derives its being.[16] His existence is one immutable now without past or future, without a cause, without antecedents, without the least shadow of imperfection. Our inquiry must take us to *finite* beings.

Summing up, then, the grades of finite beings as we have viewed them, we can readily see the general position in that sweep of beings in which the present thesis will locate its field of labor. Aristotle's "non-being which in some way is" will be found to be in the class of Thomas' "relative non-being" precisely in its distinction from "absolute non-being."[17] We would tentatively indicate, therefore, the three following grades of being for particular investigation in ascertaining just what are the antecedents of being: possible essence, potential or undetermined subjects and prime matter.

In the XII *Metaphysics* Aristotle makes mention of the causes and principles of things. He says:

> The causes and the principles, then, are three: two being the pair of contraries of which one is definition and form, and the other is privation; and the third being the matter.[18]

Saint Thomas accepts these as a threefold division of "principles of nature," as he states in *De Principiis Naturae*.[19] He does not, however,

---

16. "Esse namque divinum proprie est ratio creandi; quia per creationem omnes res communiter accedunt ad participandum esse quantum est eis possibile, non autem naturam divinam: ipsa enim non participatur a creatura...." *De Quat. Op.*, c. 4. (Opusc. 33, p. 520, Vives.)

17. "...non-ens, non simpliciter quod est nihil, sed in genere." *De Quat. Op.*, c. 4, fi.

18. *Metaph.* XII, 2, 1069 b 33. Cf. *Phys.*, I, 7, 191 a 12-20.

19. "Ad hoc autem quod sit generatio, tria requiruntur: scilicet ens in potentia quod est materia: et non esse actu quod est privatio; et id per quod fit actu quod est forma:...Sunt igitur tria principia naturae, scilicet materia et forma et privatio, quorum scilicet forma, est id propter quod fit generatio; alia duo sunt ex parte ejus ex quo est generatio." *De Princ. Nat.*, col. 3. Cf. *In XII Metaph.*, lect. 2, init.; 3.

pretend that they adequately explain the coming to be of things.[20] In his commentary on the XII *Metaphysics*, Saint Thomas indicates a threefold classification of non-being, namely, *nihil, privatio* and *materia*.[21] We shall plumb the depths of these "non-beings" to see how far they are found to coincide with the "causes and principles" of Aristotle. Can we find therein one or two basic antecedents of being? Can we find in them the "non-being which in some way is"?

Thus from the positive aspect of causes and principles, as well as from the negative aspect of the denial of being, we have possible subjects for immediate investigation. Moreover, "matter" and "privation" have been yielded from both sources, thereby presenting us with a double motive for analyzing their nature and rôle in the dynamic notion of being. Further, from the affirmation of being rather than from its negation, that is, from our own cursory overview of the grades of being, there were yielded to us three very likely candidates for meeting the requirement for antecedents of being. How will these three, namely, possible essences, potential or undetermined subjects and prime matter, hold place with the Aristotelian causes and principles as well as with the Thomistic threefold non-beings? Prime matter has made its appearance under every aspect noted above. An analysis of these concepts, of their similarities and differences, their absolute and their relative aspects, their interrelations and interpenetrations, in the hope of reaching definite conclusions not at variance with traditional Thomistic thought, will constitute the first portion of this dissertation.

Opposed to the general notion of being there is the notion of non-being. The opposition between them is that of contradiction, which

---

20. "... ex dictis ergo patet tria esse principia naturae: scilicet materiam, formam, et privationem; sed non sunt haec sufficientia ad generationem. Quod enim est in potentia, non potest se reducere ad actum.... Forma etiam non potest se extrahere de potentia in actum: et loquor de forma generati, quam dicimus esse terminum generationis: forma enim non est nisi in facto esse: quod autem operatur est in fieri, dum res fit. Oportet ergo praeter materiam et formam aliquid principium esse quod agat; et hoc dicitur causa efficiens vel agens, vel unde principium motus...." *De Princ. Nat.*, col. 6.

21. "Dicitur enim non ens tripliciter. Uno modo quod nullo modo est... alio modo dicitur non ens ipsa privatio... tertio modo dicitur non ens ipsa materia...." *In XII Metaph., lect.* 1, fi.

Saint Thomas calls the greatest opposition.[22] "Being and non-being are infinitely separated," he says.[23] An analysis of the notion of contradiction yields the concept of absolute nothingness as opposed to absolute being. Between the terms of this opposition the whole range of being extends, from pure potency to Pure Act. In the present study we will consider the nature of these two terms in themselves, in their relation to each other, and to the several types of lesser opposition mentioned by Aristotle and Thomas. These last partake of the nature of opposition to a greater or a lesser degree in proportion as they approximate the nature of contradiction, or fall short of it. They are the oppositions of privation and contrariety, and are basic principles upon which are founded the concepts of relative non-being. They are the wells from which flow the substantial and accidental changes of generation and alteration.

Inextricably bound up in all the foregoing concepts and forming a vast network of orderly interpenetration, are many other concepts, determinations and modalities which must not be omitted if our study is to lay even moderate claims to adequacy in its treatment of being and non-being. Chief among this ganglia-like mass of principles working outward from the nucleus of being, we find the principles of non-contradiction, of sufficient reason and finality, of substance, of change and motion, with its very definite problem of the becoming of things by generation and alteration; these involving in turn the principle of causality and the fourfold causes of becoming. These require other fundamental principles, such as that basic one of potency and act applied to all beings in general and that of matter and form applied to substantial beings only.

We should not have completely mapped out the scope of our subject were we to omit taking some cognizance of the problem of creation *ex nihilo*. What are its antecedents? Creation, Saint Thomas says, is the coming to be of a being in the wholeness of its substance.[24] At once this is seen to differ radically and irreconcilably from substantial change, which necessitates a determinable subject. Nothing but creation can be set over against absolute nothing as the source of its origin,

---

22. *De Quat. Op.*, c. 1.
23. "Ens et non ens in infinitum distant." *De Pot.*, q. 3, 4.
24. *Sum. Th.*, I, q. 45, aa. 1, 2, 5; esp. a. 1, *ad* 2; q. 65, a. 3; III, q. 75, a. 8.

Saint Thomas reminds us.²⁵ It is precisely in this philosophical attainment of the notion of creation *ex nihilo* that the Thomistic doctrine of production surpasses that of the Aristotelian doctrine, which seems never to have reached the idea of a pure creation.²⁶

Our aim is not only to bring to light from his own texts Saint Thomas' synthesis of reality, but to restate the principles and to make a critical application of them to modern and contemporary philosophies. We are concerned especially with those systems which perpetuate the inadequate aspects of reality surviving from the early Greeks and found impregnating Hegel's philosophy of Absolutism and Bergson's philosophy of Flux. These two modern philosophies revive the fundamental errors of Parmenides and Heraclitus and present them to us in a new form. The Scholastic concept of the absolutely dichotomous division between being and non-being, when laid over against the Hegelian reconciliation of being and nothing, ought to prove at least an enlightening contrast if not a convincing argument for the common-sense value of the doctrine of becoming which we present under the names of Aristotle and Aquinas. For the last-named doctrine makes becoming an aspect of being rather than the state or function of repose to which it is logically forced in a philosophy which refuses to consider it as an aspect of reality.²⁷

In Bergsonism, the "intuition of becoming" has been substituted for the Scholastic "abstractive intuition of being."²⁸ The Scholastic "sub-

---

25. "Sicut ergo cum per naturam fit aliquid ex suo opposito, sicut esse animal fit ex non esse animal, ita *necesse est esse simpliciter quod est proprius Dei effectus, emanare ex non esse simpliciter;* et hoc est alterum extremum contradictionis...." *De Quat. Op.,* c. 4, *init.*

26. For an interesting defense of Aristotle by Saint Thomas, cf. opusculum *De Aeternitate Mundi contra Murmurantes.* (Opusc. 27, p. 450, Vives.) For references to Aristotle bearing on the eternity of the world, of matter, of time and of motion, cf. *De Caelo, I,* 10, 279 b 4; *Phys. VIII,* 1, whole chapter, especially 251 a 9 - 252 a 4; *ibid.,* 5, 256 b 12; *ibid.,* 10, 267 b 24; *ibid.;* I, 9, 192 a 28 *sqq.; Metaph. XII,* 10, 1075 b 33-34; *ibid.,* 6, 1071 b 7, 8; 1072 b 20-23; *De Gen. et Corrup.,* II, 10, 336 b 25 *sqq.* For Eternal Unmoved Mover and Eternal Motion, cf. *De Caelo, II,* 6, 288 a 29 - 288 b 5.

27. Cf. Garrigou-Lagrange, *loc. cit.,* I, p. 169. R. G. Bandas, *Contemporary Philosophy* and *Thomistic Principles,* p. 195.

28. Bandas, *loc. cit.,* pp. 179-202. Cites H. Bergson, *Creative Evolution,* pp. 267, 8.

stance" is replaced by a perpetual "flux." Finally, "creative evolution" is the sole *raison d'être* of all reality. We shall aim to discover what, if any, points of contact can be found between Thomism, Hegelianism and Bergsonism. How neatly, for instance, will the Thomistic pattern of being versus non-being fit over the texture of Hegelian opposition? Both Thomas and Hegel admit the opposition which exists between nothing and being, but are they using the terms univocally? Does being do away with non-being, as Thomas says,[29] or do they blend and produce becoming, as Hegel asserts?[30]

Bergson denies permanency to things and sees universal mobility as the only reality. He presents the Heraclitean doctrine in a new form. "There are no things; there are only actions. Things and states are but views taken of becoming by the mind."[31] Against the Thomistic doctrine of substances, the Bergsonian flux is a movement without anything that moves. Aristotle warns us that the admission of a movement without a thing that is moved destroys the notion of substance and leaves all as accidents only.[32] Saint Thomas assures us that change must always occur in a changeable thing, as in a subject.[33] Is there any reconciliation possible here? To what extent, if any, are the Aristotelian four causes of becoming put to work in the evolutionary process of creative evolution? Such is our proposed line of investigation. We hope to draw conclusions concerning the adequacy of the Thomistic synthesis of being and non-being, and to answer the problems raised by modern and contemporary philosophies; and we hope, further, to evaluate all three systems in a critical way.

In conclusion, let us say that we must plumb the depths not only of the real, but also of the unreal; of being and of its negation, nothingness, which is the only thing that can differentiate being and which can itself be known only through being. We must try to reach

---

29. "Hoc autem quod est affirmationem et negationem esse simul, rationem entis habere non potest, nec etiam non entis; quia esse tollit non esse, et non esse tollit esse." *De Pot.*, q. 1, a. 3.
30. "Being determinate is the union of being and nothing." *Encycl.* No. 89, cited by Calkins, *Persistent Problems of Philosophy*, p. 575.
31. *Creative Evolution*, p. 248.
32. *Metaph.* IV, 4, 1007 a 20.
33. "Motus autem semper est in mobili ut in subjecto." *De Quat. Op.*, c. 4.

an understanding of a notion of which a notion (strictly speaking) is impossible, and we must do this as far as purely human equipment can penetrate its nothingness; whence looking upward through all the hierarchy of beings to the Pure Being Who is the First Uncaused Cause of them all, we are forced to cry out in wonderment, "Oh the depths of the wisdom, and the knowledge, and the power, and the goodness of God!"

2. HISTORICAL ASPECTS

Parmenides was right. Being is. Non-being is not. Heraclitus was right. Being becomes. This is not an attempted Hegelian-like reconciliation of opposites, but a suggestion of the Aristotelian synthesis of being and becoming. Being is and being becomes.

Parmenides was right. That is, he was right in his recognition of the principle of identity: Being is being. And Heraclitus was right when he trusted to his senses to reveal the changing world around him. Each was right as far as he went. The trouble is, both views were one-sided and they listed badly. Each was wrong in that it was a partial view only, and the illusion of becoming for Parmenides and the illusion of being for Heraclitus have given rise to two streams of philosophy which have carried these inadequate theories of reality right to our very door.

Partial views of reality can never reveal the real. Their errors lie radically in the very incompleteness of their comprehension; in the partiality of the truth of their premises. We grant with Parmenides that nothing can come from being, since whatever is, already exists, and what is becoming, before it becomes, does not exist.[34] Further, only one of two contradictories can be true, said Parmenides, and since nothing can come from nothing, then if at any given moment nothing

---

34. "We ourselves are in agreement with them (the early philosophers) in holding that nothing can be said without qualification to come from what is not. But nevertheless we maintain that a thing may 'come to be from what is not' — that is, in a qualified sense. For a thing comes to be from the privation, which in its own nature is not-being — this not surviving as a constituent of the result." Aristotle, *Phys.*, I, 8, 191 b 13. Oxford translation used throughout.

exists, nothing will ever come into existence. This we grant.³⁵ But we ask: Is "nothing" an univocal term? One does not hesitate to declare that it is not. Something can come into existence from the nothingness of itself, as by generation, man from not-man. Something also can be brought into existence from the nothingness of itself *and* a pre-existing subject, *ex nihilo sui et subjecti*, which coming-to-be of anything in the whole of its substance is by way of creation. The former "nothing" is relative nothing; the latter is absolute nothing.

However, such comings-to-be demand a metaphysics not attained by the Eleatic School. Even by Aristotle this second type of production, namely, from the nothingness of itself and a pre-existing subject, was not attained, at least philosophically.

For Heraclitus, on the other hand, the whole of reality was only what his senses reported, namely the change, the becoming of things. Being and non-being were but mental abstractions; everything becomes. Sense perception revealed everything in flux, therefore *that* was the real. Something is and it is not. Being and non-being existed simultaneously; things were constantly changing into their opposites; in fact there was no reality but the "becoming-ness" of things.

We grant to the followers of the Heraclitean School that becoming is a reality; but that it is the whole of reality we would question very seriously. Common sense is against it. Such a theory demands the destruction of the principle of contradiction and that is disastrous to any system.³⁶

35. "Invenimus enim in rebus quaedam quae sunt possibilia esse et non esse: cum quaedam inveniantur generari et corrumpi, et per consequens possibilia esse et non esse. Impossibile est autem omnia quae sunt talia esse: quia quod possibile est non esse, quandoque non est. Si igitur omnia sunt possibilia non esse, aliquando nihil fuit in rebus. Sed si hoc est verum, etiam nunc nihil esset: quia quod non est, non incipit esse nisi per aliquid quod est. Si ergo nihil fuit ens, impossibile fuit quod aliquid inciperet esse: et sic modo nihil esset; quod patet esse falsum." *Sum. Th.*, I, q. 2, a. 3.

36. "For it is impossible for anyone to believe the same thing to be and not to be, as some think Heraclitus says.... It is impossible for the same man at the same time to believe the same thing to be and not to be; for if a man were mistaken on this point he would have contrary opinions at the same time." Aristotle, *Metaph.*, IV, 3, 1005 b 23. "The first indemonstrable principle is that the same thing cannot be at the same time affirmed and denied; this is based on

Being is and being becomes. To this we hold. To this we must hold, because we perceive that the "is-ness," the permanence, as well as the "becoming-ness," the flux, are each in themselves only partial aspects of reality. The One Immobile of Parmenides required the Many Mobile of Heraclitus before there could emerge on the metaphysical stage a complete enactment of the rôle of reality. Merged into one doctrine, the two apparently disparate theories synthesize into a satisfying whole.

Being is. Non-being is not. Between being and non-being there can be no middle term. The principle of excluded middle forbids it. Being exhausts the universe of the real. The opposition of contradiction holds fast,[37] and in such oppositions there can be no middle term for, says Saint Thomas, "one of the extremes is absolutely non-being outside any genus."[38] Becoming therefore is not a middle term. However, becoming is everywhere apparent to our senses. What status, if any, has it? Do we perceive the real in perceiving becoming? Or must it be for us, as it was for Parmenides, only an illusion? Must not the principles of identity and contradiction give way before the testimony of our senses? An acorn becomes an oak. Water becomes warm, then hot. The human mind becomes what it knows. However, reason holds fast to those necessary first principles upon which it establishes all its knowledge of reality. A thing is what it is as long as it is what it is. A being, viewed under the same aspect, cannot at the same time exist and not exist. This is a natural, spontaneous, immediate intuition of human intelligence, and reason insists upon its retention.

The principle of contradiction, then, cannot go. As the alternative, the testimony of our senses errs. The mobility, growth, movement, change surrounding us everywhere must be illusory. Sense knowledge is no knowledge; it is an illusion. Here we hark back to Zeno. The arrow wings its way, traverses a given distance and reaches its mark, but yet it never moves; it is fixed, permanent.

The dilemma: Everything is mobile and everything is immobile. But only one of two contradictories can be true. Ancient thought stood

the notion of being and non-being, and *on this principle all others are based."* Saint Thomas, *Sum. Th.*, I-II, q. 94, a. 2.
37. Cf. *Categories*, 11 b 17.
38. *De Quat. Op.*, c. 1.

nonplused before the seeming dichotomy, as if the solution had to be found in *either one* and *only one* of these alternatives: Being is *or* being becomes. The solution needed an Aristotle, who took the center of the stage and by the simple enunciation of his doctrine of act and potency restated the propositions: Being is *and* being becomes. He wedded the permanence of a being to its very changeableness, thus presenting subsequent thought with being and becoming as dual rôles of the notion of the real.

If being is being, then as long as it is being it is not non-being; likewise non-being, as long as it is non-being, is not being. Now being is something, but non-being is nothing. In becoming, something becomes something other than what it was, therefore it would seem that becoming belongs to any being as an aspect of its being. Thus reasoned Aristotle. He drew his conclusion: Becoming is the passage from undetermined being to determined being. Being is retained as the common note of the essentially determined and the essentially undetermined.

Examples are not difficult to provide. We find them in the difference between the acorn and the oak; between the water that was first cold and then hot; and between the mind that is capable of becoming all things and the mind in possession of the knowledge that it acquires. And thus, by attributing to being a dual aspect, the Philosopher exposed the true dichotomy, namely, being is that which *is* or *can be;* non-being is that which *is not*.

It is to the genius and pertinacity of Thomas of Aquin that the philosophical world owes its treasured storehouse of Aristotelian thought *secundum exactam, veram, genuinam Aristotelis mentem*. The Arabians had distorted it and the Parisian Averroists had further mutilated it. In this sorry state, Thomas came to the rescue of "The Philosopher" and his doctrines. From early public life Thomas had risked a promising career to devote his energies to the restoration, explication, and amplification of the Peripatetic. It is chiefly to the texts of Saint Thomas as the synthesis and interpretation of Aristotelianism, that we shall have recourse in our proposed treatment of the problem: How can being be and yet become? What are the antecedents of being?

CHAPTER ONE

PRIMARY CONCEPTS AND OTHER BASIC NOTIONS

1. THE CONCEPT OF BEING

Ens est id quod non est nihil absolutum.[1] In this one sentence we are introduced to the two notions which lie at the very root of our problem. Any attempt to discover a non-being which in some way is being, has to do with the analysis of the primary and secondary concepts of the human mind. The first is all-inclusive; the second, all-exclusive. The former exhausts all reality; the latter negates it. The first notion is that of being; the second, of non-being. That being is our primary concept is expressed frequently in Saint Thomas. "That which presents itself first of all to the intellect as the best known, is the concept of being, and it is into this concept of being that it resolves all other concepts."[2]

The notion of being is followed by that of non-being. This Saint Thomas expressly states: "For that which first comes into the mind is being, and the next is the negation of being. Now from these two results, in the third place, the concept of division."[3] Again: "The first of all notions reached by the human mind is that of simple being,

---

1. Simple notions are usually defined by negation. Cf. *Sum. Th.*, I, q. 10, a. 1, *ad* 1.

2. "Illud autem quod primo intellectus concipit quasi notissimum, et in quo omnes conceptiones resolvit, est ens." *De Verit.*, q. I, a. 1. Cf. also *Sum. Th.*, I-II, q. 42, a. 2; *ibid.*, I, q. 5, a. 2.

3. "Primum enim quod in intellectum cadit, est ens; secundum vero est negatio entis; ex his autem duobus sequitur tertio intellectus divisionis ex hoc enim quod aliquid intelligitur ens, et intelligitur non esse hoc ens, sequitur in intellectu quod sit divisum ab eo; quarto autem sequitur in intellectu ratio unius, prout scilicet intelligitur hoc ens non esse in se divisum; quinto autem sequitur intellectus multitudinis, prout scilicet hoc ens intelligitur divisum ab alio, et utrumque ipsorum esse in se unum." *De Pot.*, q. 9, a. 7, *ad* 15.

and then not-being, division and unity follow in logical order."[4] Our definition (descriptive rather than essential) of being, then, includes the first and second concepts of the human mind. It is our immediate purpose to analyze each of these concepts.

The notion of being is susceptible of various modes of analysis. It is only by analysis and explication rather than by definition that a knowledge of this concept can be attained. Being is not a class name, but is that notion which, in itself transcending all classes, includes within its periphery beings of every actual and possible class. For this reason it is not subject to definition, by which to a particular class name is added, as a differentiating note, some notion not contained in the class name, thereby essentially constituting members of that class into various species within it. For example, the note "rationality" specifies members of the class "animal," thus distinguishing rational animals from other members of the class. On this point Saint Thomas says that we cannot conceive of anything which accrues to the notion of being by which it would be diversified, because what accrues to being is extraneous to it, and what is of this kind is nothing.[5] Since apart from being there is nothing, and all differentia would necessarily be being (which is contrary to the requirements of differentia, for a genus cannot enter into the essential nature of the difference), it follows that the notion of being is undefinable. It cannot be diversified by differences extrinsic to it. "Rationality" is not an essential constituent of "animal," for other beings are rational, as for instance, angels. There can be found no difference for being into which the notion of being does not enter as an essential element.[6] Being is a notion which transcends all categories.

The notion of being in general is a strictly simple notion. It presents us with being as absolutely indeterminate, without modification or determination of any kind whatsoever, without a single note enter-

---

4. "Primo igitur intelligitur ipsum ens, et ex consequenti non ens, et per consequens divisio, et per consequens unum quod divisionem privat, et per consequens multitudo, in cujus ratione cadit divisio, sicut in ratione unius indivisio...." *In IV Metaph., lect.* 3.

5. Cf. *De Verit.*, q. 1, a. 1. Also *In I Metaph.*, 5, *lect.* 9; *Sum. Th.*, I, q. 3, a. 5; *Con. Gen.*, l. I, c. 25.

6. Cf. *Sum. Th.*, I, q. 3, a. 6.

ing into the concept which might limit the notion to a "this kind" of being. It is the notion of *ens simpliciter*. In its broadest significance it is quiddity. It can be conceived purely as an essence, apart from its existence or non-existence. Actually, however, it cannot be anything without either one or other of the notes *actual* or *potential*. In its fullest sense it connotes existence, to which it stands as potency to act, for existence is the first act of essence. For this reason we find the notion of being described as "that which has reference to existence." To this we shall return shortly.

As viewed from various aspects, being may be analyzed by means of its determinations, among which are substance and accident, the infinite and the finite, the necessary and the contingent, the real and the ideal. Taken in its abstract meaning in the essential order, it is absolute existence as opposed to its contradictory, absolute non-existence. It serves our purpose best to consider being here, not in its various determinations, but in its relations to existence simply, since existence is the first perfection of being.

"The first perfection of being consists in its existence."[7] Existence is the principle in virtue of which being is made actual. "Along with the essence given by God, He produces that which the essence receives," says Saint Thomas.[8] In the *Summa Theologica* he refutes the objection that existence seems most imperfect because it is most universal and receptive of all modification. His reply is, rather, that existence is the most perfect of all things since it is to essence as act to potency.[9] We do not intend to enter here into a discussion of the problem: Does the actual existence of existing being really, logically or only virtually differ from its essence? Our present concern is to view being under whatsoever aspects it is revealed to us in relation to its formal act, existence.

The notion of being as "that which has reference to existence" contains two distinct elements which, in contingent beings, are to each other as potency to act. The first element is, as we suggested above,

7. *Ibid.*, I, 6, 3.
8. "Deus simul dans esse, producit id quod esse recipit." *De Pot.*, q. 3, a. 1, *ad* 17.
9. Cf. *Sum. Th.*, I, q. 4, a. 1, *ad* 3; I, q. 4, a. 1. Also Harper, *The Metaphysics of the School*, I, pp. 101, 2.

that of quiddity or essence, the subject which has being; the second element is that of existence, the *actus essendi*, the form or first act by which the subject has being. The act of essence (existence) is the *actus* viewed as coming upon a being as it passes from the realm of possibility to actuality. Existence is to essence as act to potency in finite beings whose existence is distinct from the actual essence into which it is received and by which it is limited.[10] The combination of these two principles, essence and form or first act, constitutes a composite essence. The composite essence and second act or form give actual existence. In the first instance the potency is pure, it is *materia prima;* in the second, the potential element, though still a subjective potency as in the first instance, is not pure potency since it already has received essential act. However, the composite essence, itself consisting of *materia prima* and first act or substantial form, may be said to be in potency to entitative act. In other words, it has subjective potency, but subjective potency that is relative or entitative potency.

Confining our attention now to being precisely in its relation to existence, we find even here a variety of possible distinctions. The notion of being in general, in relation to existence, may be viewed in its distinctions of nominal and participial being. Here being is looked at substantively, on the one hand, as real and possible insofar as the notion prescinds from or positively excludes the act (though not the possibility) of existence from our abstract thought. On the other hand, being may be viewed in its participial meaning as existent being, either actual or potential. Being is determined to these two distinct concepts within it, and to be anything real it must be either actually existing or potentially so. Here we have departed from the simple notion of being, for existent being is specifically determined to actual existence here and now, and so it constitutes a determination of transcendental being.

As noted previously, the actual and the possible might be called divisions of being, if being strictly could be divided. It is perhaps more accurate to say that being is proximately determined to be either

---

10. "Secundo, quia esse est actualitas omnis formae vel naturae; non enim bonitas vel humanitas significatur in actu, nisi prout significamus eam esse. Oportet igitur quod ipsum esse comparetur ad essentiam quae est aliud ab ipso, sicut actus ad potentiam." *Sum. Th.*, I, q. 3, a. 4.

actual or potential being. Act and potency are determinations of being in general, as distinct from the concepts of matter and form which are determinations of substantial being only.[11] Hence an analysis of the concept of being from this aspect will further unfold the nature of transcendental *ens* and the importance the concepts of act and potency play in its understanding.

The division of being which we shall follow here is not that of nominal and participial, but rather that of actual and possible. This seems most consonant with our attempt to probe the notion of being to find therein the antecedents of being. Our concern will be with real as opposed to logical being.[12] Real being bifurcates into actual and possible being. A further bifurcation of actual being yields Pure Act and mixed act. The second member under actual being, namely, potency mixed with act, claims our attention. Viewed entitatively, we find herein essence and existence — essence which receives and limits existence, and existence which determines the essence and which is in turn limited by it. They are the two distinct elements spoken of previously, the *id quod* or the essence which is said to exist, and the *id*

---

11. "Et prima principia maxime universaliter significata sunt actus et potentia; nam haec dividunt ens inquantum hujusmodi.... Sicut autem actus et potentia sunt universaliter principia omnium quia consequuntur ens commune, ita oportet quod secundum quod descendit communitas principiorum." *In XII Metaph.*, lect. 3.

"In substantiis autem compositis ex materia et forma est duplex compositio actus et potentiae: prima quidem ipsius substantiae, quae componitur ex materia et forma; secunda vero, ex ipso substantia jam composita et esse; quae etiam potest dici ex *quod est* et *esse,* vel ex *quod est* et *quo est.* Sic igitur patet quod compositio actus et potentiae est in plus quam compositio formae et materiae; unde materia et forma dividunt substantiam materialem, potentia autem et actus dividunt ens commune." *Con. Gen.*, l. II, c. 54.

12. Logical being is that which has no extramental entity. "Illud quod habet esse objective tantum in intellectu, seu ... id quod a ratione excogitatur ut ens, cum tamen in se entitatem non habeat." Coffey, *Ontology*, p. 33. Notions of non-being and privation are of this kind. "Non ens est cognoscibile nisi secundum quod fit per intellectum cognoscibile, id est, *ens rationis.*" *Sum. Th.*, I, q. 16, a. 3, *ad* 2. "Quod non ens non habet in se unde cognoscatur, sed cognoscitur in *quantum intellectus facit illud cognoscibile;* unde verum fundatur in ente in quantum non ens est quoddam ens rationis, apprehensum scilicet a ratione." *Sum. Th.*, I, q. 16, a. 3, *ad* 3.

quo or the principle in virtue of which the thing exists.[13] Reverting once more to Saint Thomas' proportion, namely that existence is to essence as act is to potency,[14] we clearly see the relation between the two principles in the entitative order.[15]

Beings of mixed potency and act may be viewed essentially as well as entitatively. This is a more fundamental aspect, for we come upon the constitutive notes which make its essence; in material substance, for example, we penetrate to the intrinsic principles of prime matter and substantial form and we find here again the basic doctrine of potency and act.[16] We do not, in fact we cannot, shake off the notes of potency and act except when we cross the threshold of finiteness into the realm of infinity, the abode of Pure Act.

Our first bifurcation of reality yielded the actual and the possible. We have already explored the territory of the actual and found that with the sole exception of Pure Act, the notions of potency and act dominated the scene. It remains now for us to pursue the second branch of the bifurcation of real being, that of the possibles. Potency and act pervade this field, too. Since all real being includes in some way or other the idea of existence, and since existence is the first act of being, it follows that in the realm of possible beings there shall be found a principle by which possible beings (the subject) are

---

13. Cf. *Con. Gen.*, l. II, c. 54. Footnote 11, p. 21, *infra*.
14. *Infra*, p. 20, footnote 10.
15. "Primo quidem, quia quidquid est in aliquo, quod est praeter essentiam ejus, oportet esse causatum vel a principiis essentiae, sicut propria consequentia speciem, ut risibile consequitur hominem, causatur ex principiis essentialibus speciei; vel ab aliquo exteriori, sicut calor in aqua causatur ab igne. Si igitur ipsum esse rei sit alius ab ejus essentia, necesse est quod ipsum esse illius rei sit causatum ab aliquo exteriori, vel a principiis essentialibus ejusdem rei. Impossibile est autem quod esse sit causatum a principiis tantum essentialibus ei; quia nulla res sufficit quae sit sibi causa essendi, si habeat esse causatum. Oportet ergo quod illud cujus esse est aliud ab essentia sua habeat esse causatum ab alio. Hoc autem non potest dici de Deo: quia Deum dicimus esse primam causam efficientem. Impossibile est ergo quod in Deo sit aliud esse, et aliud ejus essentia. Secundo, quia esse est actualitas omnis formae vel naturae; non enim bonitas vel humanitas significatur in actu, nisi prout significamus eam esse. Oportet igitur quod ipsum esse comparetur ad essentiam quae est aliud ab ipso, sicut actus ad potentiam." *Sum. Th.*, I, q. 3, a. 4.
16. Cf. *infra*, p. 21, footnote 11.

constituted real beings, and hence there must be involved here, too, the principles of act and potency. Thus possible beings as well as actual contingent beings may be viewed entitatively as well as essentially. Habitude of terms, or the non-impossibility of blending its essential intrinsic notes, is the essence of possible beings. Possible quiddity is real only insofar as it contains no interior contradiction. The *actus* comes upon this non-impossibility inasmuch as it is referrible to existence. The content of the notion "possible being," that is, the sociability of notes, has by its very nature a transcendental relation to actual existence which is, after all, its point of origin as far as the human mind is concerned, and it is susceptible of recovering the existence of which the notion has been deprived through the process of abstraction. Though it does not actually exist, nevertheless the possible conceivably may exist.

In concluding this section, we note that the notion of being is that which has reference to existence. It is the primary concept of the human mind, and the basis of its other concepts. The notion may be viewed under the aspects of real or logical; the real divides into the actual and the possible, while the two latter notions are conceived under essential as well as entitative aspects.

2. THE NEGATION OF BEING

This is the second concept acquired by our minds as we have already noted, and it is based on the concept of being. We deem that we have presented a sufficiently adequate survey of the general notion of being to enable us profitably to plumb the depths of its opposite, absolute non-being. From the simple notion of being we attain, by opposition, that of non-being. On these two concepts Saint Thomas bases all our knowledge, since from them, as he points out, are derived the first principles of thought and reality:

> The first and indemonstrable principle is that the same thing cannot be at the same time affirmed and denied; this is based on the notion of being and non-being and on this principle all others are based, as is stated by the Philosopher in the IV *Metaphysics*, c. 3.[17]

17. "Nam illud quod primo cadit in apprehensione, est ens, cujus intellectus includitur in omnibus quaecumque quis apprehendit. Et ideo primum prin-

This is the principle of non-contradiction in the form it assumes in Logic. In its metaphysical formula it might read: "A being viewed under the same aspect cannot at the same time exist and not exist." In the former formula, we see the inconceivability of the absurd; in the latter, its objective impossibility.

Opposed to being conceived precisely as being whose first act is existence, the mind grasps the notion of its negation, the denial of that being and its first act, and this opposing notion is non-being, non-existence. The opposition between our primary and our secondary notion is so complete that even all potentiality to existence is removed from the latter,[18] which means that the lower extreme of the opposition is precisely nothing, *nihil absolutum*. This is the prime opposition, that of contradiction, characterized as it is by absolute incompatibility of terms so that the extremes never meet in a middle term. So incompatible with being is the notion of absolute non-being that in itself this latter notion is unknowable, since a thing is knowable insofar as it is actual.[19] Nothing has logical being only, and as such is incapable of objective reality.[20]

It will add to an understanding of the nature of being and non-being if we pursue further the nature of the opposition of contradiction. We do well to remember that being and non-being are taken in a universal sense.[21] Saint Thomas' treatment of opposition is adopted from Aristotle's *Metaphysics*.[22] The Angelic Doctor comments on

cipium indemonstrabile est quod non est simul affirmare et negare, quod fundatur supra rationem entis et non entis: et super hoc principio omnia alia fundatur, ut dicitur in *IV Metaph.*" *Sum. Th.*, I-II, q. 94, a. 2. Cf. *De Verit.*, q. 1, a. 1, for intelligibility of things in function of being.

18. "Rationi autem entis repugnat oppositum entis, quod est non-ens. Omnia igitur Deus potest quae in se rationem non entis non includunt. Haec autem sunt quae contradictionem non implicant." *Con. Gen.*, l. II, q. 22.

19. "Unumquodque sit cognoscibile secundum quod est in actu." *Sum. Th.*, I, q. 12, a. 1. Cf. *Sum. Th.*, I, q. 16, a. 3.

20. Cf. *Sum. Th.*, I, q. 16, a. 3, *ad* 2. Also, p. 21, footnote 12, *infra*.

21. "In contradictione absoluta ens et non ens accipiuntur universaliter." *De Quat. Op.*, c. 2.

22. *Liber X*, 1054 a 20 to 1059 a.

Aristotle,[23] treats of contradiction in the *First Book of the Sentences*, and devotes the opusculum *De Quatuor Oppositis* to the question of opposition.[24]

It is in this latter work that Saint Thomas gives us his most lengthy and complete exposition of the nature of contradiction. Opposition, according to the Angelic Doctor, consists in the removal of potency from being actualized. Applied to the notions now under consideration, the removal of all potency to actualization results in absolute negation, non-being left utterly devoid of any potentiality to being.[25] The opposition of contradiction is greatest, for the extremes have least in common and are most opposed. The terms are mutually repugnant, mutually exclusive, the one affirming what the other denies; each is indefinable and apart from a genus. We have already seen how absolute being transcends all genera, requiring no subject. Now the more noble extreme in terms of opposition draws the less noble to its subject if the former has a subject. But absolute being requires no subject, therefore neither is absolute non-being found in a subject.[26]

In the preceding paragraphs we have culled the essence of this opposition which has for its extremes the first two notions attained by the human mind. For in the opposition of contradiction there can be no middle term, because such a middle term would imply the meeting of the opposed terms, but between absolute being and absolute nothing there is absolute incompatibility excluding all possibility of the terms meeting.[27] The logical principle paralleling this is that of Excluded

23. *In X Metaph., lect.* 6.
24. Opusculum 33. Vol. 27, Vives.
25. "Sciendum est etiam quod dupliciter elongat aliquid potentiam removendo, ita quod nihil ejus relinquatur; et isto modo in oppositione contradictoria elongatur potentia ab actu, quia in non ente simpliciter nihil potentiae est ad esse." *De Quat. Op.*, c. 1, *fi.*
26. "In ipsa enim oppositione contradictionis alterum extremum est nihil simpliciter, et simpliciter nihil sibi determinans tamquam subjectum, quia nobilius ejus extremum, scilicet ens, nullum subjectum requirit: quod manifestum est ex eo in quo salvatur ratio ejus perfecta, quod est substantia, cujus est non esse in subjecto, secundum Philosophum." *Ibid*, c. 2, *init.*
27. "In contradictoriis vero nihil horum reperitur: non enim habent medium sui generis, cum alterum extremum sit non ens simpliciter extra omne genus: nec in subjecto convenire possunt, cum non ens subjectum habere non possit,

Middle, which flows as a self-evident principle from the prior principles of identity and contradiction. Every concept which approaches the nature of non-being will find in itself a greater or lesser degree of opposition insofar as it falls short of absolute being. Hence to this notion of opposition we shall have occasion to return again in exploring the notion of relative non-being.

3. IMPORTANCE OF THE NOTIONS OF BEING AND NON-BEING

Here we have fundamentally the basic notions from which we derive our first judgments. It is the very nature of a thing to be what it is, and hence from the primary notions of being and non-being we derive the primary judgments, Being is being. Non-being is nothing. A thing cannot be and not be at the same time and under the same aspects. Everything that is, is, as long as it is what it is. Whatever is not, is not. The "first principles" here enumerated are naturally known by the mind whenever it understands the meaning of the terms in the subject and predicate.[28] The importance of these primary principles, based as they are on a proper understanding of our primary notions, can be understood when we realize the basic principles which flow from them. From the principle of identity is derived that of sufficient reason through the principle of contradiction. The process, briefly, is this: Everything that is must have a sufficient reason for its existence. The sufficient reason may be found either in the thing itself or in an-

---

nec etiam illud in quo salvatur perfecta ratio entis, quod est substantia; nec conveniunt secundum dependentiam suorum intellectuum, sicut relativa: ens enim non ponit suum oppositum; scilicet non ens, sicut pater ponit filium. Et ideo contradictio simpliciter est secundum se non habens medium: unde minime conveniunt contradictorie opposita, et maxime opponuntur." *Ibid*, c. 1, *init*.

28. "Si igitur notum sit omnibus de praedicato et de subjecto quid sit, propositio illa erit omnibus per se nota; sicut patet in primis demonstrationum principiis, quorum termini sunt quaedam communia quae nullus ignorat, ut ens et non ens, totum et pars, et similis." *Sum. Th.*, I, q. 2, a. 1. "Ad secundum dicendum, quod intellectus semper est rectus, secundum quod intellectus est principiorum, circa quae non decipitur ex eadem causa qua non decipitur circa quod quid est. Nam principia per se nota sunt illa quae statim intellectis terminis cognoscuntur ex eo quod praedicatum ponitur in definitione subjecti." *Sum. Th.*, I, q. 17, a. 3, *ad* 2.

other. According to the principle of contradiction, a thing cannot both be and not be at the same time and in the same respects. That is, a thing cannot have the sufficient reason for itself in itself and at the same time and under the same aspect, have its sufficient reason in another. If in itself, it is its own sufficient reason; if in another, then its sufficient reason is found in an extrinsic cause. Thus the principles of identity, contradiction and sufficient reason bring us to that of causality.[29]

The universal first principles under discussion govern all modes of being and nothing escapes them. A possible being is a possible being and an actual being an actual one, nor is a possible being an actual one nor an actual being a possible one at the same time and under the same aspects. Hence we repeat here that nothing is intelligible except in terms of being and of the principle of non-contradiction, and upon this all other principles draw for their validity.[30]

We have presented some idea of the notion of being and non-being, together with the importance of these two notions in the field of metaphysics and for that matter in all phases of knowledge, since they are the notions upon which are founded the first principles of thought and being. Real being is either actual or possible being; its contradictory is absolute non-being, the impossible. Since possible beings as possibles do not exist in the objective order, but may conceivably so exist, the notion of possibility may well claim our attention next in our search for the antecedents of being.

4. POSSIBILITY AND IMPOSSIBILITY

From absolute nothingness we step into the boundless realm of possibility. In the essential order possibility is to impossibility what in

---

29. Cf. *Con. Gen.*, l. II, c. 83, No. 30.

30. "Respondeo dicendum, quod ita se habent in doctrina fidei articuli fidei, sicut principia per se nota in doctrina quae per rationem naturalem haberetur; in quibus principiis ordo quidem invenitur, ut quaedam in aliis implicite contineantur, sicut omnia principia reducuntur ad hoc sicut ad primum: 'Impossibile est simul affirmare et negare.'" *Sum. Th.*, II-II, 1, 7. Also *Sum. Th.*, I-II, q. 9, a. 4, *ad* 2; *In IV Metaph.*, lect. 6; *Post Anal.*, 2, 20; *I Sent.*, d. 35, q. 1, a. 3, *ad* 2.

the existential order being is to non-being. Our justification for an immediate treatment of possibility and impossibility is found in the statement of Saint Thomas, that from absolute nothingness comes absolute creation. It would seem from this that absolute nothing is an antecedent of being, and that *ex nihilo aliquid fit*, Parmenides notwithstanding.[31]

"The proper causality of God reaches the extremes of the opposition of contradiction which are outside any genus," says Saint Thomas,[32] consequently creation is from the not-being which is nothing.[33] Now if creation is a fact, it must first have been a possibility; if creation is production from nothing, that is, from no matter presupposed, then possibility must have been its only prerequisite.[34] That there exists some relation between possibility and the antecedents of being even in the order of generation and corruption, must appear evident, for the production of composites through the transmutation of matter presupposes the creative act which in its turn presupposes the possibility of creation.[35] Just what place possibility has will be made clear as we proceed to discuss the production of being in the wholeness of its substance, which act is called creation.

---

31. "Sicut ergo cum per naturam fit aliquid ex suo opposito, sicut esse animal fit ex non esse animal, ita necesse est, esse simpliciter quod est proprius Dei effectus, emanare ex non esse simpliciter; et hoc est alterum extremum contradictionis; non quod ipsum non esse necesse sit duratione praecedere ipsum esse, sed natura tantum." *De Quat. Op.*, c. 4, *init.* Cf. also *Con. Gen.*, l. II, c. 6; c. 15; *Sum. Th.*, I, q. 65, a. 3; *De Pot.*, q. 10, a. 1, *ad* 3; *De Verit.*, q. 5, a. 9, *ad* 7.

32. "Propria ergo causalitas Dei attingit extrema contradictionis, quae extra genus sunt: et ideo actio sua nihil supponit necessario: et haec actio est creatio." *De Quat. Op.*, c. 4, *init.*

33. "Creatio, quae est emanatio totius esse, est ex non ente, quod est nihil." *Sum. Th.*, I, q. 45, a. 1.

34. "Creatio autem est productio alicujus rei secundum suam totam substantiam, nullo praesupposito, quod sit vel increatum, vel ab alio creatum." *Sum. Th.*, I, q. 65, a. 3. Also, *II Sent.*, d. 1, q. 1, a. 3, *ad resp.* and *ad* 2; *Con. Gen.*, l. II, c. 16; *Sum. Th.*, I, q. 41, a. 3; — I, q. 104, a. 1; — I, q. 65, a. 3, *ad* 3; *De Pot.*, q. 3, a. 1, c; — q. 10, a. 1, *ad* 3.

35. "Unde in operibus naturae non admiscetur creatio, sed praesupponitur aliquid ad operationem naturae." *Sum. Th.*, I, q. 45, a. 8.

Possibility is sometimes described negatively as non-impossibility. Saint Thomas makes use of this *via negativa* as when he introduces a refutation with such words as these: "Just as we call a thing possible whose existence is not impossible...." In the two notions of possibility and impossibility we seem to have reverted once more to our notions of being and non-being, of existence *simpliciter* and the absolute negation of existence. Possibility has to do with the very essence of being, with the habitude of terms unified in a common notion. For Saint Thomas, things were intrinsically possible, that is, possible in an absolute sense, only because of the sociability of their essential constitutive notes. It is worthwhile to quote him fully here:

> Now a thing is said to be possible in two ways: First, in relation to some power; thus, whatever is subject to human power is said to be possible to man. Secondly, on account of the relation in which the very terms stand to each other.

After indicating in what manner we are to understand God's omnipotence, he concludes:

> It remains therefore that God is called omnipotent because He can do all things that are possible absolutely, which is the second way of saying a thing is possible. For a thing is said to be possible or impossible absolutely, according to the relation in which the very terms stand to one another: possible if the predicate is not incompatible with the subject, as that Socrates sits; absolutely impossible when the predicate is altogether incompatible with the subject, as, for instance, that a man is a donkey.[36]

36. "Possibile autem dicitur dupliciter, secundum Philosophum, *V Metaph.* Uno modo per respectum ad aliquam potentiam; sicut quod subditur humanae potentiae dicitur esse possibile homini. Alio modo absolute, propter ipsam habitudinem terminorum. Non autem potest dici quod Deus dicatur omnipotens quia possit omnia quae sunt possibilia naturae creatae, quia divina omnipotentia in plura extenditur. Si autem dicatur quod Deus sit omnipotens quia potest omnia quae sunt possibilia suae potentiae, erit circulatio in manifestatione omnipotentiae, hoc enim non erit aliud quam dicere quod Deus est omnipotens, quia potest omnia quae potest. Relinquitur igitur quod Deus dicatur omnipotens, quia potest omnia possibilia absolute, quod est alter modus dicendi possibile. Dicitur autem aliquid possibile vel impossibile absolute ex habitudine terminorum. Possibile quidem absolute, quia praedictatum non repugnat subjecto, ut Socratem

Again he says, "The absolutely possible is not so called in reference either to higher causes or to inferior causes but in reference to itself."[37] "Whatsoever has or can have the nature of being is numbered among the absolutely possible things," he says in the corpus of the same article. Possibility therefore precludes the combination of contradictory terms. It is an essence whose essence requires sociability of constitutive notes. It is an *ordo* or aptitude to extramental reality.[38]

We have already suggested that even in the realm of possibility the doctrine of potency and act is put to work. That is to say, possible beings can be viewed under the aspect of potentiality and of actuality. The notions of potency and act in the essential order are as essence and existence; in the existential or actual order potency and act are as actual subject to its existence. In the order of possibility the former understanding of potency and act is applicable. In notes constituting an essence, there must be presupposed the possibility of those notes blending to form a notion which is an object of intelligible thought. For not any blending of notes is of this kind; that is, possible. Therefore in the notion of possible essence the mind sees a possibility of possible essences in the non-repugnance of such terms as are mutually sociable, as for instance, equilateral and triangle. There cannot be a possible essence where the mind conceives a repugnance to mutual sociability in the terms themselves. That aptitude of possible beings by which they admit of concordant elements in their essential constitution is said to be the "potential" aspect of the possible essence. The first act of any being is existence, as Saint Thomas frequently says; hence the first act of possible beings must be some

sedere; impossibile vero absolute, quia praedicatum repugnat subjecto, ut hominem esse asinum." *Sum. Th.*, I, q. 25, a. 3. Cf. also *De Pot.*, q. 1, a. 3, wherein Saint Thomas gives a threefold meaning to the words possible and impossible.

37. "Possibile absolutum non dicitur neque secundum causas superiores, neque secundum causas inferiores, sed secundum seipsum. Possibile vero quod dicitur secundum aliquam potentiam, nominatur possibile secundum proximam causam." *Sum. Th.*, I, q. 25, a. 3, *ad* 4.

38. "Ordo (non actualis) ad esse, aptitude ad esse seu aptitudo ad suscipiendam existentiam." J. Gredt, *Elementa Philosophiae Aristotelico-Thomisticae*, II, p. 115.

relation of the possible essence to existence; not that possible beings actually exist, but that they conceivably may exist. It is in this conceivability based on the capacity of their terms to coalesce that possible essences have a relation to existence. In other words, possible beings are real insofar as the non-repugnance of notes in the essence permits a referribility to existence, and this referribility is its first act constituting the potentially possible essence actually a possible essence.

In enumerating kinds of possibility Saint Thomas speaks of a possibility which is "in relation to some power." This is extrinsic or relative possibility as contrasted with intrinsic or absolute possibility as just described. This extrinsic possibility has as an essential constituent of its nature a transcendental relation to some power capable of reducing the intrinsically possible essence to the actual order. It can be seen that the extrinsically possible requires by its essence this relation to some agent, and that it necessarily presupposes intrinsic possibility, for no agent can produce what is intrinsically impossible.

It is not difficult to see what kind of existence the possible essence has. If it is correct to define it as a being capable of existing (and this is certainly Saint Thomas' understanding of it), it follows that it cannot possibly exist, as a possible essence, outside the objective representation of it in the mind. We say "as a possible essence," because though the essence conceived as possible may afterward actually exist in objective reality, it does so at the cost of losing its capability and hence its nature of possible essence. A thing *can be* so long as it is not; when it *is*, then it no longer *can be* in the same respect, and at the same time. In objective reality there are only actual essences. As existing in the mind only, an essence is real though only possible. As existing in reality outside the mind, the essence is real and actual. This recalls our early classification of real being into actual and possible.

As a proper understanding of the notion of being makes more intelligible the notion of its negation, so do the characteristic notes of possibility, namely the habitude of terms and their referribility to actual existence, make more clear the concept of impossibility. Impossibility brings us once again face to face with the notion of nothingness, for in the strict sense this latter concept means nothing other than intrinsic impossibility. These two negative concepts imply not alone the negation of existence (which is as its *actus*) but also the negation of that very real thing, habitude of terms, intrinsic possibility (which is as the potency).

In his treatments of possibility and impossibility, Saint Thomas repeatedly takes into consideration the question whether God's omnipotence extends even to the impossible. We introduce this question here in order to indicate further Saint Thomas' identification of impossibility with absolute nothing, as well as to dispose of the question of the power of God with respect to possible and impossible things, before we apply to creation the concept of possibility.

Saint Thomas' argument that God's power does not extend to the impossible is based on the very notions of being and non-being. We quote it here as taken from three distinct important works of the Angelic Doctor. In the *Contra Gentiles* he says:

> Now God's power is the *per se* cause of being, and being is its proper effect.... Therefore it extends to all that is not incompatible with the notion of being.... Now the opposite of being, which is non-being, is incompatible with the notion of being. Wherefore God can do all things but those which include the notion of non-being: and such are those that imply a contradiction. It follows, therefore, that God can do whatever does not imply a contradiction.[39]

In the *Book of the Sentences*, the argument assumes a formula more logical than metaphysical. Substantially it is the same argument:

> One must necessarily, then, attribute to the power itself absolutely regarded (seeing that it is infinite) the possibility of whatever is in itself something and does not imply a deficiency of power. I say advisedly, what is in itself something, because a union of affirmation and negation is nothing; and (to take an example) to say in one breath that something is at the same time

---

39. "Virtus autem divina est per se causa essendi, et esse est ejus proprius effectus, ut ex supradictis (c. 21) patet. Ergo ad omnia illa se extendit quae rationi entis non repugnant; si enim in quemdam tantum effectum virtus ejus posset, non esset per se causa entis in quantum hujusmodi, sed hujus entis. Rationi autem entis repugnat oppositum entis, quod est non-ens. Omnia igitur Deus potest quae in se rationem non-entis non includunt. Haec autem sunt quae contradictionem non implicant. Relinquitur igitur quod quidquid contradictionem non implicat Deus potest." *Con. Gen.*, l. II, c. 22.

a man and not a man, does not excite any intelligible idea. Wherefore, the power of God does not extend to the point of causing that an affirmation and negation should be verified at the same time. And the same may be said of all those cases which include a contradiction.[40]

In the *Summa Theologica* the argument again is taken from the notions of being and non-being. The Angelic Doctor writes:

> Now nothing is opposed to the idea of being except non-being. Therefore that which implies being and non-being at the same time is repugnant to the idea of an absolutely possible thing, within the scope of the Divine Omnipotence... because it has not the nature of a feasible or possible thing. Therefore, everything that does not imply a contradiction in terms is numbered amongst those possible beings in respect of which God is called omnipotent; whereas whatever implies contradiction does not come within the scope of divine omnipotence, because it cannot have the aspect of possibility.[41]

We conclude: Those things are possible in whose intrinsic notes there is found no repugnance. Given this sociability of notes, things are proximately possible in reference to some power through which an agent produces an effect proportionate to itself — human agents can do things humanly possible; the Divine Agent can do things possible to a Divine Being; "such a being" can give existence to "such a being," as man generates man. Being *per se* produces beings *per se,* and this act is called

---

40. "Ipsi ergo potentiae absolutae, cum infinita sit, necesse est attribuere omne id quod in se est aliquid, et quod in defectum potentiae non vergit. Dico autem in se aliquid esse: quia conjunctio affirmationis et negationis nihil est, nec aliquem intellectum generat quod dicitur homo et non homo simul acceptum, quasi in vi unius dictionis: et ideo potentia Dei ad hoc se non extendit, ut affirmatio et negatio sint simul: et eadem ratio est de omnibus quae contradictionem includunt." *III Sent.,* d. 1, q. 2, a. 3.

41. "Nihil autem opponitur rationi entis nisi non ens. Hoc igitur repugnat rationi possibilis absoluti, quod subditur divinae omnipotentiae, quod implicat in se esse et non esse simul; hoc enim omnipotentiae non subditur, non propter defectum divinae potentiae, sed quia non potest habere rationem factibilis, neque possibilis. Quaecumque igitur contradictionem implicant, sub divina omnipotentia non continentur, quia non possunt habere possibilium rationem." *Sum. Th.,* I, q. 25, a. 2.

creation. Having discussed the nature of possibility and impossibility in relation to habitude of terms and to the omnipotence of God, we conclude that only possible essences are capable of being actualized, and that to these alone the efficient causality of God applies. We shall now proceed to show that possibility was the sole prerequisite for the coming to be of beings *per se*. The notion of possibility here includes even the notion of efficient causality, for that is implied in the notion of extrinsic possibility which is possibility in relation to some extrinsic power.

CHAPTER TWO

Production from Nothing

1. CREATION

"Just as when nature brings something out from its opposite, ... so is it necessary that absolute existence which is the proper effect of God, emanate from absolute non-existence; and this is the other extreme of contradiction. ... The proper causality of God reaches the extremes of the opposition of contradiction, which are outside any genus; consequently the divine action necessarily does not presuppose anything; and this action is creation, which is not of the genus of change, since it does not have some subject as the principle of its change; change always occurs in a changeable thing as in a subject. Hence it is that this action is God's alone, and is communicated to no creature. For the action of a thing does not exceed the principles by which it acts. Now everything created is in a genus. Whence it is impossible for a creature to have that which is not in a genus as the subject of its action. Of this sort, however, are existence and non-existence which are the extremes of contradiction and of creation. And therefore no creature can create."[1]

Thus in the opening paragraph of the fourth chapter of *De Quatuor Oppositis,* Saint Thomas sets forth his doctrine concerning creation:

1. "Sicut ergo cum per naturam fit aliquid ex suo opposito ... ita necesse est esse simpliciter quod est proprius Dei effectus, emanare ex non esse simpliciter; et hoc est alterum extremum contradictionis; non quod ipsum non esse necesse sit duratione praecedere ipsum esse, sed natura tantum. Propria ergo causalitas Dei attingit extrema contradictionis, quae extra genus sunt: et ideo actio sua nihil supponit necessario: et haec actio est creatio, quae non est de genere motuum, cum non habeat aliquod subjectum tanquam principium motus sui: motus autem semper est in mobili ut in subjecto. Inde est quod haec actio sua solummodo est, et nulli creaturae communicatur. Actio enim rei non excedit principia ipsius per quae agit. Omnia autem res creata in genere est. Unde impossibile est creaturam ad id quod non est in genere attingere tanquam subjectum suae actionis. Hujusmodi autem sunt esse et non esse, quae sunt extrema contradictionis et creationis. Et ideo nulla creatura creare potest." *De Quat. Op.,* c. 4.

1. Creation is the production of a thing in its whole being from absolute non-existence. 2. It presupposes no pre-existing passively potential subject, such as *materia prima*.² 3. It is not a change or movement (except metaphorically, as he shows elsewhere). 4. God alone is capable of giving absolute existence. 5. No creature can create. Completing the picture from other passages in Saint Thomas, we note further that: 6. Through creation all things together come to participate in the Divine existence; and 7. Productivity presupposes productibility and so possibility of existing is a prerequisite for the act of creation. In *De Potentia* Saint Thomas gives a concise explanation of what he considers to be the nature of the possibility which is antecedent to creation. It is not due, he says, to some pre-existing matter in potency, but rather it is founded in the non-repugnance between the terms themselves: *Quia non erat repugnantia inter praedicatum enuntiabilis et subjectum.* We have, therefore, number 8: The possibility of any created thing depends radically upon the non-repugnance of the essential notes constituting its essence.

Creatio est productio rei ex nihilo sui.... We shall discuss these characteristics of the act of creation to see what light they throw on the antecedents of being. First: Creation is the production of a thing in its whole substance.³ Things come to be in several ways. A universe can be brought into existence from non-existence; an animal can come to be from another animal; an oak can come to be from an acorn; air can come to be heated by fire. Only the first kind of coming to be is an instance of creation, for only in the first instance is something brought into being in its whole substance from nothing. By creation substantial beings are given existence with all their principles concreated with

---

2. In *De Potentia* Saint Thomas says: "Antequam mundus esset, possibile erat mundum esse; non tamen oportet quod aliqua materia aliquid aliquando dici possibile, non secundum aliquam potentiam, sed quia in terminus ipsius enuntiabilis non est aliqua repugnantia, secundum quod possibile opponitur impossibili. Sic ergo dicitur, antequam mundus esset, possibile mundum fieri, quia non erat repugnantia inter praedicatum enuntiabilis et subjectum. Vel potest dici, quod erat possibile propter potentiam activam agentis, non propter aliquam potentiam passivam materiae." *De Pot.*, q. 3, a. 1, *ad* 2. Cf. also *Con. Gen.*, l. II, c. 37; *Sum. Th.*, I, q. 25, a. 3; — I, q. 46, a. 1. *ad* 1.

3. Cf. *Sum. Th.*, I, q. 64, a. 3; — q. 104, a. 1; — I, q. 41, a. 3; *Con. Gen.*, l. II, c. 16; *De Pot.*, q. 10, a. 1, *ad* 3.

them; for example, their form, their matter (in material substances), their proximate and remote principles of activity, their finality, *et cetera*, come into being simultaneously with their being. Armed warriors spring up, as it were, endowed with being *in actu*, at the will of a Divine Cause.[4] The self-subsisting thing is the creature; the act by which it is given existence is creation.

Being is most fundamentally inherent in all things, and since existence is the first act of being, it may be well to pause here to question, with Saint Thomas, whether the term of creation be *the existence of the thing created* or *the thing which exists*. This opens up immediately the question of creation as a relation.[5] Creation actively considered, that is, on the part of God, is the divine action; passively considered, that is, on the part of creatures, is the reception of existence,[6] an increase of beings by which God's Infinite Being, potentially imitable in finite perfections, is made actually so in a multiplicity of beings. Creation is simply a pure relation. It is an act of God, the Eternal Cause. The effect is the world in *esse*, not in *fieri*.

Considering creation on the part of creatures, it is a relation insofar as the creatures are referred to God as to the principle upon which they essentially depend.[7] Now relation is a predicamental accident whose essence it is that it subsist not in itself but in another as in its subject. In what subject, then, does the relation which is creation inhere? Is exist-

4. "Omnia quae a Deo sunt facta dicuntur esse Dei creaturae. Creatio autem terminatur ad esse: prima enim rerum creatarum est esse, ut habetur in lib. De Causis." *De Pot.*, q. 3, a. 5, *ad* 2. "Creatio non dicit constitutionem rei compositae ex principiis praeexistentibus: sed compositum sic dicitur creari, quod simul cum omnibus suis principiis in esse producitur." *Sum. Th.*, I, q. 45, a. 4, *ad* 2. For Saint Thomas' contrast of the actions of a natural with those of a Divine Agent, cf. *De Pot.*, q. 3, a. 1, c. *post meo*.

5. "In creatione non importatur aliquis accessus ad esse, nec transmutatio a creante, sed solummodo inceptio essendi, et relatio ad creatorem a quo esse habet; et sic creatio nihil est aliud realiter quam relatio quaedam ad Deum cum novitate essendi." *De Pot.*, q. 3, a. 3. Cf. *Sum. Th.*, I, q. 45, a. 3.

6. "Creatio non est factio quae sit mutatio proprie loquendo, sed est quaedam acceptio esse." *II Sent.*, d. 1, a. 2, *ad resp.*

7. "Creatio ponit aliquid in creato secundum relationem tantum; quia quod creatur non fit per motum vel per mutationem. Quod enim fit per motum vel mutationem, fit ex aliquo praeexistente. Quod quidem contingit in productionibus particularibus aliquorum entium." *Sum. Th.*, I, q. 45, a. 3.

ence itself the subject of creation, or the creature which exists? The essence of accidents, as we said, is to inhere in another; the essence of substance is self-subsistence. Indeed, substance is defined by Saint Thomas as that whose essence demands that it subsist in itself and not in another. Setting to work with this principle, our conclusion is evident. If creation is a relation which is an accident and therefore not self-subsistent, then creation requires a substance in which to inhere, since the term of creation is the coming to be of substance, not accident.[8] The subject of creation must be something subsisting, something which exists *per se*, and this is the *compositum*, not its essence alone, nor its existence alone, but the whole substance, the thing which is created. Hence creation has for its subject the creature itself which exists. This, however, could not be unless the creature really had existence, since existence is the first act of things created;[9] therefore, in a thing having existence the relation pertains to the very existence of the thing which exists, through which the thing is referred to God.[10]

In generation the case is different. Through generation a thing participates not in the existence, but in the nature of the one generating. Hence a man who generates a man does not share his existence but his nature; the nature is common to both, their existences are distinctly each individual's own.[11] Whereas in creation, the nature of the Creator

---

8. "Si vero nomen creaturae accipiamus magis stricte pro eo tantum quod subsistit (quod proprie fit et creatur, sicut proprie habet esse), tunc relatio praedicta non est quoddam creatum, sed concreatum, sicut nec est ens proprie loquendo, sed inhaerens. Et simile est de omnibus accidentibus." *De Pot.*, q. 3, a. 3, *ad* 2.

9. "Esse enim est prima rerum creaturarum, secundum auctorem lib. *De Causis*: non quod creatio sit ut in subjecto in ipse esse, cum creatio passiva sit accidens, cujus est habere subjectum; sed ut in subjecto est in ipsa creatura." *De Quat. Op.*, c. 4.

10. Saint Thomas is careful to explain the meaning in which "being" is to be understood. In the *Summa Theologica* he says: "Ad primum ergo dicendum, quod cum dicitur 'Prima rerum creaturarum est esse,' 'esse' non importat substantiam creatam sed importat propriam rationem objecti creationis. Nam ex eo dicitur aliquid creatum quod est ens, non ex eo quod est hoc ens, cum creatio sit emanatio totius esse ab ente universali." *Sum. Th.*, I, q. 45, a. 4, *ad* 1.

11. "In generatione vero non ducitur generatum ipsum ad participandum esse generantis, sed ad participandum naturam ejus: aliter, cum esse sit suppositi, in tali natura foret participatio in supposito, et sic Socrates generaret

is not common with but absolutely distinct from the nature of the creature, but the latter participates as much as is possible for it, in the Divine existence.

We have viewed creation as a relation, first, between the things themselves, namely, the terms God and creature; and second, as a participation by finite beings in the existence of the Infinite Being. In the first sense, the term of creation is the thing itself which exists; in the second, it is the existence itself of the thing which exists, and ultimately in the thing itself through its existence. Creation, therefore, is the act by which God produces the entire subsisting thing together with its principles from which the thing has its existence, and this is the object of creation.[12]

Creatio est productio rei ex nihilo sui et subjecti. Creation, as the emanation of a whole substance, implies that the thing itself did not exist before; that there is nothing which now is in a different state than it was before; that there was no pre-existing matter out of which some new thing was fashioned. This issue of whether something or nothing is presupposed has decided relevance to our focal question, namely: What are the antecedents of being? Anterior to creation, the thing itself did not exist. It is not before it is produced. The created

---

Socratem: ideo in generatione Socrates non generat Socratem, cum suppositum non habeat nisi unum esse incommunicabile, sed homo generat hominem: natura enim manet una secundum rationem naturae, cum definitio sit una. Deus vero non creat Deum: Deus enim nomen naturae est, sicut homo: ens tamen creat ens; ideo relatio creaturae ad Deum fundatur super esse creaturae." *De Quat. Op.*, c. 4. Cf. *Con. Gen.*, l. II, cc. 11, 12.

12. "Actio Dei qua producit totam rem simul constitutam ex suis principiis, ad ipsum esse terminatur quod est intimum est maxime formale in re, cum in ipso esse rei salvetur alterum extremum relationis, ut dictum est. Ex dictis ergo manifestum est quod actio Deo, quae dicitur creatio, totam rem producit simul cum principiis suis, ex quibus res constituitur in esse suo quod est objectum creationis, ut dictum est." *De Quat. Op.*, c. 4.

That creation terminates in the existence of the thing created and in the thing through its existence is found expressed by Saint Thomas repeatedly. Besides the opusculum mentioned, cf. *Sum. Th.*, I, q. 44, a. 1; — I, q. 45, a. 3, *ad* 2; — *ad* 3; *Con. Gen.*, l. II, c. 18; *De Pot.*, q. 3, a. 16, *ad* 21; — q. 3, a. 3, *ad* 3; — q. 10, a. 1, *ad* 3; *II Sent.*, d. 1, q. 1, a. 2, *ad* 4.

thing is not a transformed antecedently existing thing having some being before and having being otherwise after creation. For if it had previous being, whence would be the origin of the supposed antecedent of being? Ultimately, even if we postulated a series of previous beings *ad infinitum,* the answer would be creation.

What then did pre-exist creation? Certainly no material principle, for that would necessitate a previous production by which the matter would be created; in which process not even the production of the matter could strictly be called creation, for creation is not the production of a principle alone, as the material or the formal principle, but it is the production of a substance with all its principles, and this includes the material principle in question. Principles are concreated with the creation of the substance.[13] The act of creation would offer no explanation for the origin of things if there were any pre-existing subject independent of the creative act.

Ex nihilo, nihil fit. True, Saint Thomas says, for finite productions, but creation is the effect of an Infinite Being, since creation "is the cause of the being of the creatures, whereas other causes are causes of the becoming of the effect only."[14] That from nothing, nothing comes, is concerned only with finite beings, not with the emanation of beings from the Universal Principle of all beings.[15] To say that creation does not presuppose matter is to repeat the definition of creation, namely, *Creatio est productio rei ex nihilo sui et subjecti,* which is to put in another way the statement that creation, which is the production of existence, emanates from absolute non-existence. References to this

---

13. "Accidentia et formae, sicut per se non sunt, ita nec per se creantur, quum creatio sit productio entis; sed, sicut in alio sunt, ita in aliis creatis creantur." *Con. Gen.,* l. II, c. 18. Cf. *Sum. Th.,* I, q. 45, a. 8.

14. For distinction between the cause of the being of a thing and the cause of the becoming of a thing, cf. *Sum. Th.,* I, q. 104, a. 1.

15. "Antiqui philosophi, sicut supra dictum est, non consideraverunt nisi emanationem effectuum particularium a causis particularibus, quas necesse est praesupponere aliquid in sua actione; et secundum hoc erat eorum communis opinio 'ex nihilo nihil fieret.' Sed tamen hoc locum non habet in prima emanatione ab universali rerum principio." *Sum. Th.,* I, q. 45, a. 2, *ad* 1.

abound in the works of Saint Thomas. We cite one of his many arguments concerning this point, as he has it in the *Contra Gentiles:*

> For if a thing is an effect of God, either something exists before it or not. If not, our point is proved, namely that God produces an effect from no pre-existing thing. If, however, something exist before it, we must either go on to infinity — which is impossible in natural causes, as the Philosopher proves (II *Metaph.*) — or we must come to some first thing that presupposes no other. And this can only be God. For it was shown in the First Book (C. XVII), that He is not the matter of anything, nor can there be anything other than God the being of which is not caused by God, as we have proved (C. XV). It follows therefore that God in producing His effects requires no prejacent matter out of which to produce His work.[16]

Finally, creation is not a movement, strictly speaking, for movement requires passive potentiality, which is matter.[17] For movement is movement of the *modes* of being rather than of being itself, hence not even substantial becoming is properly a movement. Movement, further, is said to be "the act of anything existing in potency,"[18] and this presupposes an existing subject, a starting point, a *terminus a quo;* but creation is not such, but the production of a thing in its whole substance. Creation is metaphorically considered a movement, but that is due to the human mind, which attributes to an Infinite Being a power patterned after its own. But, Saint Thomas says, the term movement

---

16. "Si enim est aliquid effectus Dei, aut praeexistit aliquid illi, aut non. Si non, habetur propositum, scilicet quod Deus aliquem effectum producat ex nullo praeexistente. Si autem aliquid illi praeexistit, aut est procedere in infinitum, quod non est possibile in causis materialibus, ut Philosophus probat (*Metaph.*, II); aut erit devenire ad aliquod primum quod aliud non praesupponit; quod quidem non potest esse ipse Deus. Ostensum est enim (I, 17) quod ipse non est materia alicujus rei, nec potest esse aliud a Deo, cui Deus non sit causa essendi, ut ostensum est (c. 15). Relinquitur igitur quod Deus, in productione sui effectus, non requirit materiam praejacentem ex qua operetur." *Con. Gen.*, l. II, c. 16, No. 1. Cf. also *Con. Gen.*, l. II, cc. 18; 21; 22; 40, ff; 85; *ibid.*, l. III, c. 66; *De Pot.*, qq. 3, 4, *passim;* — q. 10, a. 1, *ad* 3; *II Sent.*, d. 1, q. 1, a. 3, *ad* 5.

17. Cf. *Con. Gen.*, l. II, c. 37.

18. *In III Phys.*, 1, *lect.* 5.

when applied to creation can be no other than a metaphor, inasmuch as the created thing is conceived of as having being after non-being.[19]

Since creation is the production of a substance with all its principles, without pre-existing matter, without any change or movement of passive potentiality, it follows that the explanation of existence must be sought elsewhere. According to the law of sufficient reason, everything that exists has a sufficient reason for its existence, and this principle is based directly on the principle of identity. Creation is a fact. Beings exist. What is their sufficient reason? What does their existence presuppose? Neither in material things nor in finite agents can be found the sufficient reason for existence as such. It must be in the action that is God's alone that we find the *raison d'être* of all beings. There are at least three texts in Saint Thomas, among many of the same nature, that are almost identical in their wording concerning the prerequisites of existence as such. They are found in the *Summa Theologica,* in the *Contra Gentiles,* and in *De Potentia.*[20] We shall quote in full the first reference; later we shall meet the second. A reference to the third text has already been made.[21]

> Before the world existed it was possible for it to be, not indeed according to a passive power which is matter, but according to the active power of God; and also according as a thing is called absolutely possible, not in relation to any power, but from the sole habitude of terms which are not repugnant to each other; in which sense the possible is opposed to the impossible, as appears from the Philosopher, *Meta.* V.[22]

Our conclusion must be that finite being includes in its nature an *antecedent possibility of being.* The only prerequisite for creation consists in possibility, both absolute and relative possibility which, resolved into terms of causality, may be stated as efficient (which implies final) and exemplary causes. "Deitas dicitur esse omnium effective, et exemplariter non autem per essentiam."[23]

19. Cf. *Con. Gen.,* l. II, c. 37.
20. *Sum. Th.,* I, q. 46, a. 1, *ad* 1; *Con. Gen.,* l. II, c. 37; *De Pot.,* q. 3, a. 1, *ad* 3.
21. Cf. *infra,* ch. 2, p. 36, footnote 2.
22. *Sum. Th.,* I, q. 46, a. 1, *ad* 1.
23. *Sum. Th.,* I, q. 3, a. 8, *ad* 1.

2. POSSIBILITY IN TERMS OF CAUSALITY

Efficient Cause. Saint Thomas defines a principle as "id a quo aliquid procedit quocumque modo."[24] Such procession, while having an intrinsic connection with the effect, does not necessarily have to produce a positive influence upon the effect. The process of substantial becoming proceeds from a privation of the form which is the term of the movement; the privation is a necessary and natural antecedent, but it does not exert a positive influence upon the generation of the new form. In other words, a principle is not necessarily a cause. When, however, the procession involves a real and positive influence of the principle on that which proceeds from it, then we have a cause. A cause is a principle, for it is that from which something proceeds, but it carries with it a distinguishing note which limits the principle that is a cause; that distinguishing note is "with dependence." The cause exerts a positive influence upon the generation of the new form and so there is established a relation of dependence.

Now the efficient cause of anything is that extrinsic principle which by its action produces an effect distinct from itself. That perfection or actuality by which an agent acts constitutes his active power. The scope of an agent's causality is in direct proportion to its measure of actuality, or in other words, it is an index to the agent's place in the scale of reality. The more perfect the grade of being, the higher and more perfect will be the effects achieved by the operation of its powers. Man's powers exceed those of brutes; an angel's power exceeds that of man; God's power is infinite. In this proportion will be the effects produced by the respective capacities for action.

We state that God is the efficient cause of creation. More than that, we assert that He is the sole efficient cause. Before considering the arguments advanced by the Angelic Doctor in proof of the above thesis, we shall set forth very succinctly the basic essential notes of efficient causality, either finite or infinite. There must be, as essential characteristics of efficient causality, a positive efficient influence (thus distinguishing principle from cause) on the part of the agent, the origin

---

24. *Sum. Th.*, I, q. 33, a. 1.

or production of a new actual being, with a relation of real dependence of the effect on the agent.[25]

Saint Thomas repeatedly makes the statement that God, Who is Being by His whole substance, is the sole cause of being *simpliciter*, and he advances very fundamental principles upon which his conclusion is based. In the treatise *De Homine*[26] the Angelic Doctor sets forth several principles by which he accounts for basic psychological phenomena in man. These principles can be put to work in the present problem with regard to the activity of the Infinite Agent. Though Saint Thomas offers various proofs for the existence of a single Infinite Agent, they can all be reduced to several substantial ones which in turn are rooted in a single principle which assumes various guises in different situations. The single principle which we say assumes various guises in his work, is found in his treatment of Man. We are going to apply it here to the problem of creation. In the form most frequently expressed by Saint Thomas the principle is *operari sequitur esse*:[27] the nature of one's operations follows from the nature of his being. It means simply that the ability of an agent is more or less perfect according to the degree of perfection in its essence; or again, there must be due proportion between the nature of an agent and the method of his operation. A careful sifting of the reasons Saint Thomas advanced for the necessity of a Divine Agent in the production of the universe can be summed up thus:[28]

1. The more universal effects must be reduced to the more universal and prior causes, since effects correspond proportionately to their causes. Now among all effects, the most universal one is being itself, existence, and hence it must be the proper effect of the first and most universal cause. *Omnis agens agit simile sibi.*[29]

2. Greater power is required in an agent in proportion to the dis-

---

25. "Remoto actu, actio nihil aliud importat quam ordinem originis secundum quod a causa aliqua procedit." *Sum. Th.*, I, q. 41, a. 1, *ad* 2.
26. *Sum. Th.*, I, qq. 75-102.
27. *Sum. Th.*, I, q. 75 throughout. *Ibid.*, I, q. 89, a. 1; *I Sent.*, d. 5, q. 3, a. 1, *ad* 1; *In I Metaph.*, *lect.* 1.
28. For complete arguments, cf. *Sum. Th.*, I, q. 45, a. 4; *Con. Gen.*, l. II, cc. 15; 16; 20; 21.
29. *Con. Gen.*, l. II, c. 21.

tance of the potentiality from the act. The power to actualize is so much the greater according as it is able to bring into act a potentiality more distant from act. Since the power of that agent must be infinite who produces something from no presupposed potentiality, it follows that only an Infinite Being can be the efficient cause of creation. *Qualis est operatio talis est natura.*[30]

3. The order of actions is according to the order of agents, since the more excellent the agent, the more excellent the actions. Now creation presupposes no other action; therefore the first action must be proper to the first agent Who is God alone. *Operari sequitur esse.*[31]

4. Since agent and effect must be like each other, only an agent which acts by its entire substance can produce the whole substance of an effect. But God is being by His whole substance; therefore the proper mode of His action is to produce a whole subsistent thing. *Modus operandi sequitur modum essendi.*[32]

5. What is essentially being is the cause of all that have being by participation. God is being by His essence, which means He is being by His whole substance; therefore it is the proper mode of His action to produce a whole subsistent thing; hence He is the cause of being to all other things. *Omne agens agit simili sibi.*[33]

Summing up the central note in the Thomistic proofs for a Divine Creator, we may say that from Being *per se* alone can come beings *per se* as such by participation, and this is to be being *per se*, it is true, but nevertheless *ab alio*. This sharply distinguishes the *per-seity* of contingent beings from the *per-seity* of the Necessary Being. The former may be termed *per-seity ab alio* while the latter is strictly *a-seity*.[34]

30. *Ibid.*, c. 20.
31. *Ibid.*, c. 21.
32. *Ibid.*, c. 20.
33. *Ibid.*, c. 16.
34. *Ibid.*, c. 21. An analysis of the term "being *per se*" and its analogous use in reference to God and creatures would not, it seems, be out of place here. "Being" as used here is that which is not nothing; it is something existent and it is predicated analogously of the Infinite and the finite. "*Per se*" expresses its mode of being. It is being whose essence requires that it does not exist in another. This, likewise, can be predicated of all substantial beings. There is a world of difference, however, when the origin of "*per se* beings" is investigated. In the Infinite Being an added perfection, as it were, accrues to

In his distinction between substantial and accidental becoming on the one hand, and the being *per se* which results from God's creative action, Saint Thomas makes use of the illustration of the generation of a man. In substantial becoming within the power of natural agents, the contrarieties of form and privation of form are resolved into contradictories, and so we have man and not-man. From not-man, man *per se* is made, and this is effected through, first, the intrinsic principle of matter and form uniting to make the *compositum;* and second, the actualization of the *compositum* by the *actus* existence which stands to the *compositum* as act to potency. A man is constituted *per se* since he is generated from not-man. A being is made, also; but not a being *per se*, since it is not made from not-being, but because a being already existed previously, a new being is made only *per accidens*. The reason for this is found in the set of contraries upon which the making was based. The contrary forms are being *in potentia* and being *in actu*. These are contraries which are not resolved into contradictories; each is something and they exist in the same genus. There is in this case no substantial being, but only being accidentally produced, since there was a transmutation from being to being, so that the new being is nothing more than being accidentally. Summarily, we say that as man he was made from not-man and this is by way of contradictories and so he was made man *per se;* as a being he was made from a being *in potentia* to be a being *in actu*, and this is by way of alteration through contraries, and thus was he made a being *per accidens*. Applying this to creation, the Angelic Doctor points out that when a thing is made from not-being simply, a being is made *per se*. But it belongs to that alone which is *per se* Being to do this, since other things are causes of being accidentally, and of this particular being *per se*. This must be necessarily so, since effects are referred to their proportionate causes. Being *per se* and *a se* is the sole cause of beings *per se ab alio*.

His *per-seity* by reason of His origin, or more strictly, His lack of origin. This characteristic note, found only in the Divine Being, makes Him the unique *per se* being, and this is expressed by the term "*a se.*" Contingent beings, on the contrary, if substances, are *per se* beings, but they depend for their origin upon another, hence they are "*per se* beings, *ab alio.*" Thus the *a-seity* of God is distinguished from the *per-seity* common to all substances, and from the *per-seity in alio* which is characteristic of all contingent beings.

Final Cause. Omnis agens agit proper finem. This is a Scholastic axiom in which we find the reason of the purposiveness manifest in the world. In the classes of causes, the end of an action corresponds to the final cause; it is the goal of action, that which moves the agent to act. The end as realizable, not as realized, discharges its function and exerts its influence as final cause. It is first in intention, last in execution. The final end is rightly called a cause because it actually flows into and positively influences the production of the effect. Brought to bear on our present problem, namely, to determine the antecedents of creation, the final cause merely throws further light upon the nature and activity of the efficient cause and the effects of His action. God, acting, produces an act. The end, that is, the act produced, is the cause of His action by way of finality; otherwise without a goal in mind, there would be no cause for acting. Now God's action terminates in creation. Therefore the final cause, creation as realizable, prompts the activity of the efficient cause, and as realized, brings the action to rest. If efficient causality is a prerequisite for creation, so, by implication, is final causality. "Now the origin of beings from the first being is by an action directed toward an end; since it is according to intellect, as we have proved: and every agent acts for an end."[35]

Exemplary Cause. The problem of exemplary causality in creation resolves itself into the problem of the ultimate basis of the possibles. The problem has a twofold major aspect: first, What is the ultimate source of the extrinsic possibility of all contingent realities? second, What is the ultimate source of the intrinsic possibility of all contingent realities? The first we have already disposed of as far as we think it necessary in this work. We have placed the ultimate source of extrinsic possibility of created beings fairly in the Omnipotence of God. The answer was based upon Saint Thomas' statement that "before a thing was, it was possible for it to be, through the power of the agent, by which power also it began to be...."[36]

35. "Processus autem entium a primo ente, est per actionem ordinatam ad finem, quum sit per intellectum, ut ostensum est (c. 23); intellectus autem hominis propter finem agit. Si igitur, in productione rerum, sunt aliquae causae secundae, oportet quod fines earum et actiones sint propter finem causae primae, qui est ultimus finis in rebus causatis." *Con. Gen.,* l. II, c. 42; l. III, c. 2.

36. "Possibile autem fuit ens creatum esse antequam esset, per potentiam agentis per quam et esse incepit." *Con. Gen.,* l. II, c. 37, No. 3.

Since the Divine Omnipotence presupposes the intrinsic possibility of all possible things, it remains for us now to examine the question from that point of view. The exemplary cause of anything may be said to be the ideal image-cause which is in the mind of the efficient cause, according to which he produces his effects. Possibility, as a prerequisite for creation, implies the existence in the agent of archetypal ideas whose objects are real essences possible of being actualized objectively. It is necessary that the existence of possible essences be precontained in some way in that existing agent which is the real basis of their possibility, otherwise there would be no sufficient reason for the possibility, and hence the agent could not be the real basis of the possibility. An acorn does not produce a bird because there is nothing like a bird nor the rudiments of a bird in an acorn; the possible bird is not precontained in the acorn, therefore the latter is not the basis of the possibility of a bird. An acorn does produce an oak because in the acorn there is precontained in some way the essence and existence of a possible oak, and further, it has the natural power of actualizing the potential oak. The analogy, of course, is not perfect.

The possible essence and existence of the oak are not precontained formally and actually, otherwise no being could be the sufficient reason for the internal possibility of an essence which was not on an exact level with its own. A circle would be the sufficient reason for the possibility of the essence of a circle; a man would be the sufficient reason for the internal possibility of the essential notes of humanity; God would be the sufficient reason for His own essence and for no other. The possible essence pre-exists only virtually or ideally in its sufficient reason, and hence a being can be the sufficient reason of a possible essence on a level other than its own; e. g., God can be the sufficient reason of the possible essences of all reality. We propose to show that the ideally pre-existing possible essences in God's mind are the exemplars and types of all creation and hence constitute the exemplary cause of things.

Since it has already been shown that God alone is the efficient cause of the being of finite beings, our examination into the source of intrinsic possibility is immediately restricted to the Infinite Being alone.

Creation 49

By way of introducing the question we quote here directly from Saint Thomas' treatment of Creation in the *Summa Theologica:*

> God is the first exemplar cause of all things. In proof whereof we must consider that if for the production of anything an exemplar is necessary, it is in order that the effect may receive a determinate form.... Now it is manifest that things made by nature receive determinate forms. This determination of forms must be reduced to the Divine Wisdom as its first principle, for Divine Wisdom devised the order of the universe, which order consists in the variety of things. And therefore we must say that in the Divine Wisdom are the types of all things, which types we have called ideas; i. e., exemplar forms existing in the Divine Mind (XVI). And these thoughts, though multiplied by their relations to things, in reality are not apart from the Divine essence, according as the likeness to that essence can be shared diversely for different things. In this manner God Himself is the first exemplar of all things.[37]

From the foregoing, it can easily be seen that the human mind as the ultimate basis of the possibility of things, is excluded. The mind is not conscious of having "made," that is, constructed, the sum total of constitutive notes, but rather of discovering their mutual sociability. What we know as possible is possible not due to our own minds, but to the Being Who is Himself outside the field of possibility. In answer-

---

37. "Deus est prima causa exemplaris omnium rerum, ad cujus evidentiam considerandum est quod ad productionem alicujus rei ideo necessarium est exemplar, ut effectus determinatam formam consequatur. Artifex enim producit determinatam formam in materia propter exemplar ad quod inspicit, sive illud sit exemplar ad quod extra intuetur, sive sit exemplar interius mente conceptum. Manifestum est autem quod ea quae naturaliter fiunt, determinatas formas consequuntur. Haec autem formarum determinatio oportet quod reducatur, sicut in primum principium, in divinam sapientiam, quae ordinem universi excogitavit, qui in rerum distinctione consistit. Et ideo oportet dicere quod in divina sapientia sit rationes omnium rerum, quas supra diximus ideas, id est, formas exemplares in mente divina existentes. Quae quidem, licet multiplicentur secundum respectum ad res, tamen non sunt realiter aliud a divina essentia, prout ejus similitudo a diversis participari potest diversimode. Sic igitur ipse Deus est primum exemplar omnium. Possunt etiam in rebus creatis quaedam aliorum exemplaria dici secundum quod quaedam sunt ad similitudinem aliorum vel secundum eamdem speciem, vel secundum analogiam alicujus imitationis." *Sum. Th.,* I, q. 44, a. 3.

ing the objection that exemplar causes exist outside of God, Saint Thomas quoting Saint Augustine, says: "The exemplar is the same as the idea. But ideas, according to Augustine, are the master forms which are contained in the Divine intelligence. Therefore the exemplars of things are not outside of God."[38] Further, we exclude agreement or disagreement of notes as the ultimate basis of possibility, since possibility of being is not mere relationship of notes but a relationship much more basic — namely, the relation to being, to the absolutely real, to the Being of God.

The intrinsic possibility of things is founded ultimately in God. Logically we can distinguish between God's free will, His omnipotence, His intellect and His essence. Is intrinsic possibility founded upon God's free will? Are things possible because God wills to make them possible? Were we to hold to this, then possibility would be relative rather than absolute; for if some things are possible because God wills them, then others are impossible because God does not will them. This would imply that God could have willed the impossible to exist. But God could not will that a cube be a circle. No will, not even the Divine Will, can change reality. The Divine Will has full play in things that could be but are not; such, for example, as in the production of another man, but not even the will of God can make a triangular circle.

Neither is the Divine Omnipotence the ultimate source of intrinsic possibility. For if a being were said to be possible because God can make it, then a thing is impossible only because God cannot make it; hence either all combinations of notes would be sociable and therefore possible essences, or the ultimate reason of the impossibilities of things would be due to limitation of Divine Power, and lack of power in an Infinite Being is absurd. The non-incompatibility of notes does not depend upon God's power; it is not the term of God's operation. His effect is to produce, not to make only producible. The ultimate source of extrinsic possibility is the Divine Omnipotence, but it presupposes intrinsic possibility which is founded ultimately and formally elsewhere as we shall see, and virtually in the Divine Omnipotence which may at any time give them actual existence.

---

38. *Ibid., sed contra.*

What, then, is the ultimate basis of intrinsic possibility? The question has been variously answered among Scholastic writers. Some hold that the ultimate basis of intrinsic possibility is something constituted by an act of the Divine Intellect. The argument runs thus: The Divine Intellect, contemplating the Divine Essence, understands it to be imitable without limit *ad extra*. This act of understanding grounds the intrinsic possibility of essences in the Divine Intellect which would give ideal being to the intrinsically possible essences, and in addition, would make the essences formally possible, as distinct from their virtual possibility in the Divine Essence.

Others, on the contrary, hold that possible essences, though having ideal being in the Divine Intellect, nevertheless derive their intrinsic possibility from the Divine Essence itself. The defenders of this position base their argument, in part, on an analogy with human knowledge. An intrinsically possible essence, to be understood, must be intelligible, and in order to be intelligible, it must be intrinsically possible. Therefore, antecedently to the act by which the Divine Mind understands the Divine Essence as being imitable *ad extra*, they are already possible imitations of the Divine Essence itself.

Possible essences are ultimately founded in God, but whether this foundation is the Divine Intellect which, by its act, confers ideal being and formal possibility upon essences antecedently only virtually possible in the Divine Essence, or whether, antecedent to the act of the Divine Knowledge essences are intrinsically possible imitations of that essence and thereby intrinsically possible, is as we have seen, a disputed point. That intrinsically possible essences have ideal being in the mind of God is granted by all Scholastics. In the Divine Intellect are found the prototypal ideas according to which the Divine Will by the act of creation, wills to actualize extramentally the ideally existing intrinsically possible essence. The question to be considered here is, can we assert of God, Who is simplicity itself, that His understanding rather than His essence, or vice versa, is the ultimate foundation of intrinsically possible essences? Is it not rather in the very Being of God Himself, for Saint Thomas tells us that God knows all things other than Himself in Himself.[39]

39. "Cum Deus sit ipsum esse, in tantum unumquodque est, in quantum participat de Dei similitudine; sicut unumquodque in tantum est calidum, in

We draw from Saint Thomas' tract on God, *De Deo Uno*, covering questions two to twenty-six of the first part of the *Summa Theologica*, and more especially from the question concerning the knowledge of God, for our solution of the question. First, is the Divine knowledge the ultimate source of intrinsically possible essences? It seems so, for Saint Thomas says: "The knowledge of God, joined to His will, is the cause of things.... Further, it is the knowledge of God not that they be, but that they be possible."[40] Again he writes: "... In the Divine Mind are the proper ideas of all things."[41] Further: "As the world was not made by chance but by God acting by His intellect, there must exist in the Divine Mind a form to the likeness of which the world was made."[42] Moreover: "Whatever effects exist in God, as in the First Cause, must be in His act of understanding, and all things must be in Him according to an intelligible mode: for everything which is in another, is in it according to the mode of that in which it is."[43] "The knowledge of God is the cause, not indeed of Himself, but of other things. He is actually the cause of some, that is, of things that come to be in some period of time; and He is virtually the cause of others, that is, of things which He can make, and which nevertheless are never made."[44]

quantum participat calorem. Sic et ea quae sunt in potentia, etiamsi non sunt in actu, cognoscuntur a Deo." *Sum. Th.*, I, q. 14, a. 9, *ad* 2. Cf. whole article.

40. "Scientia Dei est causa rerum voluntate adjuncta. Unde non oportet quod quaecumque scit Deus, sint vel fuerint vel futura sint; sed solum ea quae vult esse, vel permittere esse. Et iterum non est in scientia Dei quod illa sint, sed quod esse possint." *Sum. Th.*, I, q. 14, a. 9, *ad* 3.

41. "Sic igitur oportet quod in mente divina sint propriae rationes omnium rerum." *Sum. Th.*, I, q. 15, a. 2.

42. "Quia igitur mundus non est casu factus, sed est factus a Deo per intellectum agente, ut infra patebit, necesse est quod in mente divina sit forma, ad similitudinem cujus mundus est factus. Et in hoc consistit ratio ideae." *Sum Th.*, I, q. 15, a. 1.

43. "Unde quicumque effectus praeexistunt in Deo, sicut in causa prima, necesse est quod sint in ipso ejus intelligere, et quod omnia in eo sint secundum modum intelligibilem. Nam omne quod est in altero, est in eo secundum modum ejus in quo est." *Sum. Th.*, I, q. 14, a. 5.

44. "Ad primum ergo dicendum, quod scientia Dei est causa, non quidem sui ipsius, sed aliorum; quorumdam quidem actu, scilicet eorum quae secundum aliquod tempus fiunt; quorumdam vero virtute, scilicet eorum quae potest facere, et tamen nunquam fiunt. *Sum. Th.*, I, q. 14, a. 16, *ad* 1.

An intellect must be specified by that which will bring it into act. What specifies the Divine Intellect which cannot be said to be in potency to act, but actually to act? Saint Thomas says:

> ... The intellectual operation is specified by that intelligible form which makes the intellect in act. And this is the image of the principal thing understood, which in God is nothing but His own essence in which all images of things are apprehended. Hence it does not follow that the Divine Intellectual Act, or rather God Himself, is specified by anything else than the Divine Essence itself.[45]

The Divine Essence is for the Divine Intellect its intelligible species. Further, the Divine Intellect and its object (God Himself) are altogether the same: "In God, intellect, the object understood, the intelligible species, and His act of understanding are entirely one and the same."[46]

"Now in contemplating Himself, God sees all possible imitations of Himself, both according to being and to mode of being.... In the Divine Mind are the proper ideas of all things.... Inasmuch as He knows His own essence perfectly, He knows it according to every mode in which it can be known."[47] Further: "We say that God sees

---

45. "Ad tertium dicendum, quod ipsum intelligere non specificatur per id quod in alio intelligitur, sed per principale intellectum in quo alia intelliguntur. In tantum enim ipsum intelligere specificatur per objectum suum, in quantum forma intelligibilis est principium intellectualis operationis. Nam omnis operatio specificatur per formam quae est principium operationis, sicut calefactio per calorem. Unde per illam formam intelligibilem specificatur intellectualis operatio, quae facit intellectum in actu. Et haec est species principalis intellecti, quae in Deo nihil est alius quam essentia sua, in qua omnes species rerum comprehenduntur. Unde non oportet quod ipsum intelligere divinum, vel potius ipse Deus, specificetur per aliud quam per essentiam divinam." *Sum. Th.*, I, q. 14, a. 5, *ad* 3.

46. "Et sic patet ex omnibus praemissis quod in Deo intellectus intelligens, et id quod intelligitur, et species intelligibilis, et ipsum intelligere, sunt omnini unum et idem. *Sum. Th.*, I, q. 14, a. 4.

47. "Unde plures ideae sunt in mente divina ut intellectae ab ipsa, quod hoc modo potest videri; ipse enim essentiam suam perfecte cognoscit; unde cognoscit eam secundum omnem modum quo cognoscibilis est. Potest autem cognosci non solum secundum quod in se est, sed secundum quod est participabilis secundum aliquem modum similitudinis a creaturis." *Sum. Th.*, I, q. 15, a. 2.

Himself in Himself, because He sees Himself through His essence; and He sees other things not in themselves but in Himself; inasmuch as His essence contains the similitude of things other than Himself."[48] Here we have definitely the teaching that the "similitude of things," namely, possible essences, are contained, or more strictly, are radicated in the Divine Essence; hence through their presence there they are known to the Divine Intellect in its knowing the Divine Essence as the object of its contemplation. Again the Angelic Doctor says: "(Now) the species of the Divine Intellect, which is God's essence, suffices to represent all things. Hence by understanding His essence, God knows the essences of all things, and also whatever can be accidental to them."[49] Possible essences are definitely included here where Saint Thomas says: "The Divine Essence, whereby the Divine Intellect understands, is a sufficient likeness *of all things that are or can be,* not only as regards the universal principles, but also as regards the principles proper to each one."[50]

There seems to be no doubt that Saint Thomas places the ultimate intrinsic possibility of things in the Divine Essence, which he says, "can be taken as the proper ratio of each thing according to the diverse ways in which diverse creatures participate in and imitate it."[51] The Divine Essence is imitable even if not known, even if God had no intellect (which is absurd), but the imitations are not producible without the will of God. The Divine Essence is not imitated until the

---

48. "Sic igitur dicendum est, quod Deus seipsum videt in seipso, quia seipsum videt per essentiam suam; alia autem a se videt non in ipsis, sed in seipso, in quantum essentia sua continet similitudinem aliorum ab ipso." *Sum. Th.,* I, q. 14, a. 5.

49. "Sed species intellectus divini, scilicet ejus essentia, sufficit ad demonstrandum omnia. Unde intelligendo essentiam suam, cognoscit essentias omnium, et quaecumque eis accidere possunt." *Sum. Th.,* I, q. 14, a. 14.

50. "Essentia autem divina, per quam intellectus divinus intelligit, est similitudo sufficiens omnium quae sunt vel esse possunt, non solum quantum ad principia communia, sed etiam quantum ad principia propria uniuscujusque, ut ostensum est; unde sequitur quod scientia Dei se extendat ad infinita etiam secundum quod sunt ab invicem distincta." *Sum. Th.,* I, q. 14, a. 12.

51. "Sed divina essentia est aliquid excedens omnes creaturas. Unde potest accipi ut propria ratio uniuscujusque, secundum quod diversimode est participabilis vel imitabilis a diversis creaturis." *Sum. Th.,* I, q. 14, a. 6, *ad* 3.

Creation

Divine Intellect constitutes an imitation of it. The Divine Will has full play in things that could be but are not. Things that neither are nor can be are not possible even to God. The Divine Knowledge illumines the Divine Will by which God wills to actualize only those essences that He sees, from comprehending His own essence, to be intrinsically possible. The plan or exemplar according to which possible things are constituted intrinsically possible and real is the Divine Essence, the Uncreated Prototype and Exemplary Cause of all contingent beings.[52]

This we think fairly represents Saint Thomas' teaching on the intrinsic possibility of essences in their ultimate foundation. Our conclusion to this first portion of the present work amounts to this: Creation presupposes nothing other than the possibility of things, and so we have in possibility the first antecedent of beings. Whether it is the sole antecedent or not is a point for further study. The production of composite beings presupposes creation; and it is to this second type of production, namely generation of substances, that we turn our attention in the following part of this work.[53]

---

52. Cf. the entire article, *Sum. Th.*, I, q. 15, a. 2.
53. Cf. *infra*, p. 47, footnote 35.

CHAPTER THREE

GENERATION: *Ens in Fieri*

It is our aim to determine the antecedents of being. This task has led us to analyze the concepts of being and nothing to discover what is the non-being which in some way is being. Thus far we have examined the nature of the opposition between these two concepts and have seen that Saint Thomas insists that so great is the opposition between them that only by the creative act of God can being *simpliciter* be brought from non-being *simpliciter*. The effect of creation whereby God produces the whole thing possessing at once all its principles from which the thing has its very existence, is the production of existence itself primarily, and the thing through its existence. The antecedents of existence *per se* can be summed up in the word "possibility"; intrinsic, depending upon the internal relations of the very terms themselves; extrinsic, depending upon an agent capable of reducing the possible essence to actual existence. Later we shall substitute another term for "possibility." Creation, then, is a *via ad esse simpliciter* and its sole prerequisite, possibility.

1. THE NOTION OF *Fieri*

Fieri est via ad esse.[1] We now present an entirely different aspect of the problem. The problem of *fieri* which we initiate in this section is one of utmost importance in Thomistic metaphysics. Its importance accrues to it from the point of view of itself, in that it resolves the dilemma of being as the mobile *versus* being as the immobile, which problem confronted ancient thought previous to Aristotle. The problem of *fieri* is important as well in the doctrines that are involved in its understanding, namely, change, opposition, generation, alteration, matter and form, potency and act, substance and accident, and such metaphysical principles. These are so inextricably bound up with the proper

---

1. *Sum. Th.*, I, q. 90, a. 2.

understanding of the process of *fieri,* that no adequate explanation of the Thomistic doctrine can be given which does not take them intimately into consideration. The problem of *fieri* is therefore important because of its historical significance and because of the use it makes of the most fundamental principles in Thomistic metaphysics.

Our present concern is with the production of composite beings, which production presupposes creation. Composite beings "become"; that is, there is involved in their production a process whereby form gives way to form; something becomes other than it was before.[2] Here the opposition is not of absolute contradiction, as non-being is opposed to being, but it is of a lesser kind, as between two states of the same being, namely, between what "is" potentially, and what "is" or "can be" actually. In his commentary on the XII *Metaphysics* of Aristotle, Saint Thomas explains three ways in which non-being may be understood. First in his enumeration is the absolute non-being which is nothing: *quod nullo modo est.* He grants with Parmenides that from this absolute non-being, nothing can come, but he qualifies it so that he may provide for his theory, philosophically arrived at, of an omnipotent First Cause. He adds *secundum naturam* to the *ex nihilo nihil fit* formula. Privation is the second *non-ens,* a non-being considered in some subject. Generation *per accidens* flows from this principle inasmuch as all change starts from a privation of form. The third *non-ens* is potential being, and generation *per se* flows from this principle inasmuch as the new form is educed from the passive potentiality of the matter which is precisely this *non ens in potentia.*[3]

We pass without any additional comment the first interpretation of non-being, having disposed of the problem *ex nihil nihil fit secundum*

---

2. "Nam de ratione mutationis est quod aliquid idem se habet aliter nunc et prius." *Sum. Th.,* I, q. 45, a. 2, *ad* 2.

3. "Generatio sit transmutatio de non ente in ens, ex quo non ente in ens fit generatio. Dicitur enim non ens tripliciter. Uno modo quod nullo modo est; et ex tali non ente non fit generatio quia ex nihilo nihil fit secundum naturam. Alio modo dicitur non ens ipsa privatio, quae consideratur in aliquo subjecto: et ex tali non ente fit quidem generatio, sed per accidens, inquantum, scilicet generatio, sed per accidens, inquantum, scilicet generatio fit ex subjecto, sui accidit privatio. Tertio modo dicitur non ens ipsa materia, quae, quantum est de se, non est ens actu, sed ens potentia. Et ex tali non ente fit generatio

naturam in the first part of the present work. In this second section we shall take up the discussion of the *non ens . . . quae non est ens actu, sed ens potentia*, which will comprise the problems of generation and of alteration, species of the genus *fieri*. The non-being which is the object of our thought in this section is not the *nihil absolutum* but *relativa* concisely summed up by Aristotle as "something spoken of both as 'being' and as 'not being.'"[4]

2. THE PROBLEM OF CHANGE

The problem of becoming is the problem of change which, in its turn, is founded on the notion of opposition. For every change proceeds from contraries. A changeable thing changes from something that it is into something other than it is, namely, into its opposite. The *terminus* of the process is the acquisition of something new, a new substantial form or a new accidental form, either of which constitutes a new state or condition of the changeable thing. There is a start, a finish and a *transitus*, and something in the point of origin or the *terminus a quo* persists throughout the *transitus* and is found in a new state or condition in the point of arrival, the *terminus ad quem*. As such, it was not before. This process constitutes a change, properly speaking. Aristotle, from whom Saint Thomas derived the notion, expresses it in this fashion:

> In one sense things come to be out of that which has no being without qualification: yet in another sense they come to be always out of what is. For coming to be necessarily implies the pre-existence of something which potentially is, but accidentally is not, and this something is spoken of both as being and as not-being.[5]

per se. Et hoc est quod dicit quod si aliquod non ens est ens in potentia, ex tali scilicet non ente, fit generatio per se." *In XII Metaph. lect.* 1.

"Secundum naturam" is an important qualification. To omit it would be to preclude the possibility of creation, for Saint Thomas tells us that *ex nihilo, nihil fit* applies to natural becomings only, and not to the action of the First Cause. Privation, not being a principle that is also a cause, is said to be not *per se* but *per accidens* a cause of generation. It is a necessary condition, but it makes no positive contribution to the final term.

4. *De Generatione et Corruptione*, I, 3, 317 b 16.
5. *Ibid.*

In the case of generation, this persisting "something" is the prime matter; in the case of alteration, it is the second matter or the actual composite. This necessary distinction is the basis for the distinction between the notions of *mutatio* and *motus* with which we shall deal later. However, it must be borne in mind that becoming, whether it be the *fieri* of generation or that of alteration, is from form to form. In making reference to Aristotle's treatment of the question, Saint Thomas has occasion to remark that this transmutation from form to form is either accidental change, as in alteration, or substantial change as in generation.

Thus the problem of *fieri* is the problem of change. The term "change" is used of several kinds of movement, instantaneous as well as successive. All becoming is a change, a *mutatio,* but not all becoming can properly be called the specific kind of change designated as *motus.* An analysis of the notion of change will constitute the particular task of the next few paragraphs.

The notion of change is a simple one and so it cannot be defined essentially, though it can be described. In this way, then, change in a broad sense is said to be the transition from one state to another. The description involves two states, a prior and a posterior, a movement from state to state, and something abiding throughout the change. "In every movement or change there must be something that is conditioned otherwise now and before."[6] The two states are positive and really different states of the same being. The *transitus* is a real process whereby something which before was merely potential now becomes actual. Note that the description of change involves two states, not two things, for the new form which results from the change was potentially present in the prior state; otherwise it could not have been actualized, for actualization is nothing more than the realization or perfection of a potency. A swan could not be actualized from the potency inherent in a tree, but a tree can be actualized from the potency inherent in an acorn. Change, therefore, involves, not two things (as

6. "In omni mutatione vel motu, oportet esse aliquid aliter se habens nunc quam prius." *Con. Gen.*, l. II, c. 17.

a tree and a swan), but two states of the same thing (as an oak in the potentiality of an acorn and the oak in the actuality of nature).[7] Something must persist throughout the *transitus* from term to term. Clearly this is not, for example, the acorn itself, but the potential subject which is in the acorn, since potentiality is said to be the very essence of prime matter, the underlying substrate (though not in the sense of substance), the permanent, enduring thing whose persistence makes possible the eduction of the new form from its potentiality. The prime matter of the acorn persists when that form yields its place, and the same prime matter is the subject of the new form constituting the oak tree.[8] If nothing persisted, it is evident that every substantial change would involve annihilation and creation rather than generation and corruption.[9]

3. ARISTOTLE ON CHANGE

From this cursory overview of a very important metaphysical process, we shall attempt a more detailed analysis of the notion of change as presented by Aristotle and accepted by Saint Thomas. From the very start it must be borne in mind that *motus*, a motion, is not strictly co-terminous with *mutatio*, a change. *Mutatio* is used generally of all changes and in such use is frequently, though inaccurately, made co-terminous with *motus*. Strictly speaking, however, *motus* or motion is merely a species of change. Saint Thomas used *mutatio* to designate change in general, with particular application to instantaneous change, and restricted *motus* to successive change.[10] Aristotle's account of

---

7. "Extrema motus vel mutationis cadunt in eumdem ordinem: vel quia sunt sub uno genere, sicut contraria, ut patet in motu augmenti et alterationis et secundum locum lationis; vel quia communicant in una potentia materiae, ut privatio et forma in generatione et corruptione." *Con. Gen.*, l. II, c. 17.
8. "In mutatione qualibet requiritur quod sit aliquid idem commune utrique mutationis termino." *De Pot.*, q. 3, a. 2.
9. "The modes of being which appear and disappear in real change, in the transitus of anything from one state to a really different state of being, do not appear *de novo, ex nihilo* as absolute beginnings out of nothingness; or disappear *totaliter in nihilum* as absolute endings or lapses of reality into nothingness." Coffey, *Ontology*, p. 61.
10. Cf. *De Verit.*, q. 28, a. 9. *Sum. Th.*, I, q. 53, a. 3. *Quod. VII*, 9 (Vol. 15, Vives).

change as presented in the XI *Metaphysics* is practically identical in content, wording and presentation as that found in the V *Physics*.[11] In the *Metaphysics* we read:

> That which changes changes either from positive into positive or from negative into negative, or from positive into negative, or from negative into positive.... Therefore there must be three changes; for that from negative into negative is not change because (since the terms are neither contraries nor contradictories) there is no opposition.[12] The change from the negative into the positive which is its contradictory is generation — absolute change absolute generation, and partial change partial generation; and the change from positive to negative is destruction — absolute change absolute destruction, and partial change partial destruction.

Note here three features of Aristotle's presentation: first, the notion of change is based on opposition; second, the terms of the opposition are contradictories or contraries; third, the opposition of contradiction is the basis of changes of generation and corruption. In the III *Physics*, Aristotle introduces his exposition of motion by distinguishing three classes of being,

> 1, what exists in a state of fulfillment only; 2, what exists as potential; 3, what exists as potential and also in fulfillment — one being a "this," another "so much," and a third "such."[13]

This prefatory classification is in view of Aristotle's definition of motion which he gives in this book. It will be noted that he here applies motion unrestrictedly to all kinds of change. The definition has become the traditional one, and we shall quote it in its entirety:

> The fulfillment of what exists potentially, insofar as it exists potentially, is motion — namely, of what is alterable, *qua* alterable, alteration; of what can be increased and its opposite, what can be

11. *Phys.*, V, 1, 224 a 20; *Metaph.*, XI, 10, 1067 b 15-25.

12. Here Aristotle prepares the way for the exclusion of generation and corruption from the category of motion, to which category he later assigns only those changes which occur between contraries. Aristotle here points out the contradictory elements of the opposition between terms of generation and negation.

13. 200 b 25.

decreased (there is no common name), increase and decrease; of what can come to be and pass away, coming to be and passing away; of what can be carried along, locomotion.... It is the fulfillment of what is potential when it is already fully real and operates not as itself but as movable, that is motion.[14]

Summarizing Aristotle's doctrine, we have seen that in respect of opposition of terms, only three kinds of change are possible: coming-to-be and perishing, and changes between contraries. Of these, Aristotle designates the change from subject to subject, or that between contraries, as the specific change of motion.[15] However, in respect to the term of the motion, Aristotle enumerates four kinds of change, namely, in respect of the "what" or of the "quality" or of the "quantity" or of the "place." He further explains them and in connection with each names the specific type of movement that each is, namely, generation and destruction as changes of the "thisness"; increase and diminution as changes of quantity; alteration as changes of an affection; and motion as changes of place. Now there is no discrepancy between the three changes mentioned above and the four changes enumerated here, one classification being with respect to the nature of the opposition between the extremes and the other with respect to the *terminus ad quem* of the movement. Grouping two of the above three changes, namely, generation and destruction, we have the "thisness" of the latter classification. It is the change affecting the substance of a thing. Aristotle then considers the remaining one of the three earlier changes mentioned, that is, changes between contraries and intermediates, and groups them into a threefold class, augmentation, alteration and local motion.[16] Elsewhere he says: "It is always with respect to substance or to quantity or to quality or to place that what changes changes."[17] It is to the threefold classification of augmentation, alteration and local motion that Aristotle applies the term motion in the strict sense.[18]

As a summarizing paragraph we have:

> Since every movement is a change, and the kinds of change are the three named above, and of these those in the way of genera-

14. 201 a 10; 201 a 28.
15. Cf. *Phys.*, 225 b 3.
16. Cf. *Metaph.*, XI, 11, 1068 a 17; XII, 2, 1089 b 10: *Phys.*, V, 1, 225 b 10.
17. *Phys.*, V, 1, 200 b 32.
18. *Metaph.*, XI, 11, 1068 a 2.

tion and destruction are not movements, and these are the changes from a thing to its contradictory, it follows that only the change from positive into positive is movement. And the positives are either contrary or intermediate, and are expressed by an affirmative term.[19]

Thus a fourth feature of Aristotle's doctrine is restriction of the term "motion" to the opposition of contrariety alone. Becoming and perishing are not motions, he states.

4. SAINT THOMAS AND THE NOTION OF CHANGE

Saint Thomas accepts Aristotle's doctrine of change, and we shall show this from a few selected references to the Angelic Doctor's work. In the *Summa Theologica* he says:

> Change means that the same thing should be different now than what it was previously. Sometimes, indeed, the same actual thing is different now from what it was before, as in motion according to quantity, quality and place; but sometimes it is the same being only in potentiality, as in substantial change, the subject of which is matter.[20]

Here is Saint Thomas' acceptance of the doctrine of substantial *versus* accidental change. When the same actual thing is different now than it was before, it is evident that the substance has remained untouched. If a hat remains the same hat now that it was before, the substance "hat" has remained unchanged. Only superficial changes may be said to have taken place, that is, changes in its accidental mode of being; e. g., it has been dyed a new color; it has been re-blocked to a new shape; it is now on the table instead of on the head. Other instances of accidental changes are a youth, first short, later tall; water, first hot, then cold; a flower, first here, then there. The same actual thing that was before is the same actual thing now under new determinations in

---

19. *Ibid.*, 1068 a 1.
20. "Creatio non est mutatio, nisi secundum modum intelligendi tantum. Nam de ratione mutationis est quod aliquid idem se habeat aliter nunc et prius. Nam quandoque quidem est idem ens actu aliter se habens nunc et prius, sicut in motibus secundum quantitatem et qualitatem, et ubi; quandoque vero est

its mode of being. But the "same being only in potentiality" implies a change which reaches down into the very nature of the thing and transforms the substance itself. The actual substance "acorn" is the potential substance "oak tree," though no one would say the acorn *is* an oak tree, but rather that the acorn *becomes* an oak tree. This latter is the coming-to-be of a substance; it is substantial becoming. The *fieri* is the transforming process at one instant of which the substance "acorn" recedes before the substantial form "oak tree" by which the oak is constituted a substance in the same *materia prima* which was the subject of the acorn. The new form simultaneously arises from the element common to each term, and that common element in which the form of one and the potentiality of the other substance resides, is the prime matter. *Motus* can be properly said of the gradual transforming process leading up to the instantaneous change, and *mutatio* of the instantaneous and simultaneous surrender of the old form and the invasion of the new. The time-consuming transforming process is alteration; the timeless interplay of forms at the term of the alteration is corruption and generation. Hence it is that *mutatio* has for its subject *ens in potentia* while *motus* has for its subject a complete entity.[21] The *motus* is successive because contraries, unlike the contradictories in generation and corruption, admit of intermediate states, as something which is first cold, then warm, and finally hot. The movement from cold to hot is gradual, and this is properly *motus* because it is successive change which requires time.[22]

idem ens in potentia tantum, sicut in mutatione secundum substantiam, cujus subjectum est materia." *Sum. Th.*, I, q. 45, a. 2, *ad* 2.

21. "Quandoque ergo contingit quod utrique mutationis termino est unum commune subjectum actu existens; et tunc proprie et motus, sicut accidit in alteratione et augmento et diminutione et loci mutatione. Nam in omnibus his motibus subjectum unum et idem actu existens, de opposito in oppositum mutatur. Quandoque vero est idem commune subjectum utrique termino, non quidem ens actu, sed ens in potentia tantum, sicut accidit in generatione et corruptione simpliciter. Formae enim substantialis et privationis subjectum est materia prima, quae non est ens actu: unde nec generatio nec corruptio proprie dicuntur motus, sed mutationes quaedam." *De. Pot.*, q. 3, a. 2.

22. *In V Phys.* 1, *lect.* 1.

In the article of the *Summa Theologica* wherein Saint Thomas defends the immutability of God, he sets forth several concise notions of the nature of change.[23] A brief survey of them will reveal how entirely he adopts the basic elements of Aristotle's doctrine. "Now everything which is in any way changed is in some way in potentiality." This axiom pertains to change in general, whether in substances or in accidents. If a thing is different now than before, it is because it was possible for it to be different; its actual new state presupposed the prior potential state. That potentiality for futher actualization is a prerequisite for and the basis of movement is evident from Saint Thomas' doctrine on creation, wherein he supports his contention that creation is not a movement, because "in this action (viz. creation) there pre-exists nothing in potentiality to receive the action."[24]

Second, "everything which is moved remains as it was in part, and passes away in part." This applies either to substantial change where the prime matter remains and takes on a new form, or in accidental changes where the substance remains the same but a qualitative or quantitative change or a change of location takes place. "In everything which is moved, there is some kind of composition to be found" merely expresses the fact that change is a quality of sensible substances, which substances are composites of matter and form. Finally, "everything that is moved acquires something by its movement, and attains to what it had not attained previously." The acquisition is the new form, substantial or accidental, which is the *terminus ad quem* of the change.[25]

23. "Omne autem quod quocumque modo mutatur, est aliquo modo in potentia.... Quia omne quod movetur quantum ad aliquid manet, et quantum ad aliquid transit, sicut quod movetur de albedine in nigredinem, manet secundum substantiam; et sic in omni eo quod movetur, attenditur aliqua compositio.... Quia omne quod movetur, motu suo aliquid acquirit, et pertingit ad quod prius non pertingebat." *Sum. Th.*, I, q. 9, a. 1.

24. "Motus enim omnis vel mutatio est actus existentis in potentia secundum quod hujusmodi. In hac autem actione non praeexistit aliquid in potentia quod suscipiat actionem, ut jam ostensum est (c. 16)." *Con. Gen.*, l. II, c. 17.

25. Another exposition of change is made by Saint Thomas in *De Verit.*, q. 28, a. 9. Cf. also *Quodlibet VII*, 9.

A schema showing the ground we are exploring will serve to clarify the view we have given of change and motion. Change is either intrinsic or extrinsic. It is with the latter that we are concerned here:

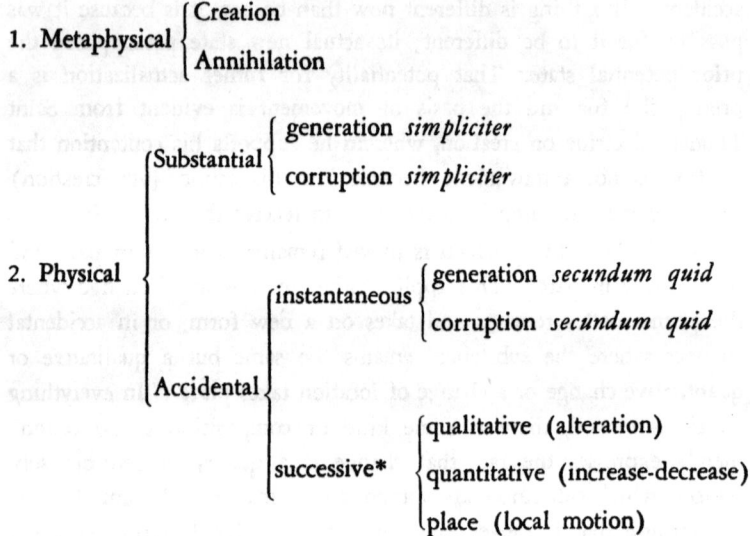

*It is successive change alone that properly is called movement.

For an accurate notion of change it is necessary to bear in mind a twofold relation on the part of the subject. In the subject there is present some degree of actuality or perfection which previously was potential. On the other hand, there is present a potentiality for further actualization. To put it in another way, some degree of potentiality has already been actualized, and a further actualization is yet acquirable, though now it is only potential. Change is the actualization or perfecting of a potency that is still in potency.[26] Enough has been said of this notion to indicate the prime importance of change in discussions of *fieri*.

26. "Considerandum est, quod aliquid est in actu tantum, aliquid vero in potentia tantum, aliquid vero medio modo se habens inter potentiam puram et

5. CHANGE BASED ON OPPOSITION

Changes of sensible substances now claim our attention, the foremost of which is the change which reaches down into the very essence of the changeable thing. The process of transmutation of substantial forms is known as substantial generation. Simply expressed, the process is this — the information of prime matter by a formal principle which constitutes a specific composite nature. The potentiality of the matter has become actualized by the substantial form and the resulting composite in its turn is as a potential principle to the *actus*, existence, which actualizes that essence in *rerum natura;* the whole activity results in a new real substance. Actually, the process is not simple, nor is it simple to describe or explain in detail.

The fundamental principle underlying the process is that there is now something which is capable of being something other than it now is. Insofar as it now is, it is in act; insofar as it is not now all that it might be, it is in potency. It is deprived of what it might be, but it is at the same time capable of becoming that which it can be. This is the non-being which in some way "is," and to it Aristotle applied the term *potentia*. But potency is not act, nor is act potency. They are contrary qualities of a single subject and thus there is set up between them a species of opposition. What the nature of this opposition is, and the part it plays in the process of generation, is now before us for consideration.[27]

---

actum perfectum. Quod igitur est in potentia tantum, nondum movetur: quod autem jam est in actu perfecto, non movetur, sed jam motum est. Illud igitur movetur, quod medio modo se habet inter puram potentiam et actum; quod quidem partim est in potentia, et partim in actu, ut patet in alteratione. Cum enim aqua est solum in potentia calida, nondum movetur: cum vero jam participat aliquid de calore sed imperfecte, tunc movetur ad calorem: nam quod calefit paulatim, participat calorem, magis ac magis. Ipse igitur actus imperfectus caloris in calefactibili existens, est motus; non quidem secundum id quod actu tantum est, sed secundum quod jam in actu existens, habet ordinem in ulteriorem actum: quia se tolleretur ordo ad ulteriorem actu, ipse actus quantumcumque imperfectus, esset terminus, et non motus: sicut accidit cum aliquid semiplene calefit." *In III Phys., lect.* 2.

27. For Aristotle's notion of the term "opposite," cf. *Metaph.* V, 10, 1018 a 20.

The Kinds of Opposition. In his opusculum *De Quatuor Oppositis* and in his commentary on the *Metaphysics* of Aristotle, Saint Thomas discusses the nature of opposition.[28] The first, and therefore the rule and measure of all other oppositions, is that of contradiction, which we discussed in the first part of this work. As a concise restatement of the opposition of contradiction, it is sufficient to say that it involves terms existing outside any genus and not subject to any created power. The termini are absolute non-being and absolute being, between which extremes there is no intermediary, and the opposition between the extremes removes all potency to being from the lower extreme, non-being.[29] All other species of opposition partake of the essential nature of contradiction insofar as they participate more or less in the nature of contradictory opposition, and hence are more or less opposed.

With the second and the third species of opposition we shall have more to do. The second species is that of privation. It approximates the nature of an opposition of contradiction insofar as its lower extreme is non-being. It is an absence, a want, a privation of form. However, this species of opposition falls short of absolute contradiction inasmuch as the terms of the opposition require a subject, though the extremes do not meet in the subject. The negation in a privative opposition is the denial of existence in a particular genus, namely, in the subject of the habitus to which the privation is opposed. There is present a repugnance between a form and the absence of a form — as between sight and the privation of sight which is blindness. In oppositions of privation the lower extreme is drawn by the more noble extreme into its own genus; consequently the privative opposites are referred to the same subject and so fall short of the nature of contradiction whose extremes do not meet in a subject, since absolute non-being cannot have a subject. Between the habitus and the privation which is opposed to it, the potency of the one extreme for the other is not removed, as in the case of the greatest opposition, but between the two termini there is interposed an irremovable obstacle which prevents the potency from being realized, because privation when it occurs takes

---

28. Opusculum 33, Vives. *In X Metaph., lect.* 3.
29. "Quia vero in creatione unum extremorum non transit in alterum, non possumus in creatione uti verbo conversionis, ut dicamus quod non ens convertitur in ens." *Sum. Th.*, III, q. 75, a. 8.

away from the subject the contrary property which it had before; as, when a man is blinded, his sight is taken away. Hence a subject under the privation of blindness, so long as the privation lasts, can in no way see. The terms which are opposites by privation are widely opposed, and they approach nearest to the opposition of contradiction.[30]

Applying the doctrine of opposition to transmutation, it can be seen that no transmutation is possible between the extremes of an opposition of contradiction nor between a privation and its habitus, for in such case there would be no change from the one terminus to the other, that is, non-being does not become being, nor does blindness become sight. Changes are between contraries for the acorn (tree *in potentia*) does become the oak (tree *in actu*).[31] It is obvious, therefore, why Aristotle and Aquinas make movement, *proprie loquendo,* to be between the extremes of an opposition of contrariety, for though in both the *Physics* and the *Metaphysics* Aristotle speaks of generation as following the opposition of contradiction, we shall see shortly in our discussion on contrariety that the contradiction implied is not absolute contradiction, but only relative, namely, the resolution of the terms of a contrariety into the form of a contradiction. The distinction between instantaneous change and successive change necessitates this distinction between the termini of contrariety and the termini of relative contradiction. This contradiction, thus restricted, is privation.

We do well to linger in our discussion of privation and to ponder its meaning, for here we find in Saint Thomas' own words a very definite trace of a "non-being which is" — the goal of our present pursuit: "From these things it is evident," he says, "that that non-existence does not mean simply non-existence outside any genus, but is the negation of the existence of something in a genus."[32]

---

30. "Et sicut res tanto perfectiores sunt quanto magis participant de ente, sicut substantia est perfectior accidente, quia in ea reperitur perfecta ratio entis; ita oppositiones rerum tanto perfectiores sunt in genere oppositionum, quanto magis accedunt ad participandam oppositionem cujus extremum est ens; et hoc reperitur in privatione et habitu quae sunt extrema primae oppositionis pertinentia ad substantiam." *De Quat. Op.,* c. 2, *fi.*
31. Cf. *De Quat. Op.,* c. 5, *init.*
32. "Ex his manifestum est, quod illud non est esse simpliciter extra genus, sed est negatio existentis in genere, ut principium est in genere." *De Quat. Op.,* c. 5, *meo.*

The third opposition of which Saint Thomas speaks is that of contrariety. This species of opposition is one between two positive forms which are in the same genus, and which are mutually repugnant. This species differs from and is lesser in nature than the two greater oppositions of contradiction and privation inasmuch as each extreme in contrariety is really *something*. Contrarieties derive their opposition from a participation in the opposition of contradiction and privation. Contrary terms may, for instance, be reduced to privation and habitus in a genus.[33] However, contraries can be resolved more radically than that; the terms approach the nature of contradiction inasmuch as contraries may be interpreted in terms of the absolutely first opposition. This at first seems not to be so, for in the opposition of contrariety each extreme is really something, and further, both extremes require the same subject. Contradiction, on the other hand, demands that one extreme be a negation, absolutely non-being, and consequently the extremes cannot meet in a subject for nothing cannot have a subject.

In contrariety, however, the opposition is due entirely to its participation in the nature of contradiction, and thus the contraries black and white can be interpreted as non-white and white, making one extreme pertain to non-being and the other to being, as in the opposition of contradiction. In this same manner, seeing and privation of seeing are sight and non-sight, even as in contradictories the opposition is between being and non-being. He would make a serious mistake who would think that this resolution of contraries and privative opposites resulted in absolute contradiction. That this is not the case will be considered at greater length shortly.

We are here confronted by the necessity of drawing together several threads that the nature of our discussion thus far has caused to be left, as it were, dangling. We have noted that physical change is a transmutation of contraries. Privation is a species of opposition approaching closest to contradictories on the one hand and, on the other hand, it is the first species of contrariety since it is the first opposition in a

---

33. "Semper tamen in contrariis omnibus alterum extremum est ut privatio, et alterum ut habitus: privatio enim et habitus faciunt contrarietatem ... et ideo omnes contrarietates oppositionem quae est in genere." *De Quat. Op.*, c. 2, *init.*

genus.[34] Contraries and privative opposites can be interpreted in terms of contradiction, though not absolute but only relative contradiction. Further, generation, we are told, is from contradictories, yet the principle stands, *ex nihilo, nihil fit secundum naturam*. Again, though we said that in contradictions absolute nothing is not in a subject because being is not in a subject, we nevertheless spoke of contradiction which participates in contraries, and which has extremes each really something, really in a genus.

It is to the task of drawing these threads, seemingly diverse, into a consistent unit, into a principle or set of principles that we now assign ourselves. Our ultimate end is to determine the antecedents of being — to find in the concepts *de nihilo* the principles from which sensible substances proceed.

6. TRANSMUTATION OF CONTRARIES

A change of physical substances is a transmutation of contraries. This is evident because the lower extremes of the opposition both of contradiction and of privation are absolutely non-being, and as such are not subject to created powers. Between contraries, however, natural transmutations can occur, since each extreme of contrariety is actually something in a genus. This is the distinguishing mark of the opposition of contrariety, that whereas contradictories are mutually repugnant terms *not in a genus,* contraries are mutually repugnant terms *in the same genus.* Aristotle calls contraries "the most different of things in the same genus."[35] Saint Thomas says: "Nothing prevents contraries from being present in the same thing as long as they are not present in the same respect."[36] Actually the different aspects in which contraries are found in the same genus are those of habitus and privation of habitus. As long as the privation persists, the acquisition of the opposite quality cannot be effected, and this is so by the very nature of privation, which removes the potency for the opposite habitus by placing in the subject an irremovable obstacle which prevents the actualization of the

---

34. "Privatio enim habitus faciunt contrarietatem, ut dicitur *I Phys*.: et ideo omnes contrarietates reducuntur in habitum et privationem tanquam in primam oppositionem quae est in genere." *Ibid.*
35. *Metaph.*, V, 1018 a 27. Cf. *Metaph.*, XI, 1067 b 12, 13; 1068 a 4-6.
36. "Nihil autem prohibet contraria eidem inesse non secundum idem." *Sum. Th.*, III, q. 46, a. 8, *ad* 1.

potency.³⁷ It is the privation which, as it were, keeps the contraries from meeting in the same respect in a subject, and thus the truth of Aristotle's statement that every contrariety depends upon privation, is evident.³⁸ Saint Thomas says that the principles of contrariety are privation and habitus.³⁹

The negation of being in the lower extreme of the opposition of contradiction is made in a universal sense, whereas in privation it is made in a particular sense only; namely, privation is asserted only of those beings which lack a quality which by nature they are capable of having. A stone is non-seeing but this is not a privation in a stone as it would be in a man. Privation, therefore, since it posits nothing, is non-being, not however universally conceived, as we have already said, but only in a particular sense, as the non-seeing in a being that is by nature entitled to see. Thus the negation in privation differs from that in contradiction, according as it regards universality and particularity.⁴⁰

Privation falls short of absolute contradiction not only on the score of the particular negation of being which is its chief characteristic, but inasmuch as it approaches in some way to being.⁴¹ It is here, in the opposition of privation, that contradictories and contraries meet, as in a middle term, for in privative opposites we have both the non-being found in contradiction and the being-in-a-genus found in contrariety.

37. "Sciendum est etiam quod dupliciter elongat aliquid potentiam removendo, ita quod nihil ejus relinquatur; et isto modo in oppositione contradictoria elongatur potentia ab actu, quia in non ente simpliciter nihil potentiae est ad esse. Alio modo interponendo obstaculum, ne potentia ducatur ad actum; sed hoc contingit dupliciter; uno modo ad tempus et mobiliter, sicut albedo facit subjectum suum distare a nigredine; alio modo immobiliter; et sic privatio removet potentiam sui subjecti ad habitum; non quod potentia omnino auferatur; sed quia obstaculum indelebile ponitur in ipso subjecto. *De Quat. Op.*, c. 1.

38. *Metaph.* XI, 1063 b 17.

39. *In X Metaph., lect.* 6.

40. *Ibid., lect.* 3.

41. "In oppositione vero privativa alterum extremum vilius nihil est simpliciter, cum sit de genere non entium; tamen aliquid sibi determinat pro subjecto: quod patet ex altero ejus extremo, quod requirit subjectum, et hoc est habitus ipse: semper enim nobilius extremum trahit ignobilius ad subjectum, si ipsum habuerit subjectum et si ipsum non habuerit subjectum, nec aliud habebit." *De Quat. Op.*, c. 2, *init*.

Contraries are drawn as it were toward contradiction and contradictories are drawn toward contrariety in a genus, and this double approach is through the medium of the opposition of privation. Sickness and health are contraries, but sickness in a body capable of being sick is negation of a particular kind, and this is privation. Sickness is the privation of health. Sickness is not a positive quality, but the negation of a habitus, and since it is drawn by the habitus of its subject into the same genus, it is said to be in a genus and in a subject, and thus contraries are explained in terms of privation.[42] But privation of health is said to be non-health as well as sickness, and thus the contraries are opposed as negation and affirmation in the manner of contradictories. However, since health and non-health are contradictories, not in the manner absolutely of non-being and being, but contradictories in a genus, they are said to be contradictories in the nature of contrariety.[43]

Always in all contraries (Saint Thomas says), one extreme is like privation, the other like a habitus for privation and habitus make contrariety, as is said in the First Book of Physics; and therefore all opposition of contrariety can be explained in terms of privation and habitus as in terms of the first opposition which exists in a genus; while all opposition of contrariety can be interpreted in terms of an opposition of contradiction as in terms of the absolutely first opposition.[44]

There is here a breaking down of the rigid distinction which at first encounter seemed to exist among the species of opposition. The demar-

42. *In X Metaph., lect.* 3.
43. "Et ideo cum dicitur, Socrates est albus, Socrates non est albus, non est contradictio absolute; sed contradictio participata in contrariis, in albo scilicet et nigro. Et ideo in omnibus tamen est genere. In contradictoriis vero absolute neutrum extremum est in genere: Hujusmodi enim sunt esse et non esse. Manifestum enim est quod ens non est in genere, nec suum oppositum. Et ideo, sicut omnes res quae sunt in genere; ita omnes oppositiones rerum in genere existentium est resolvere in oppositionem illam cujus termini non sunt in genere." *De Quat. Op.*, c. 2.
44. "Semper tamen in contrariis omnibus alterum extremum est ut privatio, et alterum ut habitus: privatio enim et habitus faciunt contrarietatem, ut dicitur *I Phys.*: Et ideo omnes contrarietates reducuntur in habitum et privationem tamquam in primam oppositionem quae est in genere: sed in oppositionem contradictionis reducitur omnis contrarietas, ut in primam oppositionem simpliciter." *Ibid.*

cation of boundaries between contradictories, privative opposites and contraries gives way so that the element of contradiction overflows into all the species, since, being the first in the genus of opposition, it is the measure of all that follow.

Somewhere in this threefold opposition can be found the basis of the principle or principles from which material or sensible substances proceed, for sensible substances are by way of generation; generation is change, and change is between opposites.

7. RESOLUTION OF CONTRARIES INTO CONTRADICTORIES

We have just seen how the transmutation of contraries accounts for all change, even in the case of generation when the change is apparently from contradictories. We shall see in what sense the terms in generation are contradictories, and in what sense they are contraries. "Change which is not accidental,"[45] says Aristotle, "on the other hand, is not to be found in everything but only in contraries, in things intermediate between contraries, and in contradictories."[46] In his metaphysical treatise, as we noted before, Aristotle specifies changes of generation and destruction as changes from a thing into its contradictory, and changes from positive subject to positive subject as changes of contrariety. This exhausts the species of change. The task here is to reconcile apparent discrepancies. The extremes of contradiction, namely existence and non-existence, are not subject to created power. Generation and corruption are changes of sensible substances, changes from form to form, from potentiality in a subject to actuality, and such changes are subject to natural agents.[47] How then can generation be changed from contradictory to contradictory, since we have shown

---

45. "Accidental" is here used by Aristotle in the sense he explains when he says: "When we say that something musical walks, that which walks being something in which aptitude for music is an accident." *Phys.* V, 1, 224 a 16. He does not refer to accidental changes such as those of quality, quantity or place as we have been discussing them here.

46. *Phys.*, V, 1, 224 b 23.

47. "Esse autem in potentia ad unum necessario adjungitur esse actu aliud, quia nunquam est in potentia pura sine aliquo actu; aliter materia esset sine forma. Et propter hoc ista extrema subsunt potentiae naturali: esse enim in potentia propter esse actu adjunctum subest agenti naturali: agens enim naturale semper requirit subjectum actu in quod agat." *De Quat. Op.*, c. 5.

that changes between contradictories are outside the power of creatures? Must every generation be said to be a creation, and every corruption an annihilation? If not, in what sense are generation and corruption said to be of the species of the opposition of contradiction? Assuredly not in the sense of absolute contradiction for in that sense Parmenides was right: *Ex nihilo, nihil fit* — provided, of course, that one adds Saint Thomas' restrictive phrase: *secundum naturam*.

The creative act of God can alone claim that power and this act is not called generation but creation. In contradiction to the statement that generation is from contradictories, we have the principle that "whatever is made from pre-existing matter must needs be made from a contrary."[48] Now all changes of generation and corruption as well as changes of quality, quantity and location are all changes of pre-existing matter, and hence of the opposition of contrariety. Our attempted reconciliation of these several principles will be sought in a principle which partakes of the natures of contradiction and of contrariety, the common denominator as it were, drawing the extremes of the genus of opposition to meet in a middle term which partakes of the nature of each extreme. Thus we have the answer — generation does proceed from contradiction, but from contradiction that participates in contraries and this is contradiction in a relative sense, i.e., contradiction whose extremes are found in a genus. The mediating factor partaking of the nature of both the greater and the lesser opposition is privation, "the principle of contrariety."

It is evident therefore, that though generation proceeds from contradictory terms, namely, non-existence and existence, they are not nonexistence and existence absolutely speaking, but only relatively. To be potentially such-and-such is to be and not to be at the same time, but not in the same respect, under penalty of denying the fundamental principle of contradiction. That the terms of generation are not absolute contradictories is best summed up by Saint Thomas in his opusculum on the species of opposition.[49]

---

48. "Omne enim quod fit ex materia praeexistente oportet ex contrario fieri." *Con. Gen.*, l. II, c. 43, No. 1.

49. "Et dictus ergo manifestum est, quod ad alterum extremum contradictionis simpliciter, ad esse scilicet, pertinent ambo extrema generationis, esse scilicet hoc, et non esse hoc, quod est esse in potentia. Esse enim in potentia

We have shown how physical generation is restricted to the extremes of the opposition of contrariety, resolved into terms of the opposition of contradiction. The conciliating element is privation, in itself nothing and able to claim only the existence of an *ens rationis*. The privation draws, as it were, the contradictories in virtue of the similarity of their lower extremes which are negations; it draws the contraries in virtue of their upper extremes which are positive, and in virtue of the fact that both contraries and contradictories can be interpreted in terms of form and privation of form. In considering the subject under privation, two characteristics impress themselves upon our mind. First, in its negative aspect, the privation itself — the absence of a form for which the subject has a natural aptitude; and second, a positive feature, the aptitude itself, a potency for possessing the form of which it is now deprived. The positive aspect spells potency, and it is precisely here that Aristotle and Aquinas said that there is to be found the non-being which in some way is being. A "non-being which in some way is" is a relative non-being, a being partly in act and partly in potency, since to be in potency implies some existence in act, as there is never a potency existing apart from some actuality.[50] To be this and not to be this is to be in potency, and to be in potency pertains in some way to existence and in some way to non-existence, for what is in potency does not exist. And so the conclusion that non-existence in a genus is the same thing as existence in potency, is

aliquo modo ad esse pertinet. Sed comparando unum eorum ad alterum, esse in potentia est quasi non esse, quia quod est in potentia non est, secundum Philosophum: et similiter esse album et non esse album, quod est esse nigrum vel medio colore coloratum, ad esse pertinent, licet non esse album vel esse nigrum comparatum ad esse album sit quodammodo non ens, cum ad vilius extremum generationis, non est non esse simpliciter, secundum Philosophum; sed illud non esse idem est quod esse in potentia. Et ideo manifestum est quod talis non esse et esse oppositi est commune subjectum, materia scilicet: et similiter est de nigro vel non albo, quod est idem, et albo. Horum enim est commune subjectum quod est ens medium. Sed contradictoria medium non habent, secundum Philosophum, ut supra dictum est. Unde ista sunt contradictoria per resolutionem aliarum oppositionum in contradictorias, quia oppositio contradictoria includitur in omnia alia oppositione, ut supra dictum est, sicut prius includitur in suo posteriori." *De Quat. Op.,* c. 5.

50. "Omne enim ens, in quantum est ens, est in actu, et quodammodo perfectum; quia omnis actus perfectio quaedam est." *Sum. Th.,* I, q. 5, a. 3.

the rational solution of the apparent insoluble antinomy between the flux revealed by the senses and the permanence recognized by the intellect. Everything that is, is being, and all created being is becoming. Saint Thomas concluded his explanation of how contradictories are resolved into contraries by saying: "... Not-to-be-this-in-act, or to-be-this-in-potency, which nevertheless implies to-be-another-in-act, is opposed to to-be-this-in-act."[51]

We are meeting here the basic term "potency" as being the positive principle which mediates between being and non-being, even as privation is the negative principle on account of which the potentiality is found in the subject. Before delving more fully into the nature of this relative non-being, since a study of it will bring us into the problems of act and potency, matter and form, substance and accident, it may serve both as a conclusion to our previous discussions and as an introduction to the following pages, to indicate concisely the general differences between creation or production from absolute nothing and generation or production from relative nothing.

8. CREATION VERSUS GENERATION

Creation is production *ex nihilo sui et subjecti*. Generation is production *ex nihilo sui* only, since generation proceeds from a subject in potency. The extremes of opposition in the creative act are absolute non-existence and existence in general; in the generative act, relative non-existence and a substance, or, in other terms, such-and-such a non-existence in a determinate species and existence of this or that composite in a determinate species. Creation results primarily in existence itself, and in the thing created through its existence. Generation results in a composite thing and, consequently, in existence which belongs to the composite. In creation, creatures participate in the existence of the Creator, but not in His nature; in generation the thing generated participates, not in the existence of the generator, which is incommunicable, but in its nature.

---

51. "Sicut ergo dicitur non album quod tamen est nigrum vel medium, opponi albo, et nullum alium non album; ita non esse actu hoc, sive esse in potentia hoc, cui tamen adjunctum est esse actu aliud, opponitur esse actu hoc." *De Quat. Op.*, c. 5.

CHAPTER FOUR

SUBSTANTIAL CHANGE: THE INTRINSIC PRINCIPLES AND RELATED NOTIONS

From the foregoing general analysis of the oppositions between whose terms sensible substances are seen to change, we proceed now to analyze the principles by which potentialities are actualized. Strictly, there is only one such intrinsic principle, namely the form; potentiality, or the material intrinsic principle, is not that *by which* but rather that *in which* the change is seen to occur. Our analysis will involve these two principles of the becoming of things which are really constitutive causes. The constitutive causes are the material and formal elements in all composite things, without which no material thing would be constituted essentially. Viewed in the light of these essential principles, material substances are seen in their static aspect, that is, as constituting a natural species. Material essences may, however, be viewed in the light of ever-changing realities as well, and this view extends beyond the limits of matter and form. It sees a substance as first in potentiality to one accidental form and then to another; and the successive provisional satisfaction of matter's potentiality to various forms, constitutes the dynamic aspect of nature. The principle of potency and act is basic here. It is the traditional explanation of the substantial and accidental becomings of material things.

1. NATURE OF THE CHANGE

Substantial becoming has a counterpart in the process of accidental becoming with these basic differences: the *terminus a quo* of the former is the primary matter of the changing substance; of the latter it is the secondary matter or the already essentially constituted composite. The *terminus ad quem* of substantial becoming is a new substantial form, a change in the essence itself; of the latter, the *terminus ad quem* is an accidental form or merely a change in the quantity, the quality, or the location of the second matter.[1] In substantial changes the mutation is instantaneous. (It is, however, preceded by a process of alteration.) The very moment, for example, that the substantial form "acorn" breaks down due to the force of the changing dispositions in the prime matter, the new substantial form "oak tree" is simultaneously educed from the potency of the matter. In accidental changes, however, the mutation is gradual, as when cold water acquires heat, there is an almost imperceptible movement from cold to lukewarm to warm to hot. There is no instant in the movement when cold gives way absolutely to hot; the whole process is one of succession requiring time for its completion. The instantaneous mutation is generation; the successive, alteration. Saint Thomas gives a brief account of the distinction between the two when, in the *Contra Gentiles* he traces the progressive stages by which the ancients attained to an understanding of being and becoming.[2]

2. PRIVATION

Basically it is the *aptitude* for other forms, and the *privation* of all forms but the *form* it has at any given moment, that is the start of the endless transmutations of material things. Form, privation of form and aptitude for other forms are the three principles from which generation proceeds. Note that it is the matter which is in potentiality, which makes possible the process of making and remaking a constant factor in nature. The change starts out from matter's lack of a form it is capable of having. If matter were perfected by any one of its potential forms there would not be that particular production but another, drawn from matter's potentiality through its lack of that other form. An acorn doesn't seek the form of an acorn, but rather of an oak. The doctrine of act and potency rules in this empire of

---

1. "Quando autem introducitur forma accidentalis, non dicitur aliquid fieri simpliciter, sed fieri hoc." "Forma accidentalis a substantiali differt quia forma substantialis facit HOC ALIQUID: forma autem accidentalis advenit rei iam hoc aliquid existenti; — si igitur prima forma per quam collacatur in genere, facit individuum esse hoc aliquid; omnes aliae formae advenient individuo existenti in actu; et ita erunt formae accidentales." *De Princ. Nat.*, col. 2 (Opusc. No. 27, Vol. 27, Vives).

2. Cf. *Con. Gen.*, l. II, c. 37.

change. Radically it is the essential potentiality of the matter and the ability of the form to reduce the potentiality to actuality that accounts for the constant surge of matter toward its perfecting principles. An acorn would remain substantially an acorn, a seed a seed, a plant a plant, hydrogen hydrogen, were their only explanation to be found in the principles of matter and form. An acorn yields its substantial form and hence its substance, to that of an oak tree, a seed to a plant, a plant to flesh, hydrogen to water, only because there is in the prime matter of acorn, seed, plant and hydrogen an aptitude for another substantial form which by its actualization of potencies is able to cross boundaries and constitute it in another determinate species. It must not be supposed, however, that matter in a determinate species has potentiality to any species. The species to which any given potential matter has an aptitude is limited. Primary matter in the abstract has capacity for all forms, but primary matter in its actual state is quite restricted.

We pause here long enough to bring forward from our introductory chapter certain principles and grades of being which we there suggested as likely candidates for the office of antecedents of being. From a cursory summing up of the metaphysical grades of being, we attached some degree of probability to possible essences as well as to a twofold potentiality, namely, relative, in an already existing actual thing, and absolute, the essential constitutive element of prime matter. From a negative point of view we sought some solution to our problem from Saint Thomas' classification of non-being into *nihil, privatio* and *materia*. From Aristotle's "principles and causes" of things, there were contributed form, privation and matter. What do we find from our analysis thus far? That, whether viewed from the aspect of grade of being or of non-being, or as principles and causes of things, our inquiry yields but a single set of correlated facts: First, that possibility of existence precedes and is presupposed by all existence. That it alone is the sole prerequisite for creation, and that from nothing nothing comes, *secundum naturam*. Second, that privation of a specific form in an already existing being, together with a potentiality for other specific or accidental forms, is the starting point of all substantial becoming. Third, that matter is the common element in both terms of substantial change, and its correlative, form, is to the potentiality of matter as its act of existence. Together, matter and form constitute a determined species and are the potential and active principles in generation and corruption. We have therefore, possibility, privation, matter and form. But privation is a negation, and form is a perfecting principle requiring a subject to be perfected, which subject is prior not in time but in nature (in one sense, though in another sense act always precedes potency); and so there remain for further consideration of the antecedents of being the two really ultimate notions of possibility and potentiality. It is our purpose now to analyze the notion of potentiality and to determine, if possible, whether or not the two above-named notions of possibility and potentiality can be reduced to a single term.

3. THE NOTION OF POTENCY

We are concerned with a closer analysis of the notion of potency. This is the third notion in Saint Thomas' threefold non-being, and from it, he declares, generation *per se* has its origin.[3] Generation is the coming to be according to nature, and such coming to be is from *ens in potentia* which, as Saint Thomas says, is "non-existence in act, not non-existence absolutely, but such-and-such a non-existence."[4] It is precisely this notion of relative non-being, or being in potency, that we are about to analyze. The term "being in potency" is an accurate expression of the nature of this notion. That the notion is of a "being" indicates a positive something, a subject; "in potency" indicates that it has not something it can have, and this spells, as we saw, privation. Thus in potential beings there is a dual aspect: First, the being lacks something, and this is negation; from it we derive a negative principle (though a real principle) of generation. Second, it can have something other than it has, and this is an affirmation, and from it we derive a positive principle of generation. The subject under privation in substantial generation, namely prime matter, exhibits in its nature this double aspect of potential beings, that is, a privation of form and an

---

3. "Tertio modo dicitur non est ens actu, sed ens potentia. Ex et tali non ente fit generatio per se." *In XII Metaph.*, lect. 1, fi.

4. "Similiter non esse, quod est terminus a quo in generatione simpliciter, non est non esse absolute, sed non esse hoc; esse tamen aliquid ut non esse actu, est esse in potentia." *De Quat. Op.*, c. 5.

aptitude for all proportionate forms other than the one at present informing it.

Since potentiality is the essence of matter, we shall first present briefly the Thomistic doctrine of the nature of matter. Since matter cannot exist without form, our analysis of *materia prima* must necessarily involve its correlative, form.[5] The distinctions between prime matter and privation, and lastly an exposition of potency itself with its correlative act, will conclude the present section of our thesis.

Numerous are the references Saint Thomas makes to prime matter throughout his works.[6] The reason is not difficult to understand. The essence of prime matter is potentiality and Saint Thomas' adoption of the Aristotelian doctrine of potency and act found repeated application throughout the philosophical and theological writings of the Angelic Doctor.

It seems beside the point to enter into a detailed account of prime matter; moreover its adequate analysis demands a separate and lengthy treatment. Our particular aim here is to do no more than to set matter forth as the subject of potentiality and privation, and as the correlative of the determining form in a given species, in order to show in how far all these concepts pertain to the antecedents of being.

5. "Materia autem secundum id quod est, est ens in potentia. Unde magis repugnat materiae esse in actu sine forma, quam accidenti sine subjecto." *Sum. Th.*, I, q. 66, a. 1, *ad* 3.

6. Saint Thomas makes numerous references throughout his works to prime matter. For the notion of what prime matter is, cf. *In VII Metaph.*, *lect.* 2; — 6; *In I Phys.*, *lect.* 11; — 12; — 15; *In XII Metaph.*, *lect.* 2; *In X Metaph.*, *lect.* 5; *I De Gen.*, *lect.* 20; *Sum. Th.*, I, q. 66, a. 1, *ad* 3; — I, q. 77, a. 1, *ad* 2; — I, q. 84, a. 3, *ad* 2; — III, q. 75, a. 3; — I, q. 4, a. 1; — I, q. 115, a. 1, *ad* 2; *IV Sent.*, d. 12, q. 1, a. 1; — d. 12, q. 3, a. 1; *III Sent.*, d. 14, q. 4; *I Sent.*, d. 3, q. 2, a. 2, *ad* 4; *De Spir. Creat.*, a. 3; *De Princ. Nat., meo.; init.; De Verit.*, q. 3, a. 5, *ad* 3; *Quodlibet*, IX, 6, 3; *De Ente et Essentia*, c. 7; *De Malo*, q. 2; *De Gen. et Corrup.*, q. 1, a. 3.

For what prime matter is not, cf. *Summa Theologica*, I, q. 76, aa. 3, 4; — I, q. 76, a. 6, *ad* 1 and *ad* 2; — I-II, q. 113, a. 8; *In I Metaph.*, *lect.* 12; — 4; — 7; *I De Gen.*, *lect.* 1; — 22; *In I Phys.*, *lect.* 9; *Con. Gen.*, l. II, c. 58; *IV Sent.*, d. 12, 1, 2; *De Natura Materiae*, cc. 1, 4, 5, 6, 7; *De Spir. Creat.*, q. 3, *ad* 19 and 20; *II De Gen. et Corrup.*, *lect.* 4; *I De Gen.*, *lect.* 10; *Quodlibet*, *q.* 1, a. 6, *ad* 2.

Prime matter, as one of the two positive constitutive elements of material bodies is, in itself, non-being, but a non-being only *per accidens*.[7] It is pure potentiality and nothing else;[8] a potentiality for the substance which the substantial form will constitute in being[9] As it has no isolated being, but exists only in conjunction with form, it is unknowable except insofar as it is joined to form.[10] In its abstract state, that is, considered universally, prime matter is essentially undetermined but infinitely determinable in respect of material bodies; it lacks privation of form as well as form when thus conceived.[11] Though it has no actual existence apart from form, it is nevertheless real,[12] is not an *ens rationis* as privation is, but a positive essential principle of corporeal beings.

From Aristotle, Saint Thomas approved and accepted two well-known definitions of matter. The positive definition is: "Matter is the first subject of each thing from which, since it is intrinsic, something which is not *per accidens* comes into being."[13] The negative definition is: "By matter I mean that which in itself is neither a particular thing nor of a certain quantity nor assigned to any of the categories by which being is determined.... The ultimate substratum is of itself neither a particular thing nor of a particular quantity nor otherwise positively

---

7. Cf. *infra*, p. 86, footnote 20.

8. "Materia autem prima non potest praefuisse per seipsam ante omnia corpora formata, quum non sit nisi potentia tantum." *Con. Gen.*, l, II, c. 43, No. 2. Cf. also *Sum. Th.*, I, q. 115, a. 1, *ad* 2.

9. "Non igitur potentia materiae est aliqua proprietas addita super essentiam ejus; sed materia secundum suam substantiam est potentia ad esse substantiale." *In I Phys.*, lect. 14. Cf. also *Sum. Th.*, I, q. 54, a. 3, *ad* 3; — I, q. 77, a. 1, *ad* 2.

10. "Quia omnis definitio et omnis cognitio est per formam; ideo materia prima non potest per se definiri nec cognosci, sed per comparationem ad formam." *De Princ. Nat.*, col. 5. "Dicere ergo quod materia sit in actu forma, est dicere contradictoria esse simul." *Quod. III*, q. 1, a. 1. Cf. also, *Sum. Th.*, I, q. 15, a. 3, *ad* 3; *De Verit.*, q. 3, a. 5.

11. Cf. *De Princ. Nat.*, col. 5.

12. For the reality of prime matter, cf. *Con. Gen.*, l. II, cc. 54, 55; *Sum. Th.*, I, q. 4, a. 1; — q. 15, a. 3, *ad* 3; — q. 66, a. 1; — q. 84, a. 3, *ad* 2; — q. 115, a. 1, *ad* 2; — III, q. 75, a. 3.

13. *Phys.* 192 a 31-34.

characterized, nor yet is it the negation of these."[14] By these definitions prime matter is seen to be excluded from the categories of both substance and accident. It is not a substance, for a substance is a self-subsisting reality, essentially so; whereas prime matter is the first subject of substance, the substrate of substantial being. Neither is prime matter an accident, for an accident is a being of being, a being whose essence it is to exist in another. Prime matter, however, is a principle of material substance and cannot be considered as an accident in any way, since, as first subject of substance, it requires no subject of inherence even though it cannot exist without the co-existence of the substantial form.

Matter, excluded from the categories of being, is not thereby non-being absolutely, since it is an essential constituent of corporeal things.[15] The union of primary matter and substantial form results in a composite substantial being, *per se* and *simpliciter unum*, and not some being *per accidens*. Primary matter "is" in some way for it is a being in potentiality.[16] Though prime matter is a non-being *per accidens* and not directly in the category of substance, yet it is reducible to it since it is an intrinsic part of corporeal substances and what is predicated of the whole, namely, substance, can be predicated of the part, namely, prime matter.[17] "Prime matter has for its genus the category of substance," says Saint Thomas, supposing one were to attempt a definition, since it is determinable to any species of corporeal substance, granted proper and commensurate efficient causality.[18]

---

14. *Metaph.* VII, 3, 1029 a 20.

15. "Materia dicitur quod habet esse ex eo quod sibi advenit, quia de se esse incompletum, immo nullum esse habet, ut dicit Commentator in II *De Anima*. Unde, simpliciter loquendo, forma dat esse materiae...." *De Princ. Nat.*, col. 2.

16. "Materia prima aliquo modo est, quia est ens in potentia." *Con. Gen.*, l. II, c. 16, *fi*.

17. "Materia enim dicitur substantis non quasi ens aliquid actu existens in se considerata, sed quasi in potentia ut sit aliquid actu haec dicitur esse hoc aliquid." *In VIII Metaph.*, 1.

18. "Materia autem si ejus essentia defineretur, haberet pro differentia ipsum suum ordinem ad formam et pro genere ipsam suam substantiam." *Quod.* IX, a. 6, *ad* 3.

Prime matter is pure potentiality; that is, it is deprived of all act; it does not contain any act as part of itself nor has it the nature of act either formally or entitatively. It enjoys no actuality in itself apart from form. This is undeniably the teaching of Saint Thomas. In itself prime matter never exists, as it is potentiality pure and simple, and as such, is too indeterminate to possess any actuality of its own. For this reason prime matter is not properly said to have an essence, since essence is determined by form and prime matter in itself is devoid of all form. Prime matter receives its existence through form, although existence, in the strict sense, comes to the composite, the resulting substance, rather than to the matter alone.[19]

Act in relation to potentiality in substantial beings is said to be twofold: first, formal act whereby essence is constituted; second, entitative act whereby existence is given to that real essence. Now in respect of prime matter *in itself*, there is neither a form constituting it an essence (no essential act), nor an act of existence giving it reality *extra causis* (no existential act). We say, *in itself*, because both formal and entitative act belongs to prime matter not in itself but insofar as it is an intrinsic principle of corporeal beings. We have said that that act or perfection whereby a thing is constituted a determinate species is said to be its formal act, or act in the order of essence.

In this sense a given form unites with prime matter to constitute some third thing, some essence. The substantial form "oak" united with prime matter constitutes the natural species "oak tree." The form determines what the prime matter shall become; thus the formal act constitutes the essence of a thing. But whereas formal act constitutes a real essence, a further act or form is necessary to give existence to that thing, placing it outside the state of mere possibility. This is entitative act; act in the order of existence. By it a thing is constituted *extra causis*. Saint Thomas held that matter in itself not only is deprived of all formal act, but enjoys no entitative act. It is not an essence

---

19. "Secundo autem quia ipsum esse non est proprius actus materiae, sed substantiae totius. Ejus enim actus est esse, de quo possumus dicere quod sit. Esse autem non dicitur de materia, sed de toto. Unde materia non potest dici quod est, sed ipsa substantia est id quod est." *Con. Gen.*, l. II, c. 54. Cf. also *Ibid.*, c. 53, No. 3.

(though it is a part of essence),[20] and it does not exist in nature apart from form.[21] It has no actuality except insofar as it shares in some actuality. Hence prime matter has existence only inasmuch as it is a constitutive cause of and shares in the actual existence of a substantial being.[22] So firm was Saint Thomas in his conviction that matter requires form as its co-existing principle, that he declares even God Himself to be incapable of giving isolated existence to prime matter.[23]

20. "Quod materia sola non sit essentia, planum est." *De Ente et Essentia*, c. 2. "Materia, proprie loquendo, non habet essentiam, sed est pars essentiae totius." *De Verit.*, q. 3, a. 5. Though Saint Thomas says in *De Veritate* that matter is only a part of essence, nevertheless in his opusculum *De Quatuor Oppositis* he says matter may be thought of as an essence with certain limitations: "Nec est etiam implicatio contradictionis cum dicitur, materia est quaedam essentia, si esse non sequitur ipsam essentiam: quia cum dicitur quod materia est essentia quaedam, idem praedicatur de se, quia materia est sua essentia quod in omnibus simplicibus invenitur. Non autem per hoc denotatu aliquod esse sequi essentiam, quia in omni re creata differt esse ab ipsa re. Nec oportet quod quandocumque in propositione aliqua ponitur 'est' aliquod esse etiam respondere in re, ut dictum est." Elsewhere in the same chapter Saint Thomas says: "Similiter cum dicitur, materia prima est non ens per accidens, non significatur quod aliquod esse sequatur essentiam materiae ipsius, quia esse actus est qui in materia prima de se non reperitur, cum sit pura potentia, sed significatur quod essentia materiae est subjecta privationi, ratione cujus dicitur non ens." *De Quat. Op.*, c. 4.

21. "Materia prima non existit in rerum natura per se ipsam, cum non sit ens in actu, sed potentia tantum." *Sum. Th.*, I, q. 7, a. 2, *ad* 3.

22. Cf. *Con. Gen.*, l. II, c. 54, for the Thomistic teaching on the composition of matter and form as distinct from the composition of essence and existence, though they both result from potency and act.

23. Cf. *Quod. III*, 1 (Vol. 15, Vives). "Cum autem Deus sit ipsum esse subsistens, manifestum est quod natura essendi convenit Deo infinite absque omni limitatione et contradictione; unde ejus virtus active se extendit infinite ad totum ens, et ad omne id quod potest habere rationem entis. Illud ergo solum poterit excludi a divina potentia quod repugnat rationi entis; et hoc non propter defectum divinae potentiae, sed quia ipsum non potest esse ens, unde non potest fieri. Repugnat autem rationi entis non ens simul et secundum idem existens: unde quod aliquid simul sit et non sit, a Deo fieri non potest, nec aliquid contradictionem includens; et de hujusmodi est materiam esse in actu sine forma. Omne enim quod est actu vel est ipse actus, vel est potentia participans actum: esse autem actu repugnat rationi materiae, quae secundum propriam rationem est ens in potentia. Relinquitur ergo quod non possit esse in actu nisi inquantum participat actum: actus autem participatus a materia

Substantial Change

There are but two remaining points to be made in the present treatment of matter. First, prime matter is neither generative or corruptible, and second, it is produced by an act of creation. "We hold," says the Angelic Doctor, "matter to be created by God though not apart from form...."[24] In changes that take place in corporeal beings, prime matter is neither brought into being nor destroyed. It remains to be the subject of the new forms, even as it was the subject of the old forms. "In whatever things there is composition of potentiality and act, that which holds the place of first potentiality or of first subject, is incorruptible; wherefore even in corruptible substances prime matter is incorruptible."[25] Hence it is the very simplicity of prime matter which guarantees its indestructibility, since corruption and generation are changes of composites.

Of itself prime matter cannot be the term of creation, but it is included in the creation of material substances which are rather "concreated" than created. "This alone is said to be created which has existence, and this is a *suppositum* or first substance whose property it is to exist in itself. Nor is matter said to exist except through such a *suppositum*, nor accidents either. And therefore they are said to be con-created rather than created."[26]

---

nihil est aliud quam forma; unde idem est dictu, materia sit in actu sine forma, est dicere contradictoria esse simul; unde a Deo fieri non potest." *Quod. III*, col. 2.

24. "Sed quia nos ponimus materiam creatam a Deo, non tamen sine forma, habet quidem materia ideam in Deo, non tamen aliam ab idea compositi; nam materia secundum se neque esse habet, neque cognoscibilis est." *Sum. Th.*, I, q. 15, a. 3, *ad* 3.

25. "Materia non est generabilis nec corruptibilis: quia omne quod generatur, ex materia generatur: et quod corrumpitur, in materiam corrumpitur; qui materia est principium primum ex quo aliquid fit et ultimum in quod abit quod corrumpitur, secundum Philosophum in *Phys*. I. Unde ipsa non nisi ex nihilo producitur, et nonnisi in nihilum desinere potest." *De Nat. Mat.*, 1. Cf. also *Con. Gen.*, 1. II, c. 5.

26. "Hoc enim solum creari dicitur quod habet esse; et hoc est suppositum, sive prima substantia, cujus est esse per se. Materia vero non dicitur esse nisi per tale suppositum, nec etiam accidentia. Et ideo concreata dicuntur potius quam creata." *De Quat. Op.*, c. 4.

4. PRIVATION AND MATTER

Privation and matter, which meet in the same subject, differ formally since privation is a principle *per accidens* but matter a principle *per se*.[27] They are intimately associated, since they meet in a common subject. Privation is a negation, not *any* negation but the negation of a form proper to a thing, and so is non-being by nature.[28] Prime matter in its actual state is subject to privation as well as to form, for inasmuch as it is informed by one form, it is deprived of all other forms for which it has potentiality, and so it is non-being but only *per accidens*.[29] Privation is an *ens rationis* only;[30] prime matter has some reality, and is capable of existing extra-mentally in *rerum natura*. The subject common to both privation and prime matter is an actual substance; in respect of privation this substance lacks a certain mode of being; in respect of prime matter this substance, while it actually is what it is, is in potency to becoming other substances.

Privation presupposes a subject with an aptitude; in other words, a potential being is the subject of privation, for if there were no subject

---

27. "Materia et privatio sunt idem subjecto, sed differunt ratione; ... unde privatio dicitur principium non per se, sed per accidens, quia scilicet coincidit cum materia." *De Princ. Nat.*, col. 3.

28. "Et quia generatio non fit ex non ente simpliciter, sed ex non ente quod est in aliquo subjecto, et non in quodlibet, sed in determinato: non enim ex quolibet non igne fit ignis, sed ex tali non igne, circa quem nata sit fieri forma ignis; ideo dicitur quod privatio est principum, et non negatio." *De Princ. Nat.*, col. 4.

29. Of this Aristotle says: "Now we distinguish matter and privation and hold that one of these, namely the matter, is not-being only in virtue of an attribute which it has, while privation in its own nature is not-being; and that the matter is nearly, in a sense IS substance, while the privation in no sense is." *Phys.*, I, 9, 192 a 1.

30. "Ens enim dupliciter dicitur, ut Philosophus docet (*Metaph.*, V): Uno modo secundum quod significat essentiam rei et dividitur per decem praedicamenta, et sic nulla privatio potest dici ens; alio modo, secundum quod significat veritatem compositionis, et sic malum et privatio dicitur ens in quantum privatione dicitur aliquid esse privatum." *Con. Gen.*, l. III, c. 9, *fi.*

in potentiality to other forms, there would be no privation; for that precisely is what privation is.[31] Prime matter does not presuppose a subject, for matter itself is the ultimate substrate of material things, the first subject of corporeal substances, itself contributing to the essential constitution of sensible bodies. Privation is a necessary and natural antecedent of generation. Though it has no positive influence in the generation of the new form, this does not mean that it is not a real principle, nor is it to be thought that it is not necessary to the process of generation.[32] It ceases with the eduction of the new form; otherwise contraries would exist at the same time and in the same respect. Prime matter is a necessary and natural antecedent *and* constituent of generated substances, thus exerting a positive influence, and is said to be a real principle that is also a cause. It does not cease, but contrariwise, it must persist under the new form or else all coming to be would be a series of annihilations and creations. The new substance which terminates a substantial change retains the prime matter of the present substance but loses the old privation and acquires new privations proper to the nature of the new substance.

"While in generation the matter or the subject perseveres, privation does not, nor does the composite which is made up of matter and privation. Therefore matter which does not imply privation is permanent,[33] that which does imply it, is transient."[34] Matter can be said to migrate from subject to subject inasmuch as it is ceaselessly informed and re-informed by the forms to which it is potential. In its abstract state, however, it is said to be in potency to existence in general, and thus it is held permanently fixed, as it were, to this one actuality so long as it is thus conceived. Neither privation nor prime matter can

---

31. "Carentia formae in eo quod est in potentia ad formam, est privatio." *Sum Th.*, I, q. 66, a. 2. Cf. *Sum Th.*, I, q. 48, a. 3.

32. "Dicitur etiam principium generationis a quo incipit generatio, et hoc modo principium vel initium generationis est privatio formae inducendae." *I Sent.*, d. 5, q. 3.

33. That is, matter in its universality; taken in an abstract sense.

34. That is, matter in its determined state under limitation of a specific form. Cf. *De Princ. Nat.*

properly be called an essence.³⁵ Privation determines its subject.³⁶ Prime matter determines form.³⁷

We have been dealing with three principles of the generation of sensible substance, namely, privation, matter and form. We noted that the essence of matter is privation of determined existence and potentiality for forms of which it is capable We therefore, in these last few pages, advanced the Thomistic teaching concerning the nature of prime matter, and we determined the differences between privation and matter. We propose to take up for special consideration the nature of potentiality in itself. Before doing so, we shall quote Saint Thomas summarily concerning the three notions of privation, form and matter:

> Three principles are required for generation, namely, potential being, which is matter; non-being in act, which is privation; and that by which a thing is, and this is form. There are therefore three principles of nature, matter and form and privation of form; of these, form is that principle by which something is generated, whereas the other two principles are principles from which generation proceeds.³⁸

The three principles are not of equal influence, for privation is a principle in *fieri* only; matter and form are principles in *esse* as well.³⁹

---

35. "Privatio autem non est aliqua essentia, sed est negatio in substantia." *Con. Gen.*, l. III, c. 7. Cf. also *De Quat. Op.*, c. 4. *Infra*, p. 86, footnote 20.

36. "Ad cujus evidentiam sciendum est quod negatio neque ponit aliquid neque determinat sibi aliquod subjectum; et propter hoc potest dici tam de ente quam de non ente; sicut non videns et non sedens. Privatio autem non ponit aliquid, sed determinat sibi subjectum; 'est' enim 'negatio in subjecto' ut dicitur, *IV Metaph.*, caecum enim non dicitur nisi de eo quod est natum videre." *Sum. Th.*, I, q. 17, a. 4.

37. "Forma vero finitur per materiam, in quantum forma in se considerata communis est ad multa; sed per hoc quod recipitur in materia, fit forma determinate hujus rei." *Sum. Th.*, I, q. 7, a. 1.

38. "Ad hoc autem quod sit generatio, tria requiruntur: scilicet ens in potentia quod est materia; et non esse actu quod est privatio; et id per quod fit actu quod est forma: ... Sunt igitur tria principia naturae, scilicet materia et forma et privatio quorum scilicet forma, est id propter quod fit generatio, alia duo sunt es parte ejus ex quo est generatio." *De Princ. Nat.*, col. 3.

39. "Privatio est principium in fieri, et non in esse; quia dum fit idolum, oportet quod non sit idolum; si enim esset non fieret, quia quicquid fit non

It remains now for us to consider potentiality itself, the most fundamental of all the notions claiming the title of antecedents of being; for Saint Thomas tells us that the subject of privation and of form is one and the same thing, which is being in *potentiality*.[40]

5. POTENCY, ACTIVE AND PASSIVE

The first subject, the ultimate material substrate of corporeal beings may be viewed under a dual aspect: first, in its inherent privation, *non-ens in genere;* second, in its essential characteristic, potentiality, *ens in potentia*. To be "this" in potency is not to be "this" in act; thus a thing in potency is to be something and not to be something under different aspects. It is the concept which fulfills Aristotle's insistence upon an indeterminate being as the only solution of the ontological dilemma. Is reality being or becoming? Commenting on the Philosopher's Book XII of *Metaphysics,* Saint Thomas says:

> The Philosopher solved their doubts (the ancients') by showing how something comes from being and from non-being. He holds that being is twofold, actual and potential. Whatever is changed, therefore, is changed from potential into actual being, as something potentially white becomes actually white. So in the genus of substance, all things come from being and non-being; from non-being accidentally insofar as something comes from a subject under privation which is said to be non-being, but the thing comes to be *per se* from being in potency.[41]

est, nisi in successivis, ut in tempore et motu sed ex quo jam idolum est, non est ibi privatio idoli, quia affirmatio et negatio non sunt simul, similiter nec privatio et habitus." *Ibid.,* col. 4.

40. Cf. *Sum. Th.* I, q. 48, a. 3.

41. "Hanc ergo dubitationem Philosophus solvit, ostendendo qualiter aliquid fit ex ente et ex non ente; dicens quod duplex est ens, scilicet ens actu, et ens potentia. Omne igitur quod transmutatur, transmutatur ex ente in potentia in actu ens; sicut aliquid alteratur ex albo in potentia in actu album. Unde et in genere substantiae fiunt omnis ex non ente et ente. Ex non ente quidem secundum accidens, inquantum fit aliquid ex materia subjecta privationi, secundum quam dicitur non ens. Sed per se fit aliquid ex ente, non autem in actu, sed in potentia." *Lect.* 1.

As a being, potency is a non-being which in a certain sense *is*. As the essential characteristic of prime matter, it is an aptitude or capacity for doing or receiving something, the principle of action and passion. Potency presents the double aspect of acting (*agendi*) and receiving (*recipiendi*) which are the basis of the twofold division of real potency into active and passive. The former is operative, is rightly called "power," and is said to be on the part of form. The latter, a passive faculty, is receptive, is properly called "potentiality," and is said to be on the part of matter;[42] which means that passive potency is proper to matter as the determinable component in the composite, and that active potency is proper to the formal cause as the determining element specifying the matter and actualizing the potentiality under the action of an adequate efficient cause.[43] In other words, active potency is a power possessed by an agent to do something proportionate to its nature; passive potency is the faculty of receiving some modification consistent with its nature. It is, for example, in the passive potentiality of snow to become water, but not to become black. A flower, to use an ever-ready illustration, is in the passive potentiality of the prime matter of the seed, and in the actual power of natural agents such as soil, air, moisture, *et cetera*. Given normal conditions, a seed can develop into a flowering plant through real distinct potentialities found in both the subject and the agents. Now potency is not actuality but its contrary, and these two notions are the basic concepts underlying all change and movement. Things between which changes are seen to occur, Saint Thomas tells us, are contraries. Potency is opposed to act as capacity for being something is opposed to the fulfillment of that capacity. But since all contraries are in a common subject, so are potency and act found in a

---

42. "Potentia ad esse non solum accipitur secundum modum potentiae passivae, quae est ex parte materiae, sed etiam secundum modum potentiae activae, quae est ex parte formae." *De Pot.*, q. 5, a. 4, *ad* 1.

43. "Sicut ea quae fiunt ex materia, sunt in potentia materiae passiva, ita quae fiunt ab agente oportet esse in potentia activa agentis. Non autem potentia passiva materiae perfecte reduceretur in actum, si ex materia fieret unum tantum eorum ad quae materia est in potentia. Ergo si aliquis agens cujus potentia est ad plures effectus faceret unum illorum tantum, potentia ejus non ita complete reduceretur in actum sicut quum facti plura. Per hoc autem quod potentia actia reducitur in actum, effectus consequitur similitudinem agentis." *Con. Gen.*, l. II, c. 45, No. 2.

given subject though under different aspects. Thus potency, which of itself is not an actual being, is nevertheless an indeterminate being, one determinable by form, a non-being which in a certain way *is*.[44] It is this indeterminateness which makes possible the changes by which the indetermined becomes determined, limited, specified. The notion of indeterminate being, or potency, is the object of our present attention.

The division of real potency into active and passive is a distinction which is founded on basic differences. The notion of active potency is that of a principle of change or movement in another, *in quantum est aliud*. It is an active power of producing an effect upon something else which is distinct from it, as the builder is distinct from the house he builds, or the soil and moisture are distinct from the tree they nourish. The notion of passive potency, on the other hand, is a principle of receptivity, a capacity for receiving a change from another insofar as it is another. Paralleling active potency, it too is distinct from the effect produced, even as the capacity for becoming an oak is distinct from the oak, or the capacity of the human mind to know is distinct from the knowledge acquired.

Active and passive potency differ as to their correlative forms. For, says Saint Thomas, act is twofold: first act which is form, and second act which is operation.[45] To this twofold act, since act and potency are correlative, there corresponds a twofold potency: one, active, the act of which is operation, and the second, passive, the act of which is form.[46] The correlative act of passive potency is movement terminating in a form, first act. The act and perfection of active potency is operation, second act, which presupposes a first act. Thus active potency is of itself an act, since it has the perfection of operation with respect

---

44. "Esse enim in potentia aliquo modo ad esse pertinet." Also "Esse in potentia est quasi non esse, quia quod est in potentia non est." Again, "Esse autem in potentia ad unum necessario adjungitur esse actu aliud, quia nunquam est esse in potentia pura sine aliquo actu; aliter materia esset sine forma." *De Quat. Op.*, c. 5.

45. "Actus autem est duplex: primus, qui est forma; secundus, qui est operatio." *De Pot.*, q. 1, a. 1.

46. "Una activa cui respondet actus, qui est operatio, alia est potentia passiva, cui respondet actus primum, qui est forma, ad quam similiter videtur secundario nomen potentia devolutum. Sicut autem nihil patitur nisi ratione potentiae passivae, ita nihil agit nisi ratione actus primi, qui est forma." *Ibid.*

to passive potency; for nothing acts, Saint Thomas says repeatedly, except insofar as it is in act. Thus active power is the principle by which potentialities are perfected in act. The opposition between passive and active potency is as the opposition between matter and form in a composite, or between act and potency in being in general.[47] Between active power and act there is no opposition, but between passive power and act there is opposition. The reason for this is found in the very fact that the active power is in some way an act, as we showed above. "Active power is not contrary to act but is founded upon it, for everything acts according as it is actual; but passive power is contrary to act, for a thing is passive according as it is potential."[48]

We must note here as we have done before that the active potency is best termed "power" and the passive potency "potentiality." This will do away with any confusion which might arise from terms, for when Saint Thomas says "no potentiality is operative,"[49] he is speaking of passive potency only; for he repeatedly tells us that active potency is the principle of action.[50] Passive potentiality, though a real capacity, is nevertheless characterized by receptivity of act, not by self-actualization; but active potency, on the other hand, tends toward activity; its object and effect is something made.[51]

Active and passive potency, or power and potentiality, are real capacities in really existing subjects and for this reason they are specified in

---

47. "Materia comparatur ad agens, sicut recipiens actionem quae ab ipso est; actus enim, qui est agentis ut a quo, est patientis ut in quo. Igitur requiritur materia ab aliquo agente, ut recipiat actionem ipsius; ipsa enim actio agentis, in patiente recepta, est actus agentis et formae, aut aliqua inchoatio formae in ipso." *Con Gen.*, l. II, c. 16, No. 6.
48. "Potentia activa non dividitur contra actum, sed fundatur in eo; nam unumquodque agit secundum quod est in actu; potentia vero passiva dividitur contra actum; nam unumquodque patitur, secundum quod est in potentia." *Sum. Th.*, I, q. 25, a. 1, *ad* 1.
49. "...nulla autem potentia operationem habet...." *Con Gen.*, l. II, c. 25.
50. "Potentia activa dicitur secundum quod est principium actionis." *De Pot.*, q. 1, a. 1.
51. "Unde cum duplex sit potentia, scilicet potentia ad esse, et potentia ad agere, utriusque potentiae perfectio virtus vocatur. Sed potentia ad esse se tenet ex parte materiae, quae est ens in potentia; potentia autem ad agere se tenet ex parte formae, quae est principium agendi, et quod unumquodque agit, inquantum est actu." *Sum. Th.*, I-II, q. 55, a. 2.

the genus of potency as real or subjective potencies. The reality of the potencies cannot be denied without violence to experience and common sense. We know from experience that an oak will result from a normal acorn under normal conditions. We likewise know that fire applied to coals will cause the latter to burn. No one of us plants an acorn in the hope that a peachtree will come forth, nor do we burn coal in the expectation that it will sprout buds or produce rain. All this is by way of saying that experience has shown us that capacities for becoming such-and-such are real in the pre-existing subject. The effect must really be in the potentiality of the matter. The effect must likewise be real in the agent. The reality of the effect is not actually in the agent but virtually. The Parthenon was not actually in the builders nor in the materials used, but virtually only; that is, in virtue of the passive potentiality of the material it was possible, by the action of the builders, to bring into actuality that which before was only potentiality. Farmers plant seeds in the firm conviction that the forces of nature have the power to produce a harvest. The active power is that by which the effect is produced; the nature of the effect lies in the passive potency of the pre-existing matter. The work of the active power is to bring that potentiality forth into actuality. Saint Thomas says of this:

> Every agent that requires prejacent matter in acting, has a matter proportionate to its action, so that whatever is in the potency (power) of the agent, is all in the potentiality (passive potency) of the matter; otherwise it could not bring into act all that are in its active power, and thus would have that power with regard to such things, to no purpose.[52]

The type of existence which prime matter has is determined by the nature of the form which informs it; for example, if the form is inorganic, then the existence which belongs to the composite of this prime matter and this substantial form is non-living existence. If the

---

52. "Omne agens quod in agendo requirit materiam praejacentem, habet materiam proportionatam suae actioni, ut quidquid est in virtute agentis, totum sit in potentia materiae; alias non posset in actum producere quidquid est in sua virtute activa, et sic frustra haberet virtutem ad illa." *Con. Gen.*, l. I, c. 16, No. 7.

composite is living, then the prime matter participates through its form in living existence. If the form is spiritual, as the soul, then this prime matter to which it is joined participates in the existence of a spiritual nature. *Forma dat esse materiae.* As a consequence of the reception of form, prime matter is restricted or limited by it. Inasmuch as it is informed by this form, it cannot at the same time be informed by another form; furthermore, its potentiality to all other forms is restricted, at least proximately, to that which can naturally be educed from its potentiality. The potentiality of the prime matter in an acorn is not in proximate potentiality to becoming a lump of coal, though it is not impossible for it, through a series of transmutations, eventually to be informed by the substantial form "coal."

Passive potency is sometimes referred to as *prope nihil.* Viewed as privation of form and lack of determination, the emphasis can well be placed on the *nihil* aspect of that expression. Viewed, on the other hand, as a subjective potency or a capacity for receiving completed act, the stress is put on the *prope* aspect. For as passive potency, prime matter is one of the two necessary components of material composites; there must therefore be a real capacity for receiving its correlative component. Passive potency therefore is something real, is *ens,* not *nihil.*

6. THE TRANSMUTATION OF FORMS: THE PROCESS OF *Fieri*

It seems advisable, if not absolutely necessary, to round out our picture of *fieri* by interpolating at this point an account of the informing of primary matter by a new substantial form. Grouped around this general question, there are questions which have to do with specific partial views of this process, and it is such as these that we shall attempt to answer in our explanation of the manner in which new forms inform matter. From them, and in addition, from what we have already learned concerning generation, we shall derive an adequate knowledge of the problem of "fieri" which Saint Thomas calls "via ad esse."[53] What is the source or origin of the new forms? Is the

---

53. "Generatio, per se loquendo, est via in esse, et corruptio via in non-esse. Non enim generationis terminus est forma, et corruptionis (terminus) privatio, nisi quia forma facit esse, et privatio non esse. Dato enim quod aliqua forma non faceret esse, non diceretur generari id quod talem formam acciperet." *Con. Gen.* l. I, c. 26, No. 5. Cf. *Sum. Th.,* I, q. 110, a. 2.

Substantial Change

proper term or final goal of the generative process the form or the composite? What is the *terminus a quo* and under how many aspects can it be conceived? What is the nature of the causality required for the production of the new substance? Finally, what contribution does matter make to the process?

With the underlying fundamental principles of act and potency, of matter and form, of creation and generation, of change and successive movement, and of the four causes of the becoming of a thing, we are already familiar. Our present treatment will have to do with the operation of these principles in the actual process of the acquisition of a new form in the primary matter of a previous substance. Saint Thomas tells us that nature produces an effect in act from being in potentiality. It is precisely the process whereby potential being is reduced to actual effect that the term generation applies.[54] Nature has been gifted with generative powers, so that the process of generation must not be confused with the act of creation whereby God alone produces existence from no pre-existing potential subject. Composite beings are within the scope of the active power of composite beings, since like is produced by like, as man by man and fire by fire.[55] Natural agents do not give existence in general, but existence of this or that composite in a determined species.[56] Further, generation takes place between con-

---

54. "Dicit ergo primo, quod trium praedictarum mutationum ille quae est de non subjecto in subjectum, existens inter contradictorios terminos, vocatur generatio. Sed hoc contingit dupliciter: Quia aut est mutatio ex non ente simpliciter in ens simpliciter, et tunc est generatio simpliciter. Et hoc quando mutabile subjectum mutatur secundum substantiam. Aut est de non ente in ens non simpliciter, sed secundum quid, sicut de eo quod non est album, in albo: et haec est generatio quaedam et secundum quid. Illa vero mutatio, quae est de subjecto in non subjectum, dicitur corruptio. Et similiter in hac distinguitur simpliciter et secundum quid, sicut in generatione." *In XI Metaph.*, lect. 11.

55. "Formae sunt ex agentibus naturalibus." *De Pot.*, q. 3, a. 8. Cf. *Sum. Th.*, I, q. 65, a. 4. For Aristotle, *Metaph.* VII, 7, 1032 a 15.

56. "Hoc autem esse non est esse in communi, sed esse hoc vel illud compositum in specie determinata: omne enim agens naturale est in specie aliqua: et ideo sua actio non extenditur ad esse quod non sit in sua specie, cujusmodi est esse in communi acceptum, quod est alterum extremum contradictionis absolutae, ut dictum est. Similiter non esse, quod est terminus a quo in genera-

traries and these imply a subject which exists,[57] so that generation is nothing other than the specifying anew of primary matter. In other words, primary matter is given a new substantial state through the acquisition of a new specific principle, and this principle is the form constituting the matter in its specific nature. The primary matter of the acorn receives a new principle which produces a new substance, namely, the form "oak" which constitutes the primary matter in the determined species "oak tree."

The most important question that can be asked in connection with this aspect of the problem is: What is the source of the new form? Whence comes it? And the answer which Saint Thomas gives, among others substantially the same, is this: The form is educed from the potency of the matter.[58] This answer means nothing other than that there is a change from being in the state of potentiality to that of being actual. This excludes creation, of course, for reasons which we need not repeat here. It excludes also the theory of Plato that the forms were introduced from without.[59] The *eductio* or drawing out of the form from the potentiality of the matter implies a pre-existence of the form in the matter. This is the crux of the question. What is the nature of that pre-existence of the form in the potency of the matter? Are the forms ready-made and concealed within the substance, ready to be pulled out as a rabbit is already existing in the magician's hat, or a trout swimming in the cool waters of the brook, awaiting "eduction" by the agent? This is the theory of Anaxagoras, and Saint Thomas refutes it in his *Commentary on the Book of Sentences of*

tione simpliciter, non est non esse absolute, sed non esse hoc." *De Quat. Op.,* c. 5.

57. "Quod autem fit, fit vel ex materiae vel ex nihilo. Quod vero ex materia fit, necesse est fieri ex materia contrarietati subjecta." *De Pot.* q. 3, a. 9. "... cum omnis generatio sit ex contrario et ex materia." *Con. Gen.*, l. II, c. 42.

58. "Nihil ergo obstat per hoc quod dicitur: per naturam ex nihilo nihil fit, quin formas substantiales, ex operatione naturae esse dicamus. Nam id quod fit, non est forma, sed compositum; quod ex materia fit, et non ex nihilo. Et fit quidem ex materia, inquantum est in potentia ad ipsum compositum, per hoc quod est in potentia ad formam. Et sic non proprie dicitur quod forma fiat in materia, sed magis quo de materiae potentia educatur." *De Pot.*, q. 3, a. 8.

59. For Plato's theory and Saint Thomas' rejection of it, cf. *II Sent*, d. 1, q. 1, a. 4, *ad* 4. Also *Sum. Th.*, I, q. 110, a. 2.

Peter the Lombard, in the same place wherein he refutes the theory of Plato.[60] According to the doctrine of Anaxagoras, the substantial forms of all substances lie hidden within every substance, so that the production of a new substance is not a generation from potentiality to actuality, but the lifting of a lid and the uncovering of the hidden form. Saint Thomas denies that such forms can *actually* exist in substances since he denies plurality of forms in a single substance. The root of the error of Anaxagoras lies in his failure to grasp the distinction between potential existence and actual existence. It is true, says Saint Thomas, that only one substantial form can inform a substance at any given time, if by that we understand *actually* informing the matter. But if we consider forms potentially present in a state of co-existence with the one actually specifying form, there is no inconsistency. Potential existence and actual existence are on distinct levels, and there can be no opposition between them other than the very basic opposition which makes them entirely different grades of reality. There is no contradiction in holding that a potential form can co-exist with an actual form in a subject. Saint Thomas says:

> Considered in itself, it (prime matter) is in potentiality in respect to all those forms to which it is common, and in receiving any one form it is in act only as regards that form. Hence it remains in potentiality to all other forms. And this is the case even where some forms are more perfect than others and contain these others virtually in themselves. For potentiality is indifferent with respect to perfection and imperfection so that under an imperfect form it is in potency to a perfect form and vice versa.[61]

Neither can it be said that the forms are in the substance imperfectly, if by imperfectly is meant partially developed.[62] For Saint Thomas, the

---

60. *Ibid.*
61. "Materia enim secundum id quod est, est in potentia ad formam. Oportet ergo quod materia secundum se considerata sit in potentia ad formam omnium illorum quorum est materia communis. Per unam autem formam non fit in actu nisi quantum ad illam formam. Remanet ergo in potentia quantum ad omnes alias formas. Nec hoc excluditur, si una illarum formarum sit perfectior et continens in se virtutes alias; quia potentia, quantum est de se, indifferenter se habet ad perfectum et ad imperfectum." *Sum. Th.,* I, q. 66, a. 2.
62. "Ad decimum dicendum, quod forma praeexistit in materia imperfecte; non quod aliqua pars ejus sit ibi in actu, et alia desit; sed quia tota praeexistit in potentia, et postmodum tota producitur in actu." *De Pot.,* q. 3, a. 8, *ad* 10.

potential forms belong to the very nature of prime matter. They do not pre-exist as forms but only insofar as the potency of the matter may be called a beginning of form. The potential pre-existence of the forms merely consists in the existence of a previous aptitude for acquiring that which, at the time, is not in the actual possession of a thing but which, through the activity of an efficient cause, it may come to possess at some future time. It is only by keeping in mind this potential notion that generation can truly be said to be the acquisition of a new form.[63] This pre-existence Saint Thomas calls *secundum quid* or *inchoatio formae,* if by that "beginning of form" is understood nothing more than the appetite of the pre-existing matter for a new form. The term is not meant to imply the *rationes seminales* of Saint Augustine.[64]

It has been said that generation is change from form to form. Is the new form the term and final end of the generative process? What, precisely, do we mean by this "form"? Is it to be conceived in the essential or the entitative order? In other words, does the act of generation reach its term when the substantial form "oak" is introduced into primary matter and the essence oak tree is conceived? One might be led to think Saint Thomas held this were one not conversant with his doctrine of second act or form constituting the already constituted essence an actually existing thing extramentally. For of generation and form Saint Thomas says: "Forma enim *quae est terminus generationis, est per se intenta tam a natura universali quam a natura particulari.*"[65] "Nam forma geniti est terminus actionis generantis, et ipsa est etiam finis generationis."[66] "*Forma quae est generationis terminus, erat in materia ante generationem completam, non in actu, sed in potentia.*"[67]

That to Saint Thomas this form is existential or entitative form is not difficult to admit, for there is much to show that he considered the *compositum* to be the proper term of generation. It is a principle of Saint Thomas that a thing has being only insofar as it is in act, and hence to the essential being which the substantial form constitutes by its union with prime matter, there must accrue a second form in the ex-

---

63. Cf. *Sum. Th.,* I, q. 90, a. 2, *ad* 2.
64. Cf. *II Sent.,* d. 18, q. 1, a. 2.
65. *De Pot.,* q. 3, a. 6, *ad* 19.
66. *Ibid.,* q. 3, a. 4.
67. *Ibid.,* q. 3, a. 8, *ad* 8.

istential order, and the whole term of the generative process is this composite being in the actual order; for since existence is the complement of essence, it follows that existence must always be the final result of the act of generation. We had occasion to refer to this earlier in our present work when showing the distinction Saint Thomas makes between the term of creation and the term of generation.[68]

In the *Summa Theologica* Saint Thomas, refuting the theories of the Platonists and of Avicenna, says:

> They seem to be deceived on this point, through supposing a form to be something made *per se,* so that it would be the effect of a formal principle. But as the Philosopher proves (*Metaph. VII*) what is made, properly speaking, is the composite: for this, properly speaking is, as it were, what subsists. Whereas the form is called a being, not as that which is, but as that by which something is; and consequently neither is a form properly speaking, made; for that is made which is; since to be made is nothing but the way to existence.[69]

Saint Thomas repeatedly says the same thing in substance.[70]

The composite therefore is the result of generation, yet this is effected only through the form, since the composite is this matter and this form, and form is that *by which* this matter is constituted a determinate species, and form is that *by which* the composite has existence.

The question of the *terminus a quo* in generation has received considerable attention elsewhere in this work. However, insofar as it throws light upon our interpretation of Saint Thomas' terminology con-

68. Cf. *De Quat. Op.,* cc. 1, 4.

69. "Quod proprie fit est compositum. Hoc enim proprie est quasi subsistens; forma autem non dicitur ens, quasi ipsa sit, sed sicut quo aliquid est; et sic per consequens nec forma proprie fit; ejus enim est fieri, cujus est esse; cum fieri nihil aliud sit quam via ad esse." *Sum. Th.,* I, q. 110, a. 2.

70. "Unumquodque autem factum, hoc modo dicitur fieri quo dicitur esse. Nam esse est terminus factionis; unde illud quod proprie fit per se, compositum est. Forma autem non proprie fit, sed est id quo fit, id est per cujus acquisitionem aliquid dicitur fieri." *De Pot.* q. 3, a. 8. "Sicut probat Aristoteles in *VII Metaph.* id quod proprie fit, est compositum." *Sum. Th.,* I, q. 65, a. 4. Cf. also *II Sent.,* d. 1, q. 1, a. 4, *ad* 4. *Sum. Th.,* I, q. 90, a. 2; — I, q. 91, a. 2. *In VII Metaph., lect.* 7.

cerning the process by which the new form is acquired, we will set down briefly the possible *termini a quo*. We have said that *ens in potentia* is the starting point of all change. In analyzing this concept we saw that it implies three notions: first, the notion of a subject, a composite; second, the notion of a privation; third, the notion of an appetite or aptitude. Any one of these three notions may be conceived as the starting point, the *terminus a quo*. The composite may be conceived as such inasmuch as there is no privation nor potentiality unless in a subject. Further, the composite corrupts during the substantial change and a new composite is the result.[71] In this respect, the *termini* of generation may be conceived as prior composite and new composite, and the process itself in relation to the new form may be described as an "acquisition" or "reception." We have already seen in what way form is said to be the *terminus* of generation, and in that sense the prior form may be said to be the *terminus a quo*, in which case the process will be from form to form.

However, more properly, the *terminus a quo* is something more elemental than the composite substance, for the change is begun from a certain lack of form for which the prime matter has an aptitude.[72] This lack of form is accompanied by an appetite or aptitude for the form which the matter lacks,[73] and thus the double aspect of a void and a capacity are responsible for the double set of terms employed by Saint Thomas to indicate the satisfaction of the capacity and the removal of the privation.[74] Considered in the light of a privation, the process of acquiring a new form may be seen as a "filling-in" process,

---

71. "Esse autem secundum se competit formae; unumquodque enim est ens actu, secundum quod habet formam. Materia vero est ens actu per formam. Compositum igitur ex materia et forma desinit esse actu per hoc quod forma separatur a materia." *Sum. Th.*, I, q. 50, a. 5.

72. "Privatio substantialis formae est terminus a quo in generatione." *Sum. Th.*, I, q. 45, a. 1, *ad* 2. " 'Ex' nominat ordinem, tun fit aliquid ex opposito etiam per se, unde et privatio dicitur principium esse fiendi." *De Pot.*, q. 3, a. 1, *ad* 16.

73. "Carentia formae in eo quod est in potentia ad formam, est privatio." *Sum. Th.*, I, q. 66, a. 2.

74. "Ita materia dicitur vacua, quia caret forma, quae implet capacitatem et potentiam materiae." *De Pot.*, q. 4, a. 2, *ad* 31.

and in this sense the word "inductio" is used.[75] When seen as an aptitude for form[76] of which it is now deprived, the term "eductio" supplies the proper connotation — the drawing forth of that capacity to its fulfillment.[77] Privation and aptitude are two aspects of passive potentiality.

Our further exposition concerns itself with the meaning of "educed from the potentiality of matter"; and since this implies a process and a cause, these two latter notions will be taken up in their relation to substantial generation.

Quidquid movetur, movetur ab alio. Since nothing is moved unless it is moved by another, the movement from potentiality to actuality in the process of eduction of the new substantial form necessitates an agent.[78] Since like is produced from like, we must look for the cause of corporeal forms in something that is a composite,[79] and that is from natural agents[80] and not from an immaterial form. The causality

---

75. "Dicitur etiam principium generationis a quo incipit generatio, et hoc modo principium vel initium generationis est privatio formae inducendae." *I Sent.,* d. 5, q. 3. Cf. *De Pot.,* q. 4, a. 2, *aa* 31.

76. "Appetitus formae non est aliqua actio materiae, sed quaedam habitudo materiae, ad formam, secundum quod est in potentia ad ipsam." *De Pot.,* q. 4, a. 1, *ad.* 2.

77. "Nam id quod fit, non est forma, sed compositum; quod ex materia fit, et non ex nihilo. Et fit quidem ex materia, inquantum materia est in potentia ad ipsum compositum per hoc quod est in potentia ad formam. Et sic non proprie dicitur quod forma fiat in materia, sed magis quod de materiae potentia educatur." *De Pot.,* q. 3, a. 8. "Forma potest considerari dupliciter: uno modo secundum quod est in potentia; et sic a Deo materia concreatur, nulla disponentis naturae actione interveniente. Alio modo secundum quod est in actu; et sic non creatur, sed de potentia materiae educitur per agens naturale." *De Pot.,* q. 3, a. 4, *ad* 7.

78. "Cum enim nihil se educat de non-esse in esse, oportet causam aliam habere quod incipit esse." *De Pot.,* q. 3, a. 17.

79. "Et ideo cum simile fiat a suo simili, non est quaerenda causa formarum corporalium aliqua forma immaterialis, sed aliquod compositum, secundum quod hic ignis generatur ab hoc igne. Sit igitur formae corporales causantur non quasi influxae ab aliqua immateriali forma, sed quasi materia reducta de potentia in actum ab aliquo agente composito." *Sum. Th.,* I, q. 65, a. 4.

80. "Res corruptibiles desinunt esse per hoc quod earum materia aliam formam recipit, cum qua forma prior stare non potest; et ideo ad earum corruptionem requiritur actio alicujus agentis, per quam forma nova educatur de

in generation is usually conceived as twofold — namely, efficient and material. The efficient cause or natural agent has a double task, that of disposing the matter and of educing the form.[81] Now since a cause produces an effect by its own causality, the effect must of necessity be precontained in the cause in proportion to the mode of its causality.[82] To put it another way, an efficient cause is a cause that *acts*. The effect an efficient cause produces is precontained in the cause as an active power — a power *to act*. In the natural agents which constitute the efficient causes of the generation of an oak tree, namely, soil, water, sun, etc., the effect, that is, the oak tree, is precontained in them insofar as they are possessed of the power to act upon the acorn and bring about in the prime matter the necessary predisposition for the reception of the new form. This activity on the part of the agent is nothing other than the active potentiality of which we spoke before.

Again, a cause produces an effect by its own causality, and since, as we said, the effect must be precontained in proportion to the mode of the causality of the cause, it follows that the material cause differs fundamentally from the efficient cause. That this is so is evident when we consider the nature of matter. It is passive. The material cause, therefore, producing its effect by its own mode of causality, fulfills its function by being receptive. Therefore it follows

potentia in actum." *De Pot.*, q. 5, a. 3, *ad* 2. "Ex hoc autem ipso quod compositum fit, et non forma, ostendit Philosophus in *VII Metaph.* quod formae sunt ex agentibus naturalibus. Nam cum factum oporteat esse simile facienti, ex quo id quod factum est compositum, oportet id quod est faciens esse compositum, et non forma per se existens, ut Plato dicebat." *De Pot.*, q. 3, a. 8.

81. "Efficiens est causa rei secundum quod formam inducit, vel materiam disponit.... Sic igitur hujusmodi inferiora agentia corporalia, non sunt formarum principia in rebus factis, nisi quantum potest se extendere causalitas transmutationis; cum non agant nisi transmutando, hoc autem est inquantum disponunt materiam, et educunt formam de potentia materiae." *De Pot.*, q. 5, a. 1. "Si autem ponamus formas substantiales educi de potentia materiae, secundum sententiam Aristotelis, agentis naturalia non solum erunt causae dispositionum materiae, sed etiam formarum substantialium quantum ad hoc dumtaxat quod de potentia educuntur in actum." *De Pot.*, q. 5, a. 1, *ad* 5.

82. "Omne agens agit in quantum actus est; secundum igitur modum actus uniuscujusque agentis est modus suae virtutis in agendo; homo enim generat hominem, et ignis ignem." *Con. Gen.*, l. II, c. 22.

that the effect is found in the material cause as in a passive potency, which means that matter receives form. Following our established example, we can say it is because the acorn is possessed of a passive potentiality which implies at the same time a privation of form and an aptitude for form, that the prime matter in the acorn is the material cause of the eduction of the oak tree. Prime matter's predisposition for the reception of a definite specific form is its positive contribution to the generation of the new substance. This predisposition is, we repeat, the aptitude or capacity of being acted on by an efficient cause capable of disposing the matter to receive the new form.

It must not be supposed that the form plays no part in the generative act. Since, like prime matter, it is a constitutive principle of the new composite, it plays the rôle of formal cause to the prime matter. Prime matter and form are mutual causes of each other. Matter is the material cause of the form and the form is the formal cause of the matter, since matter and form are ordained to each other.[83] It must be noted that the matter must be predisposed to a certain specific form and not to just any form. The substantial form of water cannot combine with primary matter predisposed to the substantial form of fire.[84]

This brings us to our final aspect of generation — namely, the process or movement itself. "Every substantial form requires in the matter," says Saint Thomas, "its specific determination without which it cannot exist; as a result, alteration is the only way to generation and corruption."[85] This alteration is the process whereby the matter is

---

83. "Materia est causa formae, inquantum forma non est nisi in materia et similiter forma est causa materiae inquantum materia non habet esse in actu, nisi per formam; materia enim et forma dicuntur relative ad compositum sicut pars ad totum." *Con. Gen.*, l. II, c. 59.

84. "Impossibile est autem in idem convenire propriam dispositionem, quae requiritur ad formam ignis, et quae requiritur ad formam aquae, quia secundum tales dispositiones ignis et aqua sunt contraria. Contraria autem impossibile est simul esse in eodem adequate." *De Mixtione Elementorum* (Opusc. No. 29, Vol. 27, Vives).

85. "Omnis forma substantialis propriam requirit dispositionem in materia, sine qua esse non potest: unde alteratio est via ad generationem et corruptionem." *Ibid.*

disposed for the eduction of the new form.[86] It is in the last instant of alteration which is precisely that instant when the prime matter, as it were, can no longer withstand the action of the efficient cause, that the substantial change takes place. It is an instantaneous change.[87] The old form recedes into the potentiality of the matter,[88] and simul-

86. "Nulla forma substantialis suscipit magis et minus; sed solum materia per alterationem praecedentem variatur, ut sit magis et minus disposita ad formam." *De Pot.*, q. 3, a. 9, *ad* 9. "Omnes hujusmodo mutationes instantaneae sunt termini motus continui sicut generatio est terminus alterationis materiae." *Sum. Th.*, I, q. 53, a. 5. "Alteratio enim ordinatur ad generationem, sicut ad finem." *Proem. in Comment. in Lib. De Gen. et Cor.* (Vol. 23, Vives).

87. "Respondeo dicendum, quod aliqua mutatio est instantanea triplici ratione: uno quidem modo ex parte formae, quae est terminus mutationis. Si enim sit aliqua forma quae recipiat magis et minus, successive acquiritur subjecto, sicut sanitas; et ideo quia forma substantialis non recipit magis et minus, inde est quod subito fit ejus introductio in materia. Alio modo ex parte subjecti, quod quandoque successive praeparatur ad susceptionem formae, et ideo aqua successive calefit; quando vero ipsum subjectum est in ultima dispositione ad formam, subito recipit ipsam, sicut diaphanum subito illuminatur. Tertio modo ex parte agentis, quod est infinitiae virtutis: unde etiam potest materiam ad formam disponere." *Sum. Th.*, III, q. 75, a. 7.

"Forma substantialis non continue vel successive in actum producatur, sed in instanti.... Forma vero non incipit esse in materia nisi in ultimo instanti alterationis." *De Pot.*, q. 3, a. 9, *ad* 9. "Forma substantialis simul recipitur et recepta est." *II Sent.*, d. 1, q. 1, a. 2, *ad* 3.

"In ultimo instanti generationis jam inest forma." *Sum. Th.*, III, q. 75, a. 3.

"Generatio aeris est simplex, cum in tota generatione aeris non appareant nisi duae formae substantiales, una quae abjicitur et alis quae inducitur, quod totum fit simul in uno instanti.... Non educatur in actum." *De Pot.*, q. 3, a. 9, *ad* 9.

88. "Forma, quae est terminus a quo, non convertitur in aliam formam, sed una forma succedit alteri in subjecto; et ideo prima forma non remanet nisi in potentia materiae." *Sum. Th.*, III, q. 75, a. 3, *ad* 2. "Formae et accidentia non sunt entia completa, cum non subsistant.... Et tamen es modo quo sunt, non omnino in nihilum rediguntur, non quia aliqua pars eorum remanet, sed remanet in potentia materiae, vel subjecti." *Sum. Th.*, I, q. 104, a. 4, *ad* 3. "Formae et accidentia, etsi non habeant materiam partem sui ex qua sint, habent tamen materiam in qua sint et de cujus potentia educuntur; unde et cum esse desinunt, non omnino annihilantur, sed remanent in potentia materiae sicut prius." *De Pot.*, q. 5, a. 4, *ad* 9.

taneously the new form is educed.[89] The alteration requires time. This is in proportion to the power of the agent, the degree of receptivity of the matter, and the resistance which the matter and form put up against the "invading" form. The substantial change is, indeed, an offensive attack on the part of the new form which has, as its besieging vanguard, the series of alterations under the agency of the efficient cause. On the part of the prior substance the substantial change is a defense action, for the matter and form resist the incoming form.[90] It is only when the greater strength is on the side of the efficient cause and the incoming form, that the prior form capitulates and the new form captures the matter. A substance has been generated; a change has been effected. The fundamental notion behind the process and without which no change could have been possible, is the notion of passive potentiality.

7. PASSIVE POTENTIALITY AND POSSIBILITY

The reality of change, that ever-present phenomenon of sense experience, depends upon the reality of passive potentiality. The law of identity need not be sacrificed in the notion of real change. The principle of identity and the actuality of change are not only not contradictory, but the principle of identity verifies the reality of the change. It asserts: This substance, *e. g.*, iron, as long as it is what it is, is itself, viz. iron. The iron cannot be rust at the same time and in the same respect. Then, when the substantial change has been effected and what was actually iron and potentially rust now becomes actually rust, the principle of identity affirms: This rust, as long as it is what it is, is

---

89. "In mutationibus instantaneis simul est fieri et factum esse; sicut simul est illuminari et illuminatum esse: dicitur enim in talibus factum esse, secundum quod jam est; fieri autem secundum — quod ante non fuit." *Sum Th.*, III, q. 75, a. 7, *ad* 2.

90. "Per se autem fit aliquid ex subjecto, quod est in potentia. Contrarium igitur resistit agenti inquantum impedit potentiam ab actu, in quem intendit reducere materiam agens; sicut ignis intendit reducere aquam in actum sibi similem, sed impeditur per formam et dispositiones contrarias quibus quasi ligatur potentia ne reducatur in actum; et quanto magis fuerit potentia ligata, tanto requiritur major virtus in agente ad reducendam materiam in actum." *Sum. Th.*, I, q. 45, a. 5, *ad* 2.

rust. It is its own nature. A thing is what it is at any given moment and there is never a moment in the transition when there is neither iron nor rust, nor is there a moment when the same thing is both iron and rust under the same aspects. If passive potency were not real, then only what is actual would be real, for actuality and potentiality exhaust being. A thing is either actually or potentially this or that. If the actual alone is real, and passive potency is not real, then there could be no becoming, no change, no disappearance. No action could be effected were there nothing real capable of being affected by the action. Aristotle and Saint Thomas held that this real capability which is the ultimate foundation of all becoming is passive potentiality. It is more basic than the principle of actual potency since the action of the latter presupposes the former. The natural forces of soil, air, moisture and the like remain ineffective unless there is present to them a passive potentiality proportionate to their power. Passive potency is the ultimate principle of generation and the foremost antecedent of generated substances.

We have said that creation presupposes no passive potentiality. But those things which are made by movement must be previously possible in respect of a passive potentiality. Here is indicated the difference between the antecedents of creation and generation. Possibility, we noted, is the only prerequisite for creation. Passive potency in a subject, in addition to an adequate efficient cause (the active potency), is the prerequisite for generation. "Drawn out of the potentiality of matter" preserves the distinction between creation and generation.

The distinction between possibility and the active and passive potency we have been discussing is between two species of potency in general; that is, subjective or real potency, to which class belong the passive and active powers which have been the subject of our recent discussion; and secondly, the objective or logical potency, the mere possibility of our discussions in the earlier pages of this work. Objective or logical potency, mere possibility, is an aptitude or power to exist that is in a thing not yet in existence. The potency is not something really existing, as is the case of subjective potency residing in a subject, but it is conceived by the mind as capable of existing. "Haec potentia non est quidquam reale existens, concipitur tamen ad modum rei recipientis existentiam."[91]

Objective potency bifurcates into intrinsic and extrinsic possibility, being non-repugnance of constitutive notes in the first instance, and in the second, the power of an agent capable of bringing it into existence. A possible explanation is needed here insofar as possibility is included under the notion potency. In the *Contra Gentiles* Saint Thomas says:

> Before a created thing was, it was possible for it to be through the power of the agent, by which power also it began to be: or it was possible on account of the habitude of terms in which no incompatibility is found, *which kind of possibility is said to be in respect of no potentiality,* as the Philosopher says (V *Metaph.*). For this predicate being is not incompatible with this subject world or man, as measurable is not incompatible with diameter; and thus it follows that it is not impossible for it to be, *apart from all potentiality.* But in those things which are made by movement, it is necessary that they be previously possible in respect of a passive potentiality.[92]

In the expressions, "which kind of possibility is said to be in respect of no potentiality," and "it was possible for it to be apart from all potentiality," Saint Thomas is referring only to that specific potency we have called *passive* potentiality which is in an existing subject. This is implied in the closing sentence of the quotation. He does not exclude the specific potentiality we have called objective or logical which, in its intrinsic aspect, is that very non-repugnance of terms which he establishes as the basis of possibility. Creation requires no pre-existing subject, and hence as a production of something in the

---

91. Donat., J., *Ontologia,* Innsbruck, 1921.

92. "Possibile autem fuit ens creatum esse antequam esset, per potentiam agentis per quam et esse incepit vel propter habitudinem terminorum in quibus nulla repugnantia invenitur; quod quidem possibile secundum nullam potentiam dicitur, ut patet per Philosophum (*Metaph.* V): hoc enim praedicatum, quod est esse non repugnat huic subjecto, quod est mundus vel homo, sicut commensurabile repugnat diametro; et sic sequitur quod non sit impossibile esse, et per consequens quod sit possibile esse antequam esset, etiam nulla potentia existente. In his autem quae per motum fiunt, oportet prius fuisse possibile per aliquam passivam potentiam." *Con. Gen.,* l. II, c. 37.

wholeness of its substance, it is independent of any and every potential subject. Such a production necessitates, of course, an infinite power.[93]

We have gathered together within the broad periphery of the notion "potentia" the intrinsic and extrinsic requisites for creation, as well as the passive and active powers of generation. Since the process of generation presupposes the creative act, which in its turn presupposes intrinsic possibility; and since in the generative act, passive potentiality is required by the active principle, it follows that intrinsic possibility and passive potentiality, each a species of "potentia," are the ultimate antecedents of being.

---

93. "Virtus facientis non solum consideratur ex substantia facti, sed etiam ex modo faciendi; major enim calor non solum magis, sed etiam citius calefacit. Quamvis igitur creare aliquam effectum finitum non demonstret potentiam infinitam, tamen creare ipsum ex nihilo demonstrat potentiam infinitam. Quod ex praedictus patet. Si enim tanto major virtus requiritur in agente, quanto potentia est magis remota ab actu, oportet quod virtus agentis ex nulla praesupposita potentia, quale agens est creans, sit infinita; quia nulla proportio est nullius potentiae ad aliquam potentiam, quam praesupponit virtus agentis naturalis, sicut non entis ad ens. Et quia nulla creatura habet simpliciter potentiam infinitam sicut neque esse infinitum, ut supra probatum est, relinquitur quod nulla creatura possit creare." *Sum. Th.*, I, q. 45, a. 5, *ad* 3.

CHAPTER FIVE

OTHER INTERPRETATIONS OF REALITY

AMONG THE ANCIENTS

The problem of being and becoming was not new to medieval philosophy. It was not new to Aristotle. Its roots are traceable to the very beginning of philosophical thought, strictly speaking. This can be dated about the sixth century before Christ.

In the formative period of truly philosophical inquiry, the pre-Socratic period, men embarked upon true speculations as to the principles and causes of things. Water, air, fire and the fusion of contraries were all considered in turn the very stuff out of which the world was made. Those were days when men considered only the matter at hand, namely, sensible stuff, and from it they attained only a material principle as the explanation of reality. It remained for Parmenides, toward the close of the period, to be the first to reach the necessary degree of abstraction which revealed to him the fundamental notion underlying all reality, the concept of being as being. Belonging to this earlier period of which we speak, he nevertheless projected upon the philosophical horizon for later periods to objectify the certain outlines of the fundamental principle of metaphysics. Great thinkers of later days seized upon his principle of identity, recognized its validity, and reared upon it a metaphysics which outlives the centuries.

Among the thinkers of the pre-Socratic group were others less penetrating in their grasp of reality. They can be termed the Sensualists, such as Heraclitus, who did not rise above sense-experience in explaining reality. These two, Parmenides the Great, as Plato called him, and Heraclitus the Obscure, as he was known to his contemporaries, were representatives of two disparate currents of thought, monistic in character, and each held by its exponent to be the only satisfactory explanation of reality. Passing over the centuries, we shall seek in later systems traces of these early explanations of ultimate reality.

Parmenides

It is historically uncertain whether Parmenides was the predecessor or the successor of Heraclitus. In other words, it is uncertain whether the doctrine of the One Immobile of Parmenides is a refutation of the Universal Flux of Heraclitus, or whether the latter proposed to refute Parmenides' intellectualism.[1]

Parmenides erred in regard to the senses. He attributed all knowledge to intellectual knowledge. The senses which reported movement and change, generation and corruption, were to be distrusted. For it was plain, he held, that whatever is, *is*. His contemplation of being yielded only being completely one, absolute, immutable, whole and entire in its unity, equal to itself in everything, all perfections contained within it, with no becoming possible to it; and as a consequence of all these, or more strictly as the principle of them all, being was incorruptible and eternal. It was all very well for Parmenides to discover rationally the perfections of the Infinite Being and to lay them down for posterity. His refusal, however, to admit the possibility of any other being was responsible for his attributing to the world the being which belongs only to Uncreated Being.

While we can accept from him his enunciation of the principle of non-contradiction, "Being is being; non-being is nothing; what already is cannot become," we cannot accept the ultra-intellectualism that built up *a priori* this notion of infinite, eternal, immutable being with absolutely no regard for the data of the senses. Not only did Parmenides disregard the function of the senses in the acquisition of knowledge, but he rejected it, branding it as untrustworthy. He thus denied the very notion of movement and cut himself off thereby from an adequate explanation of the real.

The logical result of his doctrine could be nothing less than the absorption of all finite beings into the one infinite being. And Parmenides was logical: he refused to admit that any other being could exist, and thereby rejected being mingled with non-being, in very fact, the kind of being of every created being. Thus by his reduction of the

---

1. Cf. Uberweg, *History of Philosophy*, I, pp. 38, 41, 55; De Wulf, M., *History of Medieval Philosophy*, pp. 4 seq.

multiple to one, becoming to being, he necessarily ended in denying the existence of the world.[2]

Change, said Parmenides, is an illusion. Whatever is, *is*. If it is not, it is nothing. If it is nothing, it cannot become something, for *ex nihilo, nihil fit*. From among the fragments of Parmenides' writings, we quote a portion of his poem "On Nature":[3]

> Listen and I will instruct thee — and thou, when thou hearest,
>   shalt ponder:
> What are the sole two paths of research that are open to thinking.
> One path is: That being doth be and non-being is not:
> This is the way of Conviction, for Truth follows hard in her
>   footsteps.
> Th' other path is: That being is not, and non-being must be:
> This one, I tell thee in truth, is an all-incredible pathway.
> For thou never canst know what is not (for none can conceive it),
> Nor canst thou give it expression, for one thing are thinking and
>   being. . . .
> Speaking and thinking must needs be existent, for IS is of being.
> Nothing must needs not be; these things I enjoin thee to ponder.[4]

Here is the substance of the metaphysics of Parmenides. That he attained to the strict object of the intellect, namely, being, is undeniable.

---

2. Cf. St. Thomas, *In I Metaph.*, lect. 9; *In I Phys.*, lect. 3, 4, 5, 14.

3. The translation here given was made by Thomas Davidson and published in Vol. IV of the *Journal of Speculative Philosophy*. Cited by Bakewell, *Sourcebook in Ancient Philosophy*, pp. 13-17.

4. The excerpt continues as follows:
> "Never I ween shalt thou learn that being can be of what is not;
> Wherefore do thou withdraw thy mind from this path of inquiry;
>   . . . . And now there remains
> One path only: That being doth be — and on it there are tokens
> Many and many to show that that which is is birthless and deathless,
> Whole and only-begotten, and moveless and ever-enduring;
> Never it was or shall be; but the All simultaneously now is,
> One continuous one; for of it what birth shalt thou search for?
> How and whence it has sprung? I shall not permit thee to tell me
> Neither to think: 'of what is not'; for none can say or imagine
> How not-is becomes is; or else what need should have stirred it,
> After or yet before its beginning, to issue from nothing?
> Thus either wholly being must be or wholly must not be.
> . . . .

He was the first philosopher to reach the necessary degree of abstraction, to transcend the world of sensible phenomena and even of mathematical forms, to formulate that basic first principle of all thought: What is, is, and cannot not be. To sum up his thought, we note that it includes the following propositions: Being alone exists. There is not nor can be a void; all beings constitute but one single being. In reality there is neither origin nor decay. Change is mere appearance, an illusion. What is, cannot become. Being is eternal and immutable, a continuous and indivisible whole. It is self-sufficient, independent, absolute. There is for the thinker only the All-One in whom all individual differences are merged. The being that thinks and the being that is thought are the same. To evaluate it fairly one might say the being of Parmenides was a mere abstraction.

Of the Eleatic School, De Wulf writes:

> Conceive being in the abstract and universal, endowed with the logical attributes of unity, eternity and immobility; then transfer the object of your conception from the logical to the ontological order, and you have the cosmological system of the School of Elea.[5]

In the Eleatic denial of motion, we see but a consistent following of the fundamental tenet, that all beings merge into one undifferentiated being, continuous and indivisible. Movement there cannot be, for movement is change, and there is nothing into which the All-One could change. Here we have a key to Parmenides' basic error.

> One and the same are thought and that whereby there is thinking;
> Never apart from existence, wherein it receiveth expression,
> Shalt thou discover the action of thinking; for naught is or shall be
> Other besides or beyond the Existent....
> But since the uttermost limit of being is ended and perfect;
> Then it is like to the bulk of a sphere well-rounded on all sides,
> Everywhere distant alike from the center; for never there can be
> Anything greater or anything less, on this side or that side;
> Yea, there is neither a non-existent to bar it from coming
> Into equality, neither can being be different from being,
> More of it here, less there, for the All is inviolate ever."
>
> *Ibid.*, pp. 14-17.

5. *History of Medieval Philosophy*, p. 7.

It marks the precise notion he failed to grasp. For a denial of motion implies the denial or at best the non-recognition of the notion of potentiality, since movement is precisely the change from potentiality to actuality. According to Aristotle, as we have seen, it is the actualization of the potential insofar as it is potential. In other words, there can be no movement without a potential something presupposed. An oak tree cannot just "happen." It must "become," and it becomes from a pre-existing potency in an acorn.

Parmenides, then, failed in this, that his decidedly partial view of reality did not reveal the real. His system was obviously one-sided. Had he grasped the analogy of being instead of viewing the notion univocally, he might have achieved the metaphysics arrived at later by Aristotle, since Parmenides had rooted being, quite rightly in the primary principle of thought and being — the principle of identity. Thus the metaphysics of Parmenides absorbed becoming and the multiple in the sole and motionless being. God absorbs the world. God becomes the world. The result is Pantheism. He could draw his premises to no other consistent conclusion than that of the One Immobile.

Heraclitus

As Parmenides fastened on the notion of one and only one being, and thus gave to posterity the roots of a one-sided ontology, so Heraclitus, going to the opposite extreme, bequeathed to philosophy another inadequate explanation. As Parmenides denied motion and made immutable being the keynote of his system, Heraclitus denied immutability and made motion the pivot of his system. His vision was held by the transformations which his senses revealed to him; and so powerful was its influence upon him that he cast reason to the winds and embraced the testimony of the senses alone. He laid the foundation for all modern systems of Pantheism in which the world becomes God.

Heraclitus was as persistent as Parmenides in upholding his theory. His basic error was a denial of the principle of identity. His reasoning led him along the following lines: The sole substance of the universe is fire — fire undergoing transformations. Everything is fire;

air and water are fire in the process of extinction or of renewal; earth and solids are extinguished fire which will one day be rekindled. Universal life is an endless alternation of creations and destructions, or fire assuming its various forms. In all this eternal whirl of reality, nothing changes into being and being into nothing. Being and non-being, life and death, good and evil, are the same. If not, argued Heraclitus, how could they become each other? Therefore, he concluded, change is the only reality and contradictories are identical. Whatever exists, by the fact that it exists, changes, for change is the universal law of existence. That which is, at the same time is not. There is no permanent and abiding subject underlying the change.[6]

The perpetual flux, taught Heraclitus, for all that it is the normal mode of reality, is nevertheless a difficult process. It is a perpetual struggle between contrary forces, from which results all the vegetative, animal and intellectual life on the earth. Everything arises from this strife of opposites. All bodies are but transformations of one and the same element.[7]

Critical Evaluation

The notion of being had so fascinated Parmenides that it bound him to an inadequate and erroneous conception of reality. The notion of becoming, on the other hand, so enthralled Heraclitus that he repudiated the fundamental principle of thought and being in its favor. These two ancients, representative of schools of early Greek thought, so diametrically opposed as they were, set for all future philosophers the extremes of speculation and error. Disparate as they are, their conflicting philosophies nevertheless embrace a common characteristic which underlies much of the philosophical thought of modern times. The failure of Parmenides to conceive being other than as fixed and fully determined, and the failure of Heraclitus to recognize some stable, persisting principle of things, meet in a common root. Both systems failed to conceive that fundamental principle that all reality is divided between actuality and potentiality; that reduction from potency to act is change; that something remains permanent through-

6. Cf. Aristotle, *Metaph.* IV, 5, 1010 a 13.
7. Cf. Aristotle, *Phys.* I, 2, 185 b 19.

out the change; that both the changeable and the permanent are elements of the real. Reality, therefore, cannot be monistic, and thus it escapes the possibility of being pantheistic.

Had Parmenides embraced change and applied potency and act to his doctrine, he would have seen that the composite changing world was essentially distinct from the absolute, infinite, immutable being he postulated. Had Heraclitus embraced the doctrine of potency and act, he would have recognized the necessity of a Being, Absolute and Immutable, the Prime Unmoved Mover of moving realities. Had either of these ancients done this thing, he would have avoided monism and given to Greek thought the dualism of Aristotle, the incipient dualism of spirit and matter, of Pure Act and act mixed with potency, of Infinite, Necessary Being and distinct, contingent, finite beings.

To fill in the bold outlines of the picture historically insofar as it will give us a better grasp of the later development of the notion of being and becoming among the Greeks, we shall note briefly here Aristotle's synthesis of the disparate philosophies which had preceded him. The primary premise of Aristotle is that being is not an univocal concept, but an analogous one, and hence in being there is found more than either unchanging being or ever-changing being. For Aristotle, being is applicable not only to the actually existent but also to the possibly existent and to the changing thing as well. It is Aristotle's solution, whereby he saves the differentiation of things in being from being absorbed into one being. For Aristotle, as for Saint Thomas after him, the potency of finite beings is the very reason why the latter can never be identified with absolute being. To attempt the absorption of the many by the one is to remove from creatures their very essence, their mixture of act and potency which distinguishes them from Pure Act.

The basis for the distinction between Aristotle and the earlier philosophers whom we have evaluated, lies in this, that the sweep of Aristotelian metaphysics embraces, at its start, both reason and experience. The principle of identity, so evident to Parmenides, is not sacrificed to the principle of motion, so basic to Heraclitus. But what truth there was in the realism of Parmenides finds its metaphysical complement in what truth there was in the empiricism of Heraclitus. Aristotle needed a principle to uphold the truth of being as being, imposed by the intellect in the principle of identity. Furthermore, the principles he sought must be opposed to each other as the perfected to the perfectible; they must be complementary to each other as the actualized to the possible; they must both be included in the notion of being, for Aristotle firmly held to the principle that outside of being there is nothing. His doctrine of act and potency is his answer, and it seemed to the Angelic Doctor to be the only one capable of sustaining the empirical fact of change without destroying the validity of the principle of non-contradiction. This doctrine meets the requirements enumerated. Act is to potency as the perfected to the perfectible; as the actual to the possible; both are real being.

The doctrine in question is basic in Aristotelian thought. It is the guide for the distinction between essence and existence in finite beings; for the distinction between matter and form in material things; through it, in virtue of the principles of identity and of causality, we grasp the concept of a First Cause whose essence IS his existence, and finally, at the very peak of this metaphysics, we are brought to the absolute distinction between this Infinite Being and beings in the world of sense experience. Working with Aristotelian principles, Aquinas shows us the infinite chasm yawning between the Infinite Creator and the finite creature; nevertheless, each can be apprehended within the broad, analogous notion of being. By the doctrine of act and potency, the principle of identity is saved; the principle of change is validated; pantheism is refuted, theism established.

THE MODERNS

We pass by the intervening philosophies of being and becoming, through the myriad forms they have assumed throughout the centuries. It is apart from our purpose to enter into a detailed account of these philosophies. Our interest in Parmenides and Heraclitus is founded upon the fact that they were the first to establish for all time the antithetical relations between an all-is-being philosophy and an all-is-becoming philosophy.

There are modern versions of the philosophies of Parmenides and Heraclitus, and sometimes even an attempted synthesis, which has not, however, the merits of the Aristotelian achievement. From among the modern philosophers who have attempted to fix the nature of reality, we have selected two. Starting from poles as disparate as those of Parmenides and Heraclitus, Hegel, the intellectualist, and Bergson, the anti-intellectualist, by strange coincidence arrive at almost the same general conclusions. For each there is only one reality, and each in his concept of its nature denies the very foundation not only of his knowledge of reality but of the actual existence of reality itself. Each denies the validity of the principle of contradiction. So grievous is this error in the Scholastic tradition that it means the practical denial of all truth. It is our purpose to show, in this section of the work, how disastrous to any system of metaphysics in the light of the traditional Scholastic explanation of being and becoming, is the denial of the fundamental principle of thought and being.[8] We feel that a study of this doctrine in the philosophies of Hegel and Bergson will give further clarity and validity to the Thomistic concepts we aimed to expose in the earlier portions of the thesis.

"In every genus, worst of all is the corruption of the principles upon which the rest depends. . . . Wherefore . . . in speculative matters the most grievous and shameful error is that which is about things the knowledge of which is naturally known to man. . . . "[9] This is the censure Saint Thomas passes on corrupters of the basis of reality. Basic principles are at stake: principles of identity, of substance, of sufficient reason, of causality, of motion, of finality, all of which principles we have seen are the very supporting girders of the ontological edifice erected by Aristotle and Aquinas.

To treat all of the various aspects of Hegelianism and Bergsonism would require greater length than can be allotted to them here. We aim therefore, without any detriment to the cause of either of the philosophers, to limit our discussion of them to the most commonly known attribute of them both — the fundamental thesis that ultimate reality is not stable but changing. Ultimate reality is Process, says Hegel. It is a kind of unspringing of a taut spring. Ultimate reality, says Bergson, is Flow. It is like the noisy, babbling brook flowing swiftly past, and "things" are even less than the bubbles which float

---

8. Cf. *Sum. Th.*, I-II, q. 94, a. 2; Aris., *Metaph. IV*; Gilson, *Unity of Philosophical Experience*, p. 318.

9. *Sum. Th.*, II-II, q. 154, a. 12.

to its surface. To put it another way, for each of these modern philosophers, becoming, developing, movement, alone is reality.

Hegel

"The rational is real and the real is rational."[10] Thought and being are identical. All being is thought realized and all becoming is a development of thought. "Thought developing" gives the key to Hegel's system and method. In his own words, his philosophy is "an immanent and incessant dialectic," that is, a "thought-movement." The maze of Hegelian trichotomies may easily distract our attention from the fact that for Hegel the real can be analyzed only in terms of rational thought. We emphasize the point. From start to finish in the Hegelian dialectic, it is the absolute idea (the logical concept, the Absolute) that strives to express itself. It is at the start a mere nothing — vacuity; it is at the end a self-developed and world-developing creator. This is ultimate reality, the Absolute Spirit, the initial absolute idea which has arrived at the state of perfect self-knowledge. So much, in brief, for the introductory statement of Hegel's "reality."

Our treatment of this supremely architectonic system will consider the laws of development to which the Absolute is subject, the nature of the absolute idea and the stages of its process; and an evaluation of the ultimate nature of the development which is the Process itself, will shed additional light on our later discussions of the absolute idea in its progressive and, we might say, convulsive movement from abstract notion to concrete concept.

Hegel's system can be characterized as thought-movement: a system of concepts, each of which passes over into its successor, effecting by their union a higher and richer third concept. The synthesis does not end with the completion of the first movement. A new opposition makes its appearance, and, being supplemented by its union with *its* contrary, yields a still higher concept. Each new synthesis approaches closer to the truth, but no single concept, even the last and richest, by itself alone attains full truth; for this final concept implies the whole development preceding its formation. Reality can only be known

---

10. Preface to *Philosophy of Right*. Cited by Falckenberg, *History of Philosophy*, p. 489.

through a development of concepts, an ever-swelling dialectic. The law followed in every instance by this movement, whether of greater or lesser magnitude, is the advance from position to opposition and thence to combination. This threefold rhythm, expressed in technical language, has the moments of thesis, antithesis and synthesis. For Hegel, this is the universal law of development: immediate unity, the thesis; divergence of opposites, the antithesis; and finally, reconciliation of opposites, the synthesis.

If we are to conceive the absolute idea in its final stage as the culmination of an eternal series of developments each successive one of which is superior to its predecessor, it is evident that, as one works backward toward the early stages of the process, perfections diminish. The question is, just where in the order of perfection is the absolute idea at the start of the development? If it is something, it must have had a previous development, and then we would be forced to consider the start of that earlier development. What has been achieved at the end of the development? In other words, our inquiry here is into the nature of Hegel's Absolute.

The Absolute, first, last and always, is a concept; it is a logical notion; it is thought. It is not a passive substance but a living subject, incessantly dividing into distinctions, positing itself in otherness and restoring itself from the state of "alterity" to which it descends, and by its restoration renewing identity with itself. The Process is the Absolute manifesting itself. There are three major manifestations of it which constitute the Process. In the first manifestation, the logical concept is discovered in itself (*an sich*). It reveals itself as a system of ante-mundane concepts, a realm of eternal thoughts, God as He was before creation. But the Absolute is ever unfolding and renewing itself, and thus we find in its second manifestation that it has gone out of itself (*ausser sich*) seeking self-consciousness. It descends into the unconscious realm of nature and awakens to self-consciousness in man. This excursion out of itself enriches the Absolute, and it makes a return into itself to attain a higher absoluteness than it had at the beginning. It is now the logical concept in-itself (*in-sich*).

Thus the Absolute is a process, an eternal thinking, a dialectic. The nature of the Process clarifies our understanding of the nature of the

Absolute. We have, as we said, the infinite idea in itself as the first step. This is the region of bare thinking (*Denken-in-sich*), of empty, abstract forms. To this corresponds the first division of Philosophy, Logic.[11]

The second step is the Idea in its objective form, or in its differentiation, its alterity (*Idee in ihrem anders-sein*). This is a real part of the Process, a transition stage in the development of the Absolute. It is the Absolute idea itself that becomes nature in order to become actual, conscious spirit. It was, we remark, spirit even before it became nature, but only spirit *in-sich*, in its abstractness. It was spirit only as abstract idea. Nature, however, is spirit expressing itself in external reality, becoming concretized and conscious of itself.

From this out-of-itself existence in nature, the Process perpetually repeats itself, gaining something fresh at every pulsation, and carrying the Absolute on to its highest perfection, living spirit, perfect self-knowledge, the self-thinking Idea. This is the culmination of the third major stage of the Process, with the Absolute returned into itself. It is the God of Hegel's system. To this period of its return to itself corresponds the third division of philosophy, the philosophy of Spirit (*Geist*).

Not only are the method of Logic and the phenomena of Nature manifestations of the Absolute, but they are parts of the very process in which the Absolute itself consists. In its ultimate analysis, then, the Absolute is Process. God is Dialectic. Hegel expressly identifies God with his Absolute. In speaking of the nature of the beginning of philosophy, he says:

> The expression of the Absolute, the eternal, or God (and God has the most undisputed right that the beginning should be made with him) or the contemplation or thought of these, may contain more than pure being.... If these richer forms of presentation such as the Absolute, or God, express or contain anything beyond being, then this is, in the beginning, but an empty word and mere being, so that this simple vacancy without further meaning, is, absolutely the beginning of philosophy.[12]

11. Since thought and being are the same for Hegel, his logic is the theory of thinking and of being; it is ontology as well as logic.
12. Hegel, *Science of Logic*, translated by Johnston and Struthers, Vol. I, p. 90.

We have discussed, so far, the process or the Absolute as it follows the laws of development in the three major moments of its movement, the three divisions into which philosophy is divided. This is the major triad of the Hegelian system: Logic, Nature, Spirit. It is the series of triads within triads which gives to Hegel's philosophy its external symmetry. To understand the nature of the beginning of the developing process and to understand its "arrival" at the final peak of its self-consciousness, it is necessary to show how the trichotomic system is applied throughout from the very start of the Absolute to its crowning attainment of perfect self-knowledge. The fundamental note of the law of development, namely, the movement from position to opposition and thence to union, is effected in every triad whether of major or minor significance in the system.

Apart from the super-triad of Logic, Nature and Spirit, there are others contained within these divisions. The science of logic is divided into three parts paralleling the dialectic process: being (*Sein*), essence (*Wesen*) and notion (*Begriff*). Being and essence are thesis and antithesis respectively, while the notion is the reconciliation of them, the synthesis. Being, the thesis, is subdivided into three terms: being (*Sein*), nothing (*Nichts*) and becoming (*Werden*), the last-named term being the reconciliation of the other two, and therefore the synthesis of the triad.

In the second division of logic, namely, essence, thought appears in a more definite and independent form. It no longer is characterized by bare, empty existence but rather by real, concrete existence and gives rise to the doctrine of essence. This second movement of the logical process, as seen in the nature of things, manifests a threefold division: ground, or substratum of existence; phenomenon, as expressing the necessary qualities of objects; and finally, union of substrate and attribute, by which the conception of a real thing is attained. The real thing is in contradistinction to the universal essence of which it forms a part. In this place, the individuality of each separate thing is reconciled with the unity of the absolute essence.

So far we have traced the Process through two spheres of action within logic. From the bare idea of being we come at length to that of a distinct, essential thing. But in the attempt to get beyond this in the excursion to seek the ultimate reality, we must reach a higher region of thought. To the doctrine of notions, the synthesis of the logical triad, we now go.

The notion or concept has for its movements, subjectivity, objectivity and finally the absolute idea, the union of subjectivity and objectivity. Here are the highest reaches of the science of logic. The absolute idea now moves through three successive stages: first as life, then as intelligence, and lastly as the absolute idea returned to itself, the summit of the whole logical process. It is this latter notion which is the thesis of the super-triad of Hegel's entire system.

We are still in this final stage of logic, in the region of pure thinking. We have done no more than to trace the evolution of thought upward through its more empty and abstract forms, seeing it enriched with a greater fullness at every step, and leaving it as a more concrete concept than it was at the start.

Triad upon triad could be multiplied, but for our present purposes it would be of no avail. In every instance the thesis of a triad corresponds to the Absolute in itself; the antithesis to the Absolute out of itself; and the synthesis of every movement to the Absolute returned into itself. Hence the thesis and the synthesis of every triad throughout the whole range of development may be considered as metaphysical definitions of Infinite Being, and every antithesis, therefore, a definition of finite being. Hegel points out the fact that the concept derived from the unity of opposites might be considered as the definition of the Absolute:

> The analysis of the beginning thus yields the concept of the unity of being and not-being, or (in a more reflected form) the unity of the state of being differentiated and of being undifferentiated, or the identity of identity and non-identity. This concept might be considered as the first or purest (that is, the most abstract) definition of the Absolute; which in fact it would be were we concerned with the forms of definitions and the name of the Absolute, and all further determinations and developments would be richer and more closely determinate definitions of it.[13]

Thus finite beings are only external expressions of the one infinite being, the Absolute. To the field of Logic we shall return later, for

---

13. *Ibid.*, p. 86.

it is here that the Process begins, and to understand the nature of the Absolute in the beginning, we shall have to make a study of the very first triad in Logic. We shall now continue to show the triadic nature of the philosophy of Hegel, and at the same time note the increasing perfection of the Absolute as it ascends as the Process toward self-consciousness.

The transition from the Logic to the Philosophy of Nature is by no means a clear and intelligible step. Logic is the science of *bare* thought; the Philosophy of Nature is the science of thought externalizing itself. Nature is still thought, but thought in its objective movement, the exact opposite of logical thinking. In the Philosophy of Nature, the Absolute must descend from its original unity of subject-object identity into a state of separation. Here it assumes an objective form. The divisions here are mechanics, physics and organics, each of which is subdivided into other triads. The part of Hegel's philosophy given over to Nature is without influence at the present time, and so we pass on to the highest division of the Process, the Philosophy of Spirit. At the point where nature leaves off, having carried on her operations to the very highest pitch of perfection in human organization, the philosophy of mind begins. Here we have pure logical thought and nature combined, resulting in the synthesis of the super-triad Logic, Nature, Spirit.

In the Philosophy of Spirit, the logical concept is in-itself. The Absolute is Process, but it is real only insofar as it is becoming, so that throughout the dialectic it is gradually revealing itself until, in its final and highest reaches, it becomes self-conscious; it reveals itself not to nature as in *ausser-sich* but rather *in-sich* — it reveals itself to itself. God becomes conscious of Himself.

The Absolute, even in its final development, is true to the laws of development, so that we find the Process still mounting even after it has attained the state of living spirit. It is living spirit first *an-sich* where it finds the world; then *ausser-sich* where it is objective as free will; finally, it returns to itself in order to be all in itself, *in-sich,* as Absolute Spirit, Absolute Reality, the culmination of the science of philosophy. This last is the peak. Thought can mount no higher. The Absolute is now perfect self-knowledge. In the first of these three moments of the final movement, the living spirit in-itself finds the world. The soul first appears; then the spirit distinguishes itself from the world and attains a higher degree of consciousness; finally the spirit becomes conscious of its unity with the world, and thus we have the synthesis culminating in the consciousness of the spirit. Here is the field of Hegel's psychology.

In the second moment of this ultimate movement, namely, the spirit's objectivity as free will, the spirit brings out of itself the world of freedom, the universal rational will (not the individual will), the will which produces in individuals the moral conscience and the consciousness of right. Here is Hegel's ethical system.

The third moment is Absolute Spirit. Though it is the highest point in the Process, it nevertheless has three stages of development. First, the Absolute Spirit becomes conscious of itself in intuition and imagination. This is the standpoint of Art. The consciousness of the Absolute goes beyond this: it becomes conscious of itself in feeling and representation, the field of Religion. Finally, it becomes self-conscious in thought, and this is Philosophy. Thus we may say that the withdrawal of the Absolute Spirit from outer sensibility into the inner spirit is begun in Aesthetics, completed in Religion, and reaches perfect self-knowledge in Philosophy. In philosophy the Absolute Spirit reaches its highest peak. As the synthesis of the final triad of the Process, Spirit here becomes perfectly free from all contradictions and reconciled with itself. The break between subject and object, representation and thing, thought and being, infinite and finite, is done away with, and the infinite is recognized as the essence of the finite. The reconciliation of the highest opposition gives knowledge of the Infinite in the finite.

Hegel makes philosophy to be the goal of the world-process. Will, intuition, representation and feeling are lower forms of thought. Ethics, art and religion are preliminary stages in philosophy; preliminary because they vainly try to present the concrete concept adequately, in conceptual form, and though each successive one attains the goal more perfectly, it is philosophy that first succeeds in doing so. When man supersedes religion by philosophy, then the Absolute Spirit has attained its fullest development, for man is not dissociated from the Absolute.

We have left unexplained the beginning of the Absolute, and this deliberately. Its adequate explanation necessitates the introduction of the fundamentals of a new doctrine, that of contradiction (*Widerspruch*).

The Doctrine of Contradiction

The rhythm of the whole logical process is founded upon Hegel's doctrine of contradiction. For him, all knowledge consists in a separation or a distinguishing of one thing from another. In every thought there are two parts which stand opposed; both of which are absolutely necessary to give it a clear and actual meaning. Regardless of the form in which knowledge is viewed, whether as sensation or perception or reflection, in every instance there must be something separated, defined, distinguished, or placed in opposition to something else. For example, Hegel would say, we have no notion of finite without an infinite; no idea of cause without effect; no idea of subjective without objective. This being so, it is impossible for any notion to exist as an absolute unity; it must in every instance consist of two sides, one positive and one negative. In every idea that we form, therefore, there are two things, opposed and distinguished, which unite to give the idea. We note here the strain referred to previously: position, opposition, combination, thesis, antithesis, synthesis. The true idea consists, not in either term, but in the relation existing between them.

As an example of the way in which Hegel makes the concept pass over into its opposite, and then unite with this in a synthesis, we will use the extraordinary equation which stands at the threshold of his system: Being equals Nothing. The first concrete thought results from their combination: Becoming. Right down in this triad, namely, Being, Nothing, Becoming, which is the beginning of philosophy, we look for the Absolute and see in what state it is at the start of the dialectic. If it is already something, it is as we suggested previously, something determined and hence not the beginning, and another beginning must be sought. If it is nothing, can the Process begin? What is the content of the idea at its dawn? Hegel tells us it is vacuity, emptiness, absolute indetermination.

Parmenides would have told him, *Ex nihilo, nihil fit*. Aristotle would have agreed with the latter, provided he qualified the *nihil* by the term *absolutum*. Then Aristotle would have pointed out the analogy of being and indicated that from a certain relative non-being (potency), being could come. But of the maxim of Parmenides Hegel says:

> *Ex nihilo, nihil fit* is one of the maxims to which great importance was at one time ascribed in metaphysics. Either it is just the empty tautology, "Nothing equals nothing," or, should becoming be supposed to have real meaning in it, there is in fact no becoming contained in it, for, since only nothing comes out of nothing, nothing still remains nothing here. Becoming implies that nothing should not remain nothing but pass over into its other, into being.[14]

For Hegel the beginning of the Process is nothing:

> Nothing is there except the decision to consider thought as such. The beginning must be an absolute, or what here is equivalent, an abstract beginning: it must presuppose nothing, must be mediated by nothing, must have no foundation: itself (i. e. thought) is to be the foundation, the whole of science. It must therefore just be something immediate, or rather the immediate itself. As it cannot have any determination relatively to other, so also it cannot hold in itself any determination or content; for this would be differentiation and mutual relation of distincts, and thus mediation. The beginning, therefore, is pure being.[15]

Stirling, one of the foremost Hegelians and interpreters of Hegel, comments thus on the nature of the beginning of the Process:

> What is a beginning? A beginning implies that there at once is and is not — and how can that be named otherwise than as pure being, indefinite being? — what is, is — but as yet absolutely indefinitely? This is the true *Begriff* of the *Vorstellung* — primordial chaos. A fundamen, a fomes, a *rudimentum*, a *Grundlage*, a groundwork, a mother-matter is always postulated by the *Vorstellung;* but this postulate, translated into the lan-

14. *Ibid.*, p. 96.
15. *Ibid.*, p. 82.

guage of thought proper, amounts to the *indefiniteness that is,* pure being.

But if pure being be the first, according to the law of the notion, its own opposite, or non-being, must be the second, and the third must be a new simple that concretely contains both; or the third must be a species of which the first is the genus, and the second the differentia: but this here is just *Werden;* every becoming at once *is* and *is not,* or is at once being and non-being. Here, then, is the absolutely first triad, the absolutely germinal cell: it is impossible to go further back than to the absolute indefiniteness that at once *is* and *is not,* but *becomes.*[16]

Though Hegel equates pure being and nothing, and identifies each with the other, he nevertheless insists that they must be distinguished:

Pure being . . . is pure indeterminateness and vacuity. . . . In fact, being, indeterminate immediacy, is nothing, neither more nor less.[17]

Nothing is the same determination (or rather lack of determination), and thus altogether the same thing, as pure being.[18]

Pure being and pure nothing are the same; the truth is, not either being or nothing, but that being — not passes — but has passed over into nothing, and nothing into being. But equally the truth is, not their lack of distinction, but that they are not the same, that they are absolutely distinct, and yet unseparated and inseparable, each disappearing immediately in its opposite.[19]

The metamorphosis by which being and nothing become each other is by way of abstraction:

Being, which was made the beginning of science, is of course nothing, for we can abstract from everything and this having been done, nothing remains. . . . The result of abstracting from all beings is, first, abstract being, being in general. But we can also abstract from this pure being, being can be added on to all that from which we have already abstracted: then nothing remains. Now if we wish to forget the thinking of nothing, that is, its metamorphosis into being, or know nothing about it, we can continue further to do what we *can* do: for we can, further (heaven

---

16. J. H. Stirling, *The Secret of Hegel,* pp. 348-9.
17. Johnston and Struthers, p. 94.
18. *Ibid.*
19. *Ibid.,* p. 95.

be thanked), abstract from nothing — the creation of the world is an abstraction from nothing — and then not nothing remains, for it is just this from which we are abstracting: and so being has again been reached.[20]

In asking how a thing can begin to be, it is necessary to see its transition from nothing into being. Of it Hegel says:

> The transition from being to nothing can be imagined as something easy and trivial, or, as it is called, can be explained and made conceivable thus: Being, which was made the beginning of science, is of course nothing, for we can abstract from everything and this having been done, nothing remains.[21]

Without the idea of nothing we could never have that of being, and vice versa; so that the two stand to one another as opposites, and both together combine to form a complete notion, viz. that of bare production, or the becoming of something out of nothing. This is the first step in philosophy, the primary pulsation of the dialectic process. In it being and nothing stand as the poles, and the conjunction of them forms the notion of existence. In these three (*Sein, Nichts, Werden*) we see the type or symbol of all thought, showing us that for every complete idea there must be the combination of two opposites. Neither being nor nothing can exist as a reality of itself; each is but the opposite of the other, and it is in their indifference that the act of coming into existence first appears.

Hegel says:

> The truth of being and nothing is therefore this movement, this immediate disappearance of the one into the other, in a word, becoming: a movement wherein both are distinct, but in virtue of a distinction which has equally immediately dissolved itself.[22]

20. *Ibid.*, p. 112.
21. Stirling, *op. cit.*, pp. 352-3.
22. Johnston and Struthers, p. 95.

In speaking of the beginning of the Process, he observes:

> Were we to observe this procedure (that in any science a beginning is made by pre-supposing some idea) we should have no particular object before us, because the beginning, as being the beginning of thought, must be perfectly abstract and general, pure form quite without content: we should have nothing but the idea of a bare beginning as such. It remains to be seen what we possess in this idea.
> So far, there is nothing. Something is to become. The beginning is not pure nothing, but a nothing from which something is to proceed; so that being is already contained in the beginning. The beginning thus contains both, being and nothing; it is the unity of being and nothing, or is not-being which is being and being which is also not-being.[23]

The nature of the being to which Hegel both opposes and equates nothing, is to be utterly without determination. It is the most general concept which remains after abstracting from every determinate content of thought and from which no further abstraction is possible. Pure being is the most undeterminate and immediate concept. Thus without qualities and content, it is equivalent to nothing.

So basic is the doctrine of contradiction in the Hegelian philosophy that without it there would be no movement and no life. All reality, though full of contradiction, is nevertheless rational. The contradiction is not annulled, but rather negated and conserved. To use the author's term, it must be "sublated." This is merely to think the contradictories together in a third higher, more comprehensive and richer concept. This is the negation of negations of which he speaks. The opposition is overcome. However, the play begins anew. Again an opposition makes its appearance which in its turn seeks to be negated. Each separate concept, in its turn, is one-sided, defective, representing only part of the truth and needing to be supplemented by its contrary. By the union of the contraries a higher concept is yielded which comes nearer the whole truth. Each negation being met by another negation, the idea with which the start was made is thus restored, not in its paucity, but enriched by the very process described, so that at each turn the idea has evolved to a higher degree.

23. *Ibid.*, p. 85.

From pure being, which is the ultimate abstraction and equates nothing, upward the Process goes, affirmations, negations and negations of negations succeeding each other in rapid order; the Absolute manifesting itself at every moment, attaining newer richness, until it finally bursts with the fullness of its self-consciousness on the peak of perfect self-knowledge.

Such is the nature, the subject and the method of Hegel's Absolute. The Process is the Absolute. The Absolute is Thought. Thought is Being. Therefore for Hegel the Process is Reality. It is against this feature of Hegelian philosophy that we will later direct our criticism.

Critical Evaluation

Hegelianism is pure rationalism through and through. With Parmenides, Hegel is an intellectualist. Any system constructed on the basis of a particular notion of the philosopher's own conception, and proceeding thence by *a priori* deductions without regard to the common facts of reality everywhere surrounding one, is an intellectualistic philosophy. This is precisely what Hegel has done. Beginning from an arbitrary concept of his own choosing, divorced alike from the basic principles of being and the facts of experience, Hegel resigns himself to his law of development and follows it wherever it leads him. His philosophy is not based on formal principles apprehended in the concept of being, the cogency of which consists in the very evidence they present to the mind, nor on the material of experience and its simplest and most evident facts. His philosophy starts from two *a priori* notions and from them his whole system flows: first, the unity of contradictories, and second, the identity of thought and being.

These notions are the basis of any system of absolute identity. Such is the philosophy of Parmenides; such is that of Hegel. Grant these notions to Hegel and there follow certain necessary conclusions: Contradiction is at the root of reality; the process by which thought is developed is a process of the whole nature, since thought and being are the same; the laws of logic then become the laws of the universe; dialectic is the method by which all things come to be and subsist. The result, this rhythm of existence applied to the construction of a philosophical system, which then draws within its grasp the totality of the phenomena of man, nature and Deity. This is too much for any system. The Deity will always remain by the very nature of His unique Being outside and beyond the full comprehension of man's intellect, and so of man's philosophy.

The Hegelian philosophy is monistic, and this flows from the two basic notions of which we spoke. The strictly absolute being is literally an all-inclusive, complete, unique being. There exists an absolute self, says Hegel, and every finite reality is an expression of this all-comprehending self. Both of the fundamental notions of his system are involved, for contradiction is the very base of that system. Subject and object are one; thought and being are one. Neither alone is a reality. The only reality is their mutual relation. This mutual relation consists in the synthesis of the two terms. We have already seen this in the contraries, being and nothing, and their union in becoming. The essence of the nature of being consists, therefore, in the co-existence of the two opposites. But this is against the ordinary concepts formed by man. We generally consider, for example, that this paper is a reality and that its being measures the mind; that is, the mind forms the universal concept from given objective reality, and not vice versa. For Hegel, however, it is otherwise. Ideas are the concrete realities. The universal idea is found to contain, hidden away in it, its opposite. By drawing out this hidden term it is made to serve as the difference of the genus, and by the union of these two notions, a particular idea, a species, is obtained. Thus in Hegel's first triad, being (genus), in union with nothing (difference), yields becoming (species), the first concrete thought.

But this violates a fundamental law of logical definition. The genus actually excludes the differentia, although the latter may be potentially contained in the former, as "animal" in its capacity of a logical universal does not actually contain the differentia "rational" or "irrational" within it, but potentially only. But in Hegel's notion of the differentia actually present in the genus, particular ideas serve as objective realities in the finite order, whilst the ultimate reality is the absolute self to which the finite is both subordinate and essential. The process of the evolution of these ideas in the human mind is therefore at the same time the process of all existence, the Absolute, God.

In making finite beings essential to Infinite Being and mere manifestations of it, Hegel has failed to distinguish two totally different concepts. Being in the fullest sense of the term is that which realizes in all its fullness the reality of being, and this is the Absolute Being — the Infinite God. This Absolute Being is unique; it is the most comprehensive concept of all possible concepts, the very antithesis of being in general. Being in general is common to everything and distinguished only from nothingness.[24] Hegel failed, too, to distinguish between various modes in which relative being is dependent upon Absolute Being. God is Absolute; creatures are relative. Substance is absolute in respect of accidents which need to inhere in another. God is not thereby one all-pervading substance of which finite realities are accidental manifestations.

Further, the very notion of being upon which Hegel built his dialectic is an empty abstraction. His pure being is the being of Parmenides: "The simple idea of pure being was first enunciated by the Eleatics, as the absolute and as sole truth; especially by Parmenides whose surviving fragments... proclaim that Being alone is, and nothing is not at all."[25] He immediately takes his departure from Parmenides, however, for the being of Parmenides, he says, admits of no progress from being, and so he effects progress from the outside by determining this indeterminate being with which he started. "Being thus isolated (the being of Parmenides) is the indeterminate; it is not related to other; it therefore seems that no progress could be made from this beginning (that is, out of being itself): progress could only be effected by connecting something foreign from without."[26] He therefore makes a new beginning and effects progress by asserting that being is the same as nothing: "The progress made by asserting that being is the same as nothing, therefore, appears like a second and independent beginning — a transition dependent on itself and merely added to being from without."[27] Surely *no-thing*, which is the denial of *thing-hood*, can make an addition to *thing*. The development of being, Scholastics hold, must be made from within being itself, and

---

24. *Con. Gen.*, l. I, c. 26.
25. Johnston and Struthers, p. 95.
26. *Ibid.*, p. 107.
27. *Ibid.*

additions to it can be additions of being only. The notion of nothing is not a reality at all, and can add nothing to being.

Therefore only in the notion of being can be found the notion of its determinants. *Omnia alia includuntur quodammodo in ente unite et indistincte sicut in principio,* says Saint Thomas.[28] But Hegel insists upon an extrinsic addition, and how this is to be done we noted previously; namely, the addition of nothing as the difference to being as genus, the species being becoming. As we have already shown, any difference added in this way to being would be nothing, because whatever is, is being. But it is precisely nothing that Hegel adds to his pure being to effect, as he says, progress. But being is a transcendental notion which places it beyond categories and so incapable of extrinsic additions. All the concepts of the intellect and all additions to being *are* being and therefore, by explication, differences are found within the notion itself. These are not new entities but new modes of being not expressed by the sole term "being." Such a modality is *substance,* which does not express being different from being, but only a mode of being not expressed by "being"; substance *is* being, but being *per se.*[29] Throughout the entire first article of question one in *De Veritate,* Saint Thomas discusses the special and general modes of being, and shows that from the notion of being itself are derived the additions which are made to it — additions which are not new entities but only new relations within being itself; relations, that is, of being to itself and relations of beings to other beings.

For Saint Thomas and the Scholastics, indeterminate being — the pure being of Hegel — is not nothing, for it is a true concept of the mind derived from objective reality. For though stripped of every determination down to the point where only possibility remains, it is

28. *I. Sent.,* d. 8, q. 1, a. 3.
29. "Sed secundum hoc aliqua dicuntur addere supra ens, inquantum exprimunt ipsius modum, qui nomine ipsius entis non exprimitur. Quod dupliciter contingit: uno modo ut modus expressus sit aliquis specialis modus entis; sunt enim diversi gradus entitatis, secundum quos accipiuntur diversi modi essendi; et juxta hos modos accipiuntur diversa rerum genera; substantia enim non addit supra ens aliquam differentiam, quae significet aliquam naturam superadditam enti; sed nomine substantiae aliquam exprimitur quidam specialis modus essendi, scilicet per se ens; et ita est in aliis generibus." *De Verit.,* q. 1, a. 1.

nevertheless being — that which is or can be. To abstract beyond possibility is to negate being itself. The notion of being is applicable analogously to all reality, from prime matter to God. Beyond the notion traditional Scholasticism does not go in its rational approach to Absolute Being, Pure Act. For Hegel there is no difficulty in affirming that from an empty beginning perfection issues, since he denies the validity of the principle of contradiction. But the principle holds nevertheless as the primary principle of human reason, however much Hegel may deny it and Hegelians defend his system.

W. T. Harris, who during his lifetime, was the foremost Hegelian in the United States, says in defense of Hegel's beginning of reality:

> The absolute of the infantile thought of mankind is the starting point of Hegel's logic. Pure Being is the empty abstract. But the method of his logic is to show the impossibility of such an absolute. ... In conclusion he shows how all things presuppose by their imperfection and changeable reality a higher reality, a real absolute, self-active and self-determined. Hence Hegel does not begin his logic with the true absolute but with its opposite, the Pantheistic absolute, and makes it the sole business of his dialectic to refute every possible shape under which it masquerades. He arrives at an absolute self-activity of reason whose form is personality, instead of empty indifference or formlessness. His philosophy is the precise opposite of Pantheism. ... Brahma or the Hindu Absolute is the pure being of Parmenides, and the first or simplest pure thought and hence the beginning of logic but not its finality.[30]

Harris fails to note that Hegel identified the Absolute of his end with the Absolute of his beginning even to the extent of identifying God with the beginning which, according to Harris, "it is the sole business of his dialectic to refute" in "every possible shape under which it appears." Whence, then, we may ask Harris, is the origin of the Absolute whose form is personality? With the principle of contradiction voided, such inconsistencies present no difficulty, for everything is its opposite and contradiction is the root of all reality.

In his *History of Philosophy*, Hegel traces the development of thought according to the Process of his logic, from Parmenides at the

---

30. Harris, W. T., *Hegel's Logic*, p. 125.

lowest end (postulating bare existence) up to his own triumphant achievement through which he deduces the Absolute Idea in all the fullness of its truth and glory. The pure being of Parmenides, then, is said to be the start of the Process, but Hegel identifies pure being with pure nothing, which Parmenides most certainly did not. Parmenides arrived at his notion of pure being (being-in-general) by way of abstraction and absolutely excluded the notion of nothing.[31]

Hegel, in effect, syllogizes thus: Pure being is pure indetermination. But pure indetermination is pure non-being. Therefore pure being is pure non-being. Pure being is non-existing being. There is a fallacy hidden away in this, inasmuch as the term pure indetermination is not used univocally in both propositions. In the first proposition pure indetermination is the negation of specific and generic determinations, not of *being* which transcends all genera. Being itself is not negated in this proposition. For example, in the notion "horse" one could negate the specific and generic determinations of irrationality and animality and still retain the note "being." In the second proposition, however, pure being is the negation not only of specific and generic determinations but even of the notion "being" itself. To negate being results in only nothingness. Hence the pure indetermination in proposition one is not the pure indetermination in proposition two and the conclusion does not follow, namely, that pure being is non-existing being, is nothing.

The relation between being and nothing, says Harris, is one of identity and of difference, though the difference cannot be expressed or identified. The fact that Hegel failed to grasp is this: that the difference between being and nothing can be specified. The conception of being-in-general is obtained, as we showed above, by abstracting all differences and retaining only what is identical in the objects of our concepts. Thus, by prescinding from all the differences between Infinite Being and finite beings, we retain the notion being. In form-

---

31. Parmenides, in *On Nature* says:
"... I shall not permit thee to tell me
Neither to think: 'Of what is not'; for none can say or imagine
How not-is becomes is; or else what need should have stirred it,
After or yet before its beginning, to issue from nothing?"
Bakewell, *op. cit.*, p. 14.

ing a concept of nothing, however, we abstract even the note of being, so that nothing remains, for even the very concept of nothing is not real being but it is only conceived after the manner of being (*ens rationis*).

Hegel starts off with a vacuum,[32] and by a process of self-development it attains to infinite proportions, in fact, to infinite being itself. It would seem rather more consistent to say that a vacuum multiplied unto infinity is still a vacuum. The Process, or the charge of the Absolute through finite to infinite proportions, involves the proposition that the greater proceeds from the lesser. But why not, when the principle of contradiction has no objective significance?

Insofar as Hegel postulates reality as unique, as a single, all-inclusive and self-identical Absolute, there can be for his system, in one respect, no change as there could be none for Parmenides, for the simple reason that there is nothing for the unique being to change into. The objection may be put: In Scholastic philosophy change is possible even though all reality is united under the periphery of the term "being." What is there for being to turn into if outside of being there is no reality? If there is no other reality, there can be no passage from reality into otherness. Our answer is merely to indicate what has already been pointed out: Change is from being potentially such-and-such a thing to being actually that thing. Change operates between potential being and actual being. The Scholastic doctrine of analogy of being provides for this distinction, where Hegel's Absolute is not an analogous notion.

However, insofar as the all-of-reality is a Process whereby the unique substance, or rather, as Hegel would prefer it, the unique *subject* tends to perfect itself in consciousness, the philosophy of Hegel is a philosophy of becoming. The Process is the Becoming.[33] The Absolute is ever unfolding, yet never is unfolded. Were we to follow the interpretation of "becoming" as given by Mary Whiton Calkins,[34] we

32. "There is nothing perceivable in it (pure being) ... there is nothing thinkable in it. Being undetermined, immediate being, is in fact nothing, and is neither more or less than nothing" (*Werke*, III, p. 73). Cf. Stirling, J. H., *The Secret of Hegel*, p. 320, first ed., 1865.
33. "Becoming is a name for the dialectic process." M. W. Calkins, *The Persistent Problems of Philosophy*, p. 575.
34. *Op. cit.*

would say that the Process is no more than a series of "replacements" whereby less satisfactory conceptions of reality are replaced by more adequate ones. She says:

> By this doctrine (that pure being and nothing are each alike found to be mere becoming) Hegel seems to mean no more than the following: Pure being and nothing are each found to be an unsatisfactory expression for ultimate reality, and therefore when reflected on they are replaced — that is, they "become" — more adequate conceptions of reality.[35]

Restricting changes to changes within this Absolute Spirit by which it seeks self-consciousness, there can be no doubt of the fact that, following Heraclitus, Hegel is an evolutionist. For the former, universal life is an endless alternation of creation and destruction; for the latter, the all-of-reality is an eternal process of origination and ceasing; in the constant whirl of Heraclitus' doctrine, nothing constantly changes into being and vice versa. Being and non-being are the same. What is Hegel's doctrine but the very same, except perhaps for terms: *whirl* becomes *process?* The perpetual flow of Heraclitus is a struggle between contraries, and produced from this opposition are all vegetative, animal and intellectual life on earth. The realization of itself through the Process is for Hegel's Absolute a movement of strife and conflict, and in its excursions out of itself, it expresses itself in finite realities, in the world of nature. A fair characterization of the philosophy we have discussed can be made by the expression: Ultimate Reality is Process. It is against this point, involving as it does, the denial of the basic principle of thought and being, that we shall later direct our refutation.

Bergson

It is said that Heraclitus declared that the echo of his voice would be heard throughout the centuries. Who can doubt that this prophetic utterance has been fulfilled in the modern philosophies of change? The foremost prophet of contemporary fluxism is Henri Bergson, and it is in the Heraclitean principle of flux that we find the germ of Bergsonian creative evolution. The outstanding characteristic of this

---

35. *Ibid.*, p. 365, footnote 2.

philosophy of becoming is its anti-intellectualism. In this it is the very antithesis of the absolutistic idealism of Hegel, whom we nevertheless hope to indict conjointly with Bergson on the basis of their common denial of the objective validity of the primary principles; the identification of contradictories in becoming; and the rejection of the ontological validity of the notion of being.[36]

The philosophy of Bergson has won great renown in contemporary philosophical circles. Any one of several major aspects of this philosophy could be treated, and *de facto* has been treated elsewhere at great length. In consonance with the purpose of the present thesis, however, which has been stated previously as the analysis of the notions of being, non-being and becoming, we shall confine ourselves here to a discussion of the nature of reality as found in the writings of Bergson. The answer to the question: What is reality? in the philosophy under discussion, involves the use and understanding of several notions which are fundamental to his system. To ask of Bergson whether reality is the material thing which endures without changing or the living thing which endures by changing, would be to elicit an answer involving the fundamental terms we have in mind. Bergson would answer that reality is *the living stuff, the ever-flowing time,* and that to know it, a special faculty is required, that of *intuition,* since it is only by intuition that one can seize upon the real, that flux, change, duration, which is absolutely evasive to the intellect. Inextricably bound up, therefore, with the notion of the Bergsonian real, are the notions of intuition, life, duration. It is due to this philosopher's discrediting of the intellectual faculty that he found it necessary to postulate the existence of an intuitive power superior in degree but not in kind to the sensitive faculty of instinct. Only by flashes of this extra-intellectual intuition can the

---

36. "The anti-intellectualism of Heraclitus, revamped at the present day by Bergson, is at the opposite pole of the absolute intellectualism of Hegel which also denies the objective validity of the principle of identity. While the Sensualist philosophy of becoming reduces the rational to experimental reality, to the facts of experience ... the intellectualist philosophy of becoming, on the contrary, restores experimental reality to the rational order.... Thus Bergsonism appears like a reversed Hegelianism." Garrigou-Lagrange, *op. cit.,* I, p. 172. Cf. same work for scholarly defense of the ontological validity of primary ideas and first principles.

mind seize the reality of things, which reality is nothing other than the flow, real time, or duration. It is with these three doctrines, therefore, insofar as they reveal the nature of the Bergsonian concept of reality, that we shall deal here.

We begin, first, with the notion of reality and find that it is variously described as "the fluid continuity of the real"; "the endless flow"; "the fluid mass of our existence"; "the moving zone"; "the perpetual flux of things"; "the continual change of form"; et cetera. Reality is a perpetual growth, a creation which pursues itself unendingly. It is duration. It is a current, a wave, a rocket, a sheaf. It is life, movement, progress; it is an urge, an impulse, a constant flux, an *élan vital*.

Change is reality, and change for Bergson is so incontestable a fact that he seizes upon it as the whole fact. "There are no things but only actions," he declares, and by this he inverts the real order and gives us, not a world of changing substances, but rather a universe of substantial changes. His emphasis is all on the change, and in the eternal flux the notion of substance is washed away and only substantized accidents remain. "There is only change, but nothing which changes; change needs no support; movement does not imply anything that moves."[37] Reality, therefore, for Bergson, is not static nor is it conceived under a dual aspect of movement and rest. It is essentially, entirely kinetic. It is consciousness of living. It is intuition of life.

In the philosophy of becoming, being has been outmoded; and not only outmoded but superseded by the notion of change. For Bergson the notions becoming and being are mutually exclusive; they are the distinguishing concepts between the real and an unreal representation of the real. What does not flow is not real. Form is a snapshot view of becoming, not the perfecting principle of being; essence is merely the average of a succession of images, not *that which* makes a thing that which it is, the abiding, indivisible reality which underlies the phenomena.[38]

---

37. "Il y a des changements, mais il n'y a pas de choses qui changent; le changement n'a pas besoin d'un support.... Le mouvement n'implique pas un mobile." *Conference d'Oxford,* p. 24. Cited by F. J. Sheen, *God and Intelligence,* pp. 163-4.

38. "Now, life is an evolution. We concentrate a period of this evolution in a stable view which we call a form, and when the change has become con-

Following immediately upon his rejection of being, is the rejection of the concept of space. Space may be considered as abstract extension considered as a receptacle for bodies. An essential note in the concept is expansion in three dimensions. The notion of space as a container for bodies implies a philosophy which takes cognizance of bodies. The only *raison d'être* for the concept of space is the existence in a concrete state of bodies with the concrete attribute of extension. A philosophy that repudiates being and makes all reality to be the ever-flowing "now" has no need of the notion of space; and so we find in creative evolution that the notion of time or duration is given not only primacy but absolute supremacy to the practical annihilation of the notion of space.

The logical sequence to follow in our exposition might seem, under one aspect, to be the pursuance of Bergson's notion of reality into the domain of consciousness and life. "To exist is to change; to change is to mature; to mature is to go on creating oneself endlessly," and this is *life*.[39] However, since Bergson's concept of life and becoming involves a knowledge of his intuitive method, it seems advisable to interpolate at this point an exposition of this latter doctrine. The relation of intellect and intuition to reality can be understood from the following passage:

> Matter or mind, reality has appeared to us as a perpetual becoming. It makes itself or it unmakes itself, but it is never something made. Such is the intuition that we have of mind when we draw aside the veil which is interposed between our consciousness siderable enough to overcome the fortunate inertia of our perception, we say that the body has changed its form. But in reality the body is changing form at every moment; or rather, there is no form, since form is immobile and the reality is movement. What is real is the continual change of form: the form is only a snapshot view of a transition. Therefore, here again, our perception manages to solidify into discontinuous images the fluid continuity of the real. When the successive images do not differ from each other too much, we consider them all as the waxing and waning of a single mean image, or as the deformation of this image in different directions. And to this mean we really allude when we speak of the essence of a thing, or of the thing itself."
> *Creative Evolution*, p. 302.

39. *Ibid.*, p. 7.

and ourselves. This, also, is what our intellect and senses would show us of matter, if they could obtain a direct and disinterested idea of it.[40]

Intellect is associated with material objects; intuition with the hidden secrets of consciousness. The intellect is ordained for solids; its forces tend to transform matter into an instrument of action. The intellect is so fascinated by its contemplation of matter that it cannot *naturally* think mobility, changing forms, life itself.[41] It is intuition which reveals life.[42] What is the nature of this intuition and its distinction from intellect we shall investigate next.

The whole of life, Bergson has said, is one continuous movement. It gathers up like a snowball all its past, which it carries along with it, thrusting its way into the future, creating that future and its needs as it gnaws its way along.[43] In this creative process life had need of sense faculties and so it created them. Thus was brought into existence the line of instinct, and in its highest powers are found the kingdoms of ants and bees. Life had need, too, of intelligence, and so intellect evolved in response to nature's need for it. But since intellect is only a part of the real flow which is life, it is thereby unable to penetrate the real meaning of life in its entirety, which means, for Bergson, the real meaning of reality since the whole of life is the whole of reality.

40. *Ibid.,* p. 272.

41. "Our intelligence, as it leaves the hands of nature, has for its chief object the unorganized solids." *Ibid.,* p. 153. "All the elementary forces of the intellect tend to transform matter into an instrument of action.... The intellect always behaves as if it were fascinated by the contemplation of inert matter ... it cannot, without reversing its natural direction and twisting about on itself, think true continuity, real mobility, reciprocal penetration — in a word, that creative evolution which is life.... The intellect is not made to think evolution in the proper sense of the word — that is to say, the continuity of a change that is pure mobility.... The intellect is characterized by a natural inability to comprehend life." *Ibid.,* pp. 161, 2, 3, 5.

42. "It is to the very inwardness of life that intuition leads us." *Ibid.,* p. 176.

43. "My mental state, as it advances on the road of time, is continually swelling with the duration which it accumulates: it goes on increasing — rolling upon itself as a snowball on the snow." *Ibid.,* p. 2. Cf. also, pp. 4, 5.

Neither the senses nor the intellect can know the whole of reality; and therefore, reasons Bergson, life had need of another faculty; and to meet this need it called into existence the faculty of intuition. Its function is to *feel* the flow of life, which escapes the notice, because it escapes the power, of both pure animal instinct and the intellect. This new third faculty, however, is a continuation of the instinctive faculty, higher in degree but not differing in kind from that from which it springs, namely, animal instinct. As the intellect is given to inert matter and to activity, so intuition is given to speculation. This is Bergson's basis for the division of the sciences. The intellect has for its field of activity the natural sciences, which deal with "things"; and since it escapes the ability of intellect to grasp the meaning of reality, intuition makes up for this lack, in the field of philosophy. Continuous life and movement, therefore, so elusive to the intellect, is revealed to intuition, which Bergson variously describes as the "indistinct fringe" surrounding the "bright nucleus" of the intellect and fading off into darkness. It is a flickering lamp which burns up brightly now and then for a brief spell; its usual vacillating light, though feeble, vague and discontinuous, reveals to the individual secrets hidden from the intellect.[44] It is described at times as a sympathy which puts us in the swing of the movement; at other times it is a self-conscious, reflecting instinct.[45]

The domains of intellect and intuition are, in Bergson's philosophy, definitely distinct. Intellect finds its proper sphere of activity within the positive sciences. The aim of these is practical utility. The instru-

---

44. "It is a lamp almost extinguished which only glimmers now and then, for a few moments at most. But it glimmers whenever a vital interest is at stake. On our personality, on our liberty, on the place we occupy in the whole of nature, on our origin and perhaps also on our destiny, it throws a light feeble and vacillating, but which none the less pierces the darkness of the night in which the intellect leaves us." *Ibid.*, pp. 267, 8.

45. "By intuition is meant the kind of intellectual sympathy by which one places oneself within an object in order to coincide with what is unique in it and consequently inexpressible." *An Introduction to Metaphysics,* trans. by Hume, p. 6. "By intuition I mean instinct that has become disinterested, self-conscious, capable of reflecting upon its object and of enlarging it indefinitely." *Creative Evolution,* p. 176.

ment of utility and of action is intelligence.⁴⁶ Intuition, on the other hand, is a dip into the flow, a flash of genius in which rare moments one "sees" reality, "feels" the flow, is "bathed" in its rhythm, and forms "fluid" concepts capable of following along in the stream of this flowing reality. It is sympathy with reality's rhythms. It is an extremely difficult effort to make; it can be sustained only for the briefest of instants, but in that split second it pierces the obscurity in which intellect leaves us. It alone can seize the real, and grasp life and spirit in their unity and movement. It establishes sympathetic communication between us and all other living things; it expands our consciousness and qualifies us to enter into the ceaseless flow of life.⁴⁷ Transcending intellect despite the fact that it is only a faint, intermittent, glimmering light, a vague nebulosity beside the "bright nucleus" which is intellect, it nevertheless can grasp in one faint glimmer that which the intellect is unable to capture.⁴⁸ Though it is sprung from animal instinct, the force responsible for the impulsion by which it transcends the intellect is from the intellect itself;⁴⁹ and despite the fact that intelligence can supply the force which propels instinct to the realm of intuition and so to an understanding of vital operations, it is itself doomed to consort with material things: "Intellect is charged with matter; intuition with life."⁵⁰ So natural is it for intelligence to look outside life and fix itself on inert matter,

46. "We think only in order to act. Our intellect has been cast in the mould of action." *Ibid.*, p. 44.
47. "By the sympathetic communication which it establishes between us and the rest of the living, by the expansion of our consciousness which it brings about, it introduces us into life's own domain, which is reciprocal interpenetration, endlessly continued creation." *Ibid.*, p. 178.
48. "Intellect remains the luminous nucleus around which instinct, even enlarged and purified into intuition, forms only a vague nebulosity. But in default of knowledge properly so called, reserved to pure intelligence, intuition may enable us to grasp what it is that intellect fails to give us, and indicate the means of supplementing it." *Ibid.*, p. 177.
49. "Though it (intuition) thereby transcends intelligence, it is from the intelligence that has come the push that has made it rise to the point it has reached. Without intelligence it would have remained in the form of instinct, riveted to the special object of its practical interest, and turned outward by it into movements of locomotion." *Ibid.*, p. 178.
50. *Ibid.*

that it is a sheer unnatural process for it to look inward upon life and to think that continuous, real mobility, that creative evolution which is life.[51] Not only movement and life, but continuity itself is outside the domain of science. "Of immobility alone does the intellect form a clear idea.... Of the discontinuous alone does the intellect form a clear idea."[52]

The above is necessarily a sketchy account of Bergson's doctrine of intelligence and intuition. Summarily, we may say that intuition is held by him to be the only faculty capable of perceiving pure movement, while intellect is kept busy parceling out reality into "things," snapshots of the flow as it passes by. By discrediting intellect and so rendering it incapable of perceiving being, Bergson had no other alternative than to substitute an intuitive faculty or else professedly to restrict all knowledge to sense knowledge (which latter is, *de facto,* the actual nature of his doctrine of intuition).

We have presented thus far two basic doctrines of Bergsonism, namely, the primacy of becoming over being and the doctrine of intuition. We take up the thread once more and we seek the nature of that principle which is reality. It is extremely difficult to expose adequately Bergson's concept of reality, and much more difficult to do so briefly. However, sifting through the many varied expressions by which he tries to express his concept, one might say that *existence is the creative evolution.* Equating terms, we have: Existence in time is duration; duration is life; life is unceasing creation. In seeking the precise meaning that consciousness gives to the word "exist," Bergson finds that "to exist is to change, to change is to mature, to mature is

---

51. "Instinct is sympathy. If this sympathy could extend its object and also reflect upon itself, it would give us the key to vital operations — just as intelligence, developed and disciplined, guides us into matter. For — we cannot repeat it too often — intelligence and instinct are turned into opposite directions, the former toward inert matter, the latter toward life. Intelligence, by means of science, which is its work, will deliver up to us more and more completely the secret of physical operations; of life it brings us, and moreover claims to bring us, a translation in terms of inertia. It goes all around life, taking from outside the greatest possible number of views of it, drawing it into itself instead of entering into it. But it is to the very inwardness of life that intuition leads us." *Ibid.,* p. 176.

52. *Ibid.,* p. 154 and p. 155.

to go on creating oneself endlessly."⁵³ The prime reality, then, for Bergson is movement.

But how is the nature of this reality to be defined? What is this duration which is life? this maturing which is creative evolution? Bergson tells us that duration is more than the constant replacement of instants. It is more than the present. Duration is concrete, a prolonging of the past into the present. Past, present and future are all found in it. Hence, let us note here, can be drawn the inference which contradicts his fundamental theory. If all endures, then nothing passes away; everything *is*. "Duration is the continuous progress of the past which gnaws into the future and which swells as it advances."⁵⁴ Bergson has no need of memory. The past preserves itself.

> The past is preserved by itself, automatically. In its entirety, probably, it follows us at every instant; all that we have felt, thought and willed from our earliest infancy is there, leaning over the present which is about to join it, pressing against the portals of consciousness that would fain leave it outside.⁵⁵

If we can get no closer to a concrete conception of the prime reality than "duration," let us look to the origin of this principle which Bergson calls the "vital impulse," the *élan vital*. Is it a creature, so that we might say of it that it was created? Bergson would tell us that so our intellects erroneously inform us, but such a notion is due to obscurity in our concept of creation. "Everything is obscure in the idea of creation if we *think* of things which are created and a thing which creates, as we habitually do, as the understanding cannot help doing."⁵⁶

> It is natural to our intellect (to think of things created and a thing creating), whose function is essentially practical, made to

---

53. *Ibid.,* p. 7.
54. *Ibid.,* p. 4. Note: Duration is "the preservation of the past in the present" (p. 23); "a real persistence of the past in the present; a duration which is, as it were, a hyphen, a connecting link" (p. 22); To know a living being is to "get at the very interval of duration" (p. 22); life is "unceasing creation"; "we are creating ourselves continually" (p. 7).
55. *Ibid.,* p. 5.
56. *Ibid.,* p. 248.

present to us things and states rather than changes and acts. But things and states are only views taken by our mind, of becoming. There are no things, there are only actions.[57]

For Bergson there is no thing creating. Movement just began. It evolves along definite though unpredictable lines and in its course life has appeared. "At a certain moment, in certain points of space, a visible current has taken rise."[58] It passes from generation to generation, struggling to establish itself in the universe and is forced, of necessity, to call into being various faculties by which to establish satisfactory reactions to environment. Such a faculty is intelligence. This vital impulse which is life gnaws into the future, splitting up as it grows, forming the great highways of life. Many of these lines of development became blind alleys, life was hindered in its passage, sometimes turning back, at other times resting.[59] The highways of plants, brutes and man surged steadily forward. One of the streams of life split up into plants and animals;[60] the animal line split up into anthropoids and vertebrates; in the former line the insect was the highest form, while in the latter, the line culminated in man.

We see the one impulse breaking up into species and individuals.[61] But what causes the division? Is it from within the impulse itself or extrinsic to it? Now in view of the fact that the impulse creates as it moves along, one would expect that the sufficient reason of the bifurcations would be wholly intrinsic. But such is not the case. Bergson assigns two reasons for the division of the original impulse. The first, and he says the real cause of the division, is explained by the fact that *life is tendency* and the very essence of tendency is to develop divergent directions along which the impetus is pushed.[62] A further

---

57. *Ibid.*
58. *Ibid.*, p. 26.
59. *Ibid.*, p. 104.
60. *Ibid.*, pp. 112-114. "The same impetus that has led the animal to give itself nerves and nerve centres must have ended, in the plant, in the chlorophyllian function" (p. 114).
61. *Ibid.*, p. 87.
62. "But the real and profound causes of division were those which life bore within its bosom. For life is tendency, and the essence of a tendency is to develop in the form of a sheaf, creating, by its very growth, divergent directions among which its impetus is divided." *Ibid.*, p. 99.

cause which Bergson gives is extrinsic to the movement, and it introduces us to his close approximation to, if not the actual embrace of, monism. The second cause of life's division into species and individuals is the resistance of matter to the movement of the vital principle. Matter tends to stifle life, and hence ages of effort were required for life to conquer this obstacle. Life succeeded "by dint of humility," and so the very earliest forms of life were insignificant indeed.[63]

Let us see the relation of matter to this vital impetus. The movement is described by Bergson as an ascending current which evolves aspects of reality as it forges upward. He says:

> The impetus of life consists in a need of creation. It cannot create absolutely, because it is confronted with matter, that is to say, with the movement that is the inverse of its own.[64]

The upward impetus of life becomes the downward push of matter; the two are likened to the movement of a single arm, its rising and falling; they are seen as one, as reality making and unmaking itself.

> Let us think of an action like that of raising the arm; then let us suppose that the arm, left to itself, falls back and yet that there subsists in it, striving to raise it up again, something of the will that animates it. In this *image of a creative action which unmakes itself* we have already a more exact representation of

---

63. "The resistance of inert matter was the obstacle that had first to be overcome. Life seems to have succeeded in this by dint of humility, by making itself very small and very insinuating, bending to physical and chemical forces, consenting even to go a part of the way with them, like the switch that adopts for a while the direction of the rail it is endeavoring to leave. Of phenomena in the simplest form of life, it is hard to say whether they are still physical and chemical or whether they are already vital. Life had to enter thus into the habits of inert matter, in order to draw it little by little, magnetized, as it were, to another track. The animate forms that first appeared were therefore of of extreme simplicity... but possessed of the tremendous internal push that was to raise them even to the highest forms of life.... Ages of effort and prodigies of subtlety were probably necessary for life to get past this new obstacle." *Ibid.*, pp. 98-9.

64. *Ibid.*, p. 251.

matter. In vital activity we see, then, that what subsists of the direct movement is the inverted movement, *a reality which is making itself in a reality which is unmaking itself.*[65]

The two movements are inseparable from each other; between them organized life is brought into existence. Thus we find linked together matter, to which the intellect is ordained,[66] and the immaterial, the duration or impulse itself, to which intuition is ordained.

But how can both be said to endure if duration is the flow of the vital impulse and matter is its opponent?[67] How do matter, the intellect and the sciences with which the latter is charged, endure? Only because they are "inseparably bound up with the rest of the universe," Bergson tells us, and he adds:

> It is true that in the universe itself two opposite movements are to be distinguished, as we shall see later on, "descent" and "ascent." The first only unwinds a roll ready prepared. In principle, it might be accomplished almost instantaneously, like releasing a spring. But the ascending movement, which corresponds to an inner work of ripening or creating, endures essentially, and imposes its rhythm on the first, which is inseparable from it.[68]

Critics see in this doctrine an acceptance of monism on the part of Bergson. The "roll ready prepared" which the descending movement unwinds is none other than the ascending creating movement in conflict with matter; matter is the inversion of life. Matter has its origin in life, therefore there is one radical kind of life, for spirit and the inversion of spirit are ultimately one and the same thing. Thus the two movements are but two aspects of a single, all-embracing movement which gives rise to the organized world.

65. *Ibid.*, p. 247 (Italics Bergson's).

66. "Intellect and matter have progressively adapted themselves one to the other in order to attain at last a common form. This adaptation has, moreover, been brought about quite naturally, because it is the same inversion of the same movement which creates at once the intellectuality of mind and the materiality of things." *Ibid.*, p. 206. Cf. also p. 11.

67. *Ibid.*, p. 11.

68. *Ibid.*

> In reality, life is a movement, materiality is the inverse movement, and each of these two movements is simple, the matter which forms a world being an undivided flux, and undivided also the life that runs through it, cutting out in it living beings all along its track. Of these two currents the second runs counter to the first, but the first obtains, all the same, something from the second. There results between them a *modus vivendi*, which is organization. This organization takes, for our senses and for our intellect, the form of parts entirely external to other parts in time and space.[69]

The failure of the vital impulse in its accomplishment of infinitely varied kinds of work, is due to the limitation of its power, for the vital impulse is finite. "The impetus is finite and has been given once for all."[70]

A final feature of Bergson's prime reality must be noted. We recall that he remarked that the notion of creation is obscured if one thinks of things created and a thing creating; that there are no things but actions only. All creation is evolving, the creator as well as the created, if one may be permitted to use these terms of Bergson's evolutionary movement where everything is essentially action. Expressing his belief that there are worlds other than this one, and that they differ in no way in their movement from the movement of our world, Bergson then presents his notion of creation and of God:

> Now, if the same kind of action is going on everywhere, whether it is in unmaking itself or whether it is that which is striving to remake itself, I simply express this probable similitude when I speak of a center from which worlds shoot out like rockets in a fireworks display — provided, however, that I do not present this center as a *thing*, but as a continuity of shooting out. God, thus defined, has nothing of the already made; He is unceasing life, action, freedom. Creation, so conceived, is not a mystery; we experience it in ourselves when we act freely.[71]

---

69. *Ibid.*, pp. 249-250. Also: "The movement it (the vital impulse) starts is sometimes turned aside, sometimes divided, always opposed; and the evolution of the organized world is the unrolling of this conflict." *Ibid.*, p. 254.

70. *Ibid.*, p. 254.

71. *Ibid.*, p. 248.

Not only does the evolutionary movement have a nebulous start, a shooting out that is nothing but a continuity of shooting out and for all practical purposes a mere nowhere; it also is going nowhere. "Evolution does not mark out a solitary route; it takes directions without aiming at ends."[72] How, then, does Bergson explain life's unity? The unity which he assigns to reality is in virtue of an impetus, a push that sends it along the road of time, not a unity in virtue of an end which operates as an attractive force.[73] So the evolutionary movement takes directions without having a goal.

> As the smallest grain of dust is bound up with our entire solar system, drawn along with it in that undivided movement of descent which is materiality itself, so all organized beings, from the humblest to the highest, from the first origins of life to the time in which we are, and in all places as in all times, do but evidence a single impulsion, the inverse of the movement of matter, and in itself indivisible. All living hold together and all yield to the same tremendous push.[74]

Having given to becoming the primacy over being, Bergson finds himself involved in "torturing problems" presented by the "phantom notion of the nought." His escape from them is unique:

> Now if we could prove that the idea of the nought, in the sense in which we take it when we oppose it to that of existence, is a pseudo-idea, the problems that are raised around it would become pseudo-problems.[75]

His whole aim is to show the impossibility and absurdity of the notion of the nought.

The problem of nothing, remarks Bergson,[76] has received too little attention for "the hidden spring, the invisible mover of philosophical thinking" that it is.[77] The very nature of philosophical thinking has

---

72. *Ibid.*, p. 102.
73. "The unity is derived from a *vis a tergo:* it is given at the start as an impulsion, not placed at the end as an attraction." *Ibid.*, p. 103.
74. *Ibid.*, pp. 270-271.
75. *Ibid.*, p. 277.
76. *Ibid.*, p. 275.
77. *Ibid.*

led thinkers to question the reason of their own existence; the reason of the existence of the universe; and, granted that the universe is referred to an immanent or transcendent principle, the philosophizing is pushed backward to the reason of the principle itself:

> Whence comes it, and how can it be understood, that anything exists? Even here, in the present work, when matter has been defined as a kind of descent, this descent as the interruption of a rise, this rise itself as a growth, when finally a principle of creation has been put at the base of things, the same question springs up: How — why does this principle exist rather than nothing?[78]

The mystery surrounding existence, says Bergson, is due to a fallacious explanation of nothing peculiar to the nature of man's intellect. For to man, existence seems like a conquest over nought. Reality is represented as extending on nothing as on a carpet; being has come by superaddition to nothing:

> In short, I cannot get rid of the idea that the full is an embroidery on the canvas of the void, that being is superimposed on nothing, and that in the idea of nothing there is less than in that of something.[79]

This is a mystery which must be cleared up, the French philosopher holds, especially if the basis of reality is laid in a free-acting principle which eminently endures. For actually, he says, there is *more* and not less in the idea of a non-existent object than in the idea of this same object conceived as "existent."[80]

Bergson embarks upon his repudiation of the notion of nothing. A possible solution of the mystery of existence could be had, he says,

78. *Ibid.*
79. *Ibid.*, p. 276.
80. "In other words, and however strange our assertion may seem, there is more, and not less, in the idea of an object conceived as 'not existing' than in the idea of this same object conceived as 'existing'; for the idea of the object 'not existing' is necessarily the idea of the object 'existing' with, in addition, the representaton of an exclusion of this object by the actual reality taken in block." *Ibid.*, p. 286.

by postulating a principle at the base of everything which is eternal in the same way as the axiom $A=A$. But this he rejects as demanding too great a sacrifice. If the principle of all things exists after the manner of a mathematical formula or definition, then the principiates follow rigidly as consequences of this, and thereby destroy free efficient causality.[81] Bergson decides that the notion of nothing must be branded as false. He starts by denying that one can imagine nothing. Nought ought to be the suppression of everything, inner self as well as outer self, and this absolute suppression is impossible and absurd:

> ... We cannot imagine a nought without perceiving, at least confusedly, that we are imagining it, consequently that we are acting, that we are thinking, and therefore that something still subsists.[82]

Thought cannot form an *image* of the suppression of everything, but can the *idea* represent nothing? An idea whose elements are driven away as fast as they are assembled is not an idea at all, but a mere word, he says. Though the mind can represent any existing thing whatever as annihilated, nevertheless the application of that to include the annihilation of everything results in self-contradiction and absurdity.[83]

Action, to which the intellect is ordained, aims at getting something for which we feel a want, or creating something as yet non-existent. Thus action in this special sense goes from empty to full, from absence to presence, from the unreal to the real. This "unreal" however, is purely relative, for we are immersed in realities and cannot escape them. To express what we have as a function of what we want, is quite legitimate in the field of action,[84] but not in the field of speculation. We make use of the void to think of the full only because of the static habits contracted by the intellect in its peculiar mode of activity. The void of which we speak is basically only the absence of some definite object which, having moved or been moved, leaves behind it the void

---

81. *Ibid.*, pp. 276-277.
82. *Ibid.*, p. 279.
83. *Ibid.*, pp. 280-281.
84. *Ibid.*, p. 275.

of itself.[85] This he considers partial nought. The mind perceives the presence of an old object in a new place, or vice versa, and the idea of annihilation or partial nothingness is nothing more than the substitution thought by a mind which would prefer to keep the old in place of the new.[86] The so-called idea of the absolute nought, supposedly attained by the application of the principle of substitution which yields the partial nought, is in reality, says Bergson, the idea of everything, as full and comprehensive as the idea of All:[87]

> In a word, whether it be a void of matter or a void of consciousness, the representation of the void is always a representation which is full and which resolves itself on analysis into two positive elements: the idea, distinct or confused, of a substitution, and the feeling, experienced or imagined, of a desire or a regret.[88]

Bergson concludes, therefore, that the idea of an absolute nought in the sense of the annihilation of everything, is a self-destructive idea, a pseudo-idea, a mere word. It cannot be opposed to the All, for this would be to oppose the full to the full. The perplexing question,

---

85. "(Thus is formed) the idea of the void, or of the partial nought, a thing being supposed to be replaced, not by another thing, but by a void which it leaves, that is, by the negation of itself." *Ibid.*, p. 296. Elsewhere he says: "The idea of annihilation or of partial nothingness is therefore formed here in the course of the substitution of one thing for another, wherever this substitution is thought by a mind that would prefer to keep the old thing in the place of the new or at least conceives this preference as possible." *Ibid.*, p. 282.

86. "The conception of a void arises when consciousness, lagging behind itself, remains attached to the recollection of an old state when another state is already present. It is only a comparison of what is and what could or ought to be, between the full and the void." *Ibid.*, p. 283.

87. "If we analyze this idea of Nothing, we find that it is, at bottom, the idea of Everything, together with a movement of the mind that keeps jumping from one thing to another, refuses to stand still, and concentrates all its attention on this refusal by never determining its actual position except by relation to that which it has just left. It is therefore an idea eminently comprehensive and full, as full and comprehensive as the idea of All, to which it is closely akin." *Ibid.*, p. 296.

88. *Ibid.*, p. 283.

Why does something exist?, becomes therefore, a pseudo-problem raised about a pseudo-idea, a "phantom problem which haunts the mind with such obstinacy."[89]

Critical Evaluation

In commenting on Bergson's philosophy of becoming, first, insofar as it aims to supplant the traditional philosophy of being as taught by Aristotle and the Schoolmen, we may note that, as regards the fact of movement and becoming, there can be no doubt that Bergson and Saint Thomas are in agreement. "Speculation must begin with the fact of movement," says Bergson.[90] "Whoever is ignorant of movement is ignorant of nature," says Saint Thomas.[91] With regard to the negation of being, however, the Schoolmen are in no accord with the French philosopher. The Schoolmen might distinguish between *ens reale, ens entis* and *ens rationis,* but the *ens* existed somewhere. It is a dictate of common sense that a thing *is.* But if it is the essence of a thing always to be becoming something, then it is never itself. It is simply intellectual suicide to deny the *ens,* declare the Scholastics. Where is truth, if we cannot say of things which we see and feel and taste, that they *are?* The idea of being is one of the primary observations of human experience. Contrasting sharply with the Bergsonian descriptions of reality, the Scholastics tell us that being is "that which is or can be." Being is that which *is.* Being is being. It is almost as if we said a book is a book; a man is a man. Being cannot be explained by something other than being, because everything is being. It is a self-evident truth; that is, its nature is obvious. We see it. We grasp its nature. Reality is being. But if reality is flux, then nothing *is.* That is just where Bergson's philosophy of change brings us.

89. Cf. *Ibid.,* p. 298.

90. *Ibid.,* pp. 194-199.

91. "Ignorato motu, ignoratur natura." *III Phys., lect.* 1. Saint Thomas even speaks of the fluidity of things. "Dicitur autem creatura fluvius, quia fluit semper de esse ad non esse per corruptionem, et de non esse ad esse per generationem" (*Sermones Festivi,* No. 61). Cited by F. J. Sheen, *op. cit.,* p. 157 (*q. v.*).

We have said that being is obvious, and that it can be explained by nothing other than being. This means that being is the first notion conceived by the mind upon contact with external or internal reality. The human intelligence is commensurate with being and must always be in relation to being. Whatever our view of reality, there is no escape from the persistent and constant instinct of the intellect to affirm *that which is*. It is our primary notion, and the formal object of the intellect. From it are derived other fundamental notions as well as the primary principles of thought and reality.

Plato recognized the fallacy underlying the philosophy of flux. In his dialogue "Cratylus" he says:

> Must not the same thing be born and return and vanish while the word is in our mouths? At the moment that the observer approaches them, they (things) become other and of another nature, so that you cannot know that which has no state. Nor can we reasonably say, Cratylus, that there is knowledge at all if everything is in a state of transition and there is nothing abiding. If the very nature of knowledge changes, at the time when the change occurs there will be no knowledge; and if the transition is always going on, there will always be no knowledge, and according to this view, there will be no one to know and nothing to be known.[92]

Saint Thomas consistently held that the notion of being is absolutely the first attained by the intellect. It is implied in all other ideas and no other concept could be formed by the intellect without it. Hence the notion of becoming is dependent upon the notion of being; the kinetic has full meaning only in its right relation to the static. When a thing becomes, it is in a *state* of becoming. The two elements are mutually complementary. In order to become it must be in the state of becoming, otherwise it could not become at all. Indeed, the very reality of the flux depends upon the ultimate reality of the static concept that the flux *is*. The flux *is,* and so is real. The one enduring reality is that which is, and that which is, is being; and thus even be-

---

92. B. Jowett, *The Dialogues of Plato* — "Cratylus" (New York, 1890), I, p. 680.

coming must be conceived as an aspect of being. Saint Thomas enunciates this truth when he says:

> Every movement presupposes something immutable; for when a change of qualities occurs, the substance remains unmoved; and when there is a change of substantial form, matter remains unmoved. Moreover, the various conditions of movable things are themselves immutable; for instance, though Socrates be not always sitting, yet it is an unchangeable truth that whenever he does sit he remains in one place.[93]

It is not difficult to see Bergson's position. His denial of being forced him, as a logical consequence, to deny the intelligence, for reason attests to the primordial evidence of being. The first of all the acts of the intellect is its adherence to being; hence the repudiation of being means the repudiation of that faculty by which being is spontaneously and naturally known.

In emphasizing the reality of time, Bergson does violence to the notion of space. Both notions are conditions of material bodies. This paper, book, desk, room, all exist in time and all occupy a given space. It need not, indeed it does not, detract from the experimental fact of change, to insist upon the equally experimental fact that there are other essential elements of natural bodies. Extension is one of them; so is liability to change. To make change the sole reality is to deny extension, for all things would then be only a flowing point. The result would be no differentiation between bodies by way of extension, and so all bodies could be said, with equal truth, to have the same extension. But that would be only the extension of the flowing "now," and who could grasp it?

Whereas Bergson practically annihilates space, Saint Thomas uses it as one of the notions provided by the senses for the intellect from which the latter derives, by way of abstraction, its notion of intelli-

---

93. "Omnis motus supponit aliquid immobile. Cum enim transmutatio fit secundum qualitatem, remanet substantia immobilis; et cum transmutatur forma substantialis, remanet materia immobilis. Rerum etiam mutabilium sunt immobiles habitudines; sicut Socrates; etsi non semper sedeat, tamen immobiliter est verum quod, quando sedet, in uno loco manet." *Sum. Th.*, I, q. 84, a. 1, *ad* 3.

gible matter. For him, no space exists unless there are bodies to occupy it. Once having lifted itself beyond the sensible order, the intellect rids itself of the crutches of time and space and transcends them in the universal concept:

> Just as things actually intelligible are apart from place, so are they apart from time: because time is consequent upon local movement; wherefore it measures only such things as are somehow in place.[94]

In the reflex universal, when the intellect refers the universal concept to concrete realities, then time and space again enter in:

> In composition and division our intellect always includes time past or future, but not in understanding what a thing is. For it understands what a thing is by abstracting intelligible from sensible conditions: wherefore in respect of that operation, it understands the intelligible apart from time and all conditions of things sensible. Whereas it composes and divides by applying previously abstracted intelligibles to things, and in this application, time must of necessity be implied.[95]

This shows us precisely wherein Bergson's difficulty lies. His notion of intellect is responsible in great part for the trouble. The flow, to be sure, excludes the possibility of things being in place and so of occupying a definite space. "There are no things, but only actions," he himself declares. The nature of the intellectual faculty in his system, however, due to its inability to transcend the sensible because

---

94. "Sicut enim intelligibilia actu sunt absque loco, ita etiam sunt absque tempore; nam tempus consequitur motum localem, unde non mensurat nisi ea quae aliqualiter sunt in loco." *Con. Gen.*, l. II, c. 96, *fi*.

95. "Operationi autem intellectuali nostrae adjacet tempus, ex eo quod a phantasmatibus cognitionem accipimus, quae determinatum respiciunt tempus; et inde est quod, in compositione et divisione, semper noster intellectus adjungit tempus praeteritum vel futurum, non autem intelligendo *quod quid est;* intelligit enim *quod quid est,* abstrahendo intelligibilia a sensibilium conditionibus; unde, secundum illam operationem neque sub tempore neque sub aliqua conditione sensibilium rerum intelligibile comprehendit; componit autem aut dividit applicando intelligibilia prius abstracta ad res, et in hac applicatione necesse est cointelligi tempus." *Ibid.*

of its absorption by sense, is by that fact unable to transcend space; and therefore, for philosophical purposes, the notion of space must be destroyed.

On the point of being, then, students of Scholastic philosophy cannot agree with Bergson. Without denying the actuality of the kinetic, we refuse to surrender the static. For even a thing which is in a flux is a whole, is what it is as long as it is what it is; even the flux *is*. Everything has its own essence, unchangeable and indivisible, the abiding reality underlying the phenomena. It may change accidental parts without change of being, but if its essential parts change, then the thing ceases to be and a new thing begins to be. But the *res* is always present so long as a thing exists. There is always *ens* somewhere.

Instead of using his intellect to abstract essences from life, man must plunge into the stream of phenomena and "feel" life. Thus would Bergson substitute sensation for knowledge. In speaking of Heraclitus and the early philosophers (and the same holds true for the modern Heraclitus whom we are discussing here), Saint Thomas says:

> Because they (the early philosophers) observed that all bodies are mobile, and considered them to be ever in a state of flux, they were of opinion that we can have no certain knowledge of the true nature of things. For what is in a continual state of flux cannot be grasped with any degree of certitude, for it passes away before the mind can form a judgment thereon: according to the saying of Heraclitus, that it is not possible twice to touch a drop of water in a passing torrent, as the Philosopher relates (*Metaph.* IV; *Did.* III, 5). [96]

To Saint Thomas, certain knowledge was not only possible but the normal result of the intellect's normal activity. Not only *can* the intellect know with certitude, but it must go to the senses themselves for the matter of its activity. It goes to the very flow and finds therein,

---

96. "Primi philosophi, qui naturis rerum inquisiverunt, putaverunt nihil esse in mundo nisi corpus. Et quia videbant omnia corpora mobilia esse, et putabant ea in continuo fluxu esse, existimaverunt quod nulla certitudo de rerum veritate haberi posset a nobis. Quod enim est in continuo fluxu, per certitudinem apprendi non potest, quia prius labitur quam mente dejudicetur; sicut Heraclitus dixit, quod 'non est possibile aquam fluvii currentis bis tangere,' ut recitat Philosophus in *IV Metaph.* text. 22." *Sum. Th.*, I, q. 84, a. 1.

according to the mode of its own nature, the stable which is necessarily presupposed. Thus the intellect does know mobility, but it views it in the light of an aspect of being:

> Evolution supposes that a reality, while remaining itself in a certain fashion, becomes another thing. It postulates the analogy of being. If all is in all, if being is identical with itself, becoming is impossible.[97]

The intellect knows mobility according to its mode of knowing, and that, as we noted, is in an immaterial way. Intellect can seize the intelligibility of the flux and, penetrating the outward appearances of instability, find the stable, the constant; find, in other words, the substantial aspect of *ens*. To find the constant behind the flux, the real behind the phenomena, the *ens* behind *fieri*, one must transcend the senses, whose mode of reception is material, to the realm of intellect, whose receptive operations include the de-materializing power of abstraction. Being is primary; becoming is as one of its species. To Bergson we would say: The intellect truly reveals the real. *Abstrahentium non est mendacium.*

It will be to Saint Thomas that we shall have recourse for the corrective principles to be applied to Bergson's doctrine of intellect and intuition. In trying to make intuition a continuation of instinct, the French philosopher thought along the wrong line. He made it a sensitive faculty, whereas it is a mental one. Reflecting upon the internal senses, he recognized that operation whereby is felt the present state of the body, the flow of the "now." Seizing upon this sense perception he made it the basis of his intuitive faculty, the only faculty which for him adequately comprehends life. Thus he dragged down human knowledge to the merely sense level, and merited for himself and his system the title "anti-intellectualist."

Thomistic philosophy admits of an intuitive power of the human mind, but not at the sacrifice of the intellect. It is a function of the intellect, a more perfect function than ratiocination. *Necessitas rationis est ex defectu intellectus,* says Saint Thomas. Bergson failed to recog-

---

97. N. Balthasar, *L'Être et les Principes Metaphysiques,* p. 7. Cited by F. J. Sheen, *op. cit.,* p. 160 (*q. v.*).

nize a twofold power of man's intellect: first, reasoning, which is discursive and which he shares with no other creature; second, intelligence, which is intuitive and which he shares, though in a much less perfect way, with the angels.[98] Man and angels have intelligence. God *is* intelligence. Here is where Bergson made a fatal error, but not his only one. He confused reason with intelligence, attributing to man's intellect only one function. Thus he had no faculty for attaining to the notion of "being" and hence declared it only an artificial representation foisted upon man by his intellect. Saint Thomas, on the other hand, recognized the distinction between *intellectus* and *ratio*, and held intellective intuition, or the function whereby we derive our abstractive apprehension of being and the notions and principles which flow therefrom, to be distinct from ratiocination as the perfect from the imperfect. *Defectus quidam intellectus est ratiocinium.* Bergson then easily succumbed to the fallacy of giving to becoming the primacy over being. With its higher operation reduced to sense perception, the intellect itself was discredited by Bergson. It is an incapable faculty, he held, a deformer of reality, and fit only to operate among sensible things. Its destruction as a higher faculty was complete and it came toppling down; in its place was installed the "intuitive faculty," which is fundamentally the same as animal instinct, and this Bergson ordained to speculation. To intellect in its disgrace was said: In this realm of speculation thou shalt not enter. We would bluntly ask here: How can animal instinct (and such was Bergson's concept), ordained to practical needs as it is, be a speculative power? We prefer to keep with common sense and Saint Thomas and hold to the supremacy of the intellect, to its double operation of reasoning and intuition, and thus give the primacy to being, which is immediately intuited by intelligence; we reject the substitution of his "intuitive faculty" in place of human intelligence; of phenomena for substance; of error for truth; of finality for aimless impulse. We would save ourselves the embarrassment of reconciling these contradictory positions, namely: 1. Everything is passing, nothing remains (All is becoming); and 2. Everything remains, nothing passes (All is duration).

We would hasten to assure Bergson that it is not the human intellect in its abstractive power which falsifies; it represents the ab-

---

98. Cf. *Sum. Th.*, I, q. 79, a. 8 *corp. et ad* 3.

stract concept as true to reality, though we grant the latter does not adequately represent the particular types it represents and of which it is affirmed. Our mind is capable, however, of completing the whole view and representing the unity of the object with such-and-such individual characteristics. The simple apprehension of intelligible being and the intuition of its first principles enables the mind to acquire a more complex knowledge by way of reasoning.

Intuition, it has been well said, is inaccessible without an intellectual approach.[99] Hence the faculty which "distorts and disfigures" reality cannot be conceived as a reliable means to the end of knowing reality as it really is. Further, intuition has need of concepts to express the objects of its perception. How can one intuit the stream of life without such concepts as life, flux, existence? If springs are poisoned at their source, they will be poisoned throughout their course. If intellectual concepts distort reality, so will they distort the intuition which must use them to express what it intuits.[100]

We shall trace here the basic notions of the Thomistic concept of intuition, intellect and instinct. For Saint Thomas, intuition is an operation of the mind, properly speaking. We are not considering here the nature of sensation, which is an immediate intuition of an external object present to the senses. We are considering intellective intuition, which is intuition properly so called. Knowing by way of intuition consists in an intellectual grasp of being by an *immediate knowledge* with an intimate penetration of the real, which is seized in itself, without any process of reasoning. It is a more perfect form of knowing than reasoning, for by it the mind perceives the truth as immediately evident; as, for instance, when I perceive that I am myself and not you. That the whole is greater than its parts, and that being is being and not-being is not, are immediately evident truths. These are simple truths, facts of common sense. The supreme ideal of intelligence is that immediate act of the intellect which lays hold

99. *Contemporary Philosophy and Thomistic Principles,* pp. 191-192.
100. "Intuition, if it tries to set up alone as a sufficient way of knowing, has three defects: It cannot *define* what it perceives; for definition makes use of a concept. It cannot *communicate* what it perceives, for language is made of the common coins of concepts. It cannot *defend its truth* nor *distinguish true from false interpretation,* without the aid and criticism of the intellect." H. W. Hocking, *Types of Philosophy* (New York, 1929), p. 211.

of the innermost truth of a thing with the shining clearness of perfect vision. God, by a simple act of intuition, knows all things perfectly in their individual realities. Man's knowledge of his own *ego*, of his acts and his habits, upon reflection, is an incomplete intuition. But what of complex truths? Can the intellect see these at a glance? Or if not intellect, is there any faculty in man that can?

Instinct in man, considered as a function of organic sense, certainly is not such a faculty, for it cannot attain to even simple, abstract truths, and *a fortiori*, it can never attain the complex. Considered as an organic faculty, instinct can touch only single, concrete objects, never the abstract. It never generalizes. It is unable to make the slightest reflection. This instinct operates whenever sense phenomena present themselves — as the eye sees color and the ear hears sound. Reason is not a condition of its existence. It is shared alike by men and brute, and its function in man is to provide the sensible images from which the intellect makes abstractions. Instinct gathers up the sensible data and brings them into consciousness up to a certain point. Beyond the concrete it does not go. Intellect takes up the work and forms generalizations from the ever-recurring experiences of the senses. It is precisely at this point that instinct and intellect are seen to be diverse faculties; and precisely at the same point that brutes and human beings part company. Man shares instinct with the brutes; above and beyond it, man soars to the intelligible in the sensible; brutes are powerless. In refuting those who say that sense and intellect are the same, Saint Thomas has this to say:

> Sense is found in all animals, but animals other than man have no intellect; which is proved by this, that they do not work like intellectual agents, in diverse and opposite ways, but just as nature moves them to fixed and uniform activities; as every swallow builds its nest in the same way. . . . Sense is not cognizant except of singulars . . . but the intellect is cognizant of universals. The knowledge of the senses does not extend beyond things corporeal. . . . The intellect knows things incorporeal, for instance, wisdom, truth and the relations of things. . . . Sense neither knows itself nor sees that it sees; . . . the intellect knows itself and knows that it understands.[101]

101. "Sensus enim in omnibus animalibus invenitur. Alia autem animalia ab homine intellectum non habent; quod ex hoc apparet quia non operantur diversa

Here we see how much at variance Bergson is with Thomistic thought. For in the latter, instinct and intellect do not operate in different fields nor go in divergent directions. They operate on different planes, it is true, but the object of both is the same — sensible realities, though under different aspects; the former deals with the appearances, the latter with the object in its truest reality, its *quiddity*. Both go in the same direction but to different lengths; both tend toward knowledge, but instinct is ever the *ancilla* of intellect.

Such is the distinction between instinct and intellect; the former is a *sine qua non* condition of the intellectual functioning, but never a substitute for it. Each must act according to its own proper nature; but in Bergsonism sensation usurps the rôle of intelligence.

Just as decisively as Saint Thomas cuts off instinct from intellect, and insists that they are faculties on distinct levels, he joins reasoning and intelligence as dual functions of intellect.[102] Discursive movements toward conclusions as well as intuitive apprehensions of self-evident truths are "visions" of the intellect. There are three intellectual habits or virtues which Saint Thomas considers.[103] First, there is that of plain common sense — the easy grasp of those truths which the average person can readily understand. They are things which even children need not be taught and without their knowledge of which no teacher could instruct them. This virtue is the intellectual habit or power of understanding,[104] or knowledge, and it provides its possessor

et opposita, quasi intellectum habentia, sed sicut a natura mota ad determinatas quasdam operationes et uniformes in eadem specie, sicut omnis hirundo similiter nidificat.... Sensus non est cognoscitivus nisi singularium; cognoscit enim omnis sensitiva potentia per species individuales, quum recipiat species rerum in organis corporalibus. Intellectus autem est cognoscitivus universalium, ut per experimentum patet.... Cognitio sensus non se extendit nisi ad corporalia; quod ex hoc patet quod qualitates sensibiles, quae sunt propria objecta sensuum, non sunt nisi in corporalibus; sine eis autem sensus nihil cognoscit. Intellectus autem cognoscit incorporalia, sicut sapientiam, veritatem et relationes rerum.... Nullus sensus seipsum cognoscit nec suam operationem; visus enim non videt seipsum nec videt se videre; sed hoc superioris potentiae est, ut probatur in secundo *de Anima*. Intellectus autem cognoscit seipsum et cognoscit se intelligere. Non est igitur idem intellectus et sensus." *Con. Gen.*, l. II, c. 66.

102. Cf. *Sum. Th.*, II-II, q. 49, a. 5, *ad* 3.
103. Cf. *Sum. Th.*, I, q. 79, a. 10, *ad* 3.
104. Cf. *Sum. Th.*, II-II, q. 8, a. 1, *ad* 2.

with a set of first principles which are understood as soon as the terms involved in them are understood. That the whole is greater than its parts is a principle in question. This is the knowledge we referred to earlier as being intuitive. It provides us with an intellective intuition of being and the primary principles.

An acquired facility in handling these first principles, whereby conclusions are seen almost as easily as self-evident principles without involving long, discursive reasoning, is the second of these intellectual virtues, that of science. Columbus saw wood floating on the water. A child might have asked: How did that get here? But without long and labored reasoning from premises to conclusions, Columbus *knew* that land was near. A scientist notes that a constant result follows from a given experiment. By constant omissions of a single simple factor from the experiment, a different effect as constantly results. The intellectual virtue of science enables him to draw conclusions immediately from the results with a minimum of intellectual activity.

Science is the specific perfection of ratiocination. That is to say, the human mind proceeds from abstract and universal concepts and principles, such as we explained under the intellectual habit of understanding, and goes by way of discursive reasoning, to science. Science is its perfection. It is facility in this process of reasoning from premises to conclusions that constitutes the intellectual habit. If our intelligence were intuitive, as that of God and the angels, there would be no need of science. *Est enim aliquid scientia melius, scilicet intellectus.* In the absence of simple and intuitive intellection, science is the best available form of speculation, though it participates in the defects of reasoning. *Omnis scientia essentialiter non est intelligentia.*

The habitual, masterly manipulation of first principles, the power to study the various sciences, trace them to their ultimate sources and ordain them to man's highest happiness, the spontaneous act whereby one sums up all available evidence and assents to its resulting conclusion, is the habit of wisdom. This faculty, like those of understanding and of science can, through proper and adequate training, acquire such dexterity as to act spontaneously, and in this case its operation is of the nature of intuition. In summary, let us note that the first knowledge of the mind is a very confused knowledge of being, an imperfect intuition, an apprehension of "something as existing."

From this, by way of reasoning, it attains to science, which is the specific perfection of reasoning. Finally in its judgments the mind examines what it has found, and judges of the validity of its reasoning by referring again to the same principles by which it obtained such knowledge. Hence all reasoning starts from intuition, and ends again in this intellectual intuition by a reduction of all things to first principles.[105] The certitude of reasoning depends upon intellective intuition.

In referring the reason to intellect, we may consider the latter in one sense as the principle, and in another sense as the terminus of the operations of reason; as the principle indeed, because the human mind could not argue from one thing to another unless it started the argument by the simple acceptance of some truth, and this, of course, is the acknowledgment by the intellect of certain first principles. In like manner, by no process of reasoning could one know anything for certain, unless what the reason has thus acquired be again examined in the light of those first principles to which reason submits its findings. Thus, the intellect assumes the rôle of principle in the acquisition of truth, and becomes the terminus when it passes judgment on the same. Therefore, although human knowledge commences with the reasoning faculty, nevertheless there is inherent in this same faculty some of that simple knowledge possessed by beings of a higher order, and on this account they are said to have intellectual power.[106]

105. "Ratiocinatio hominis, cum sit quidam motus, progreditur ab intellectu aliquorum, scilicet naturaliter notorum absque investigatione rationis, sicut a quodam principio immobili; et ad intellectum etiam terminatur, inquantum judicamus per principia per se naturaliter nota de his quae ratiocinando inveniuntur. Constat autem quod sicut ratio speculativa ratiocinatur de speculativis, ita ratio practica ratiocinatur de operabilibus. Oportet igitur naturaliter nobis esse indita sicut principia speculabilium, ita et principia operabilium." *Sum. Th.*, I, q. 79, a. 12.

106. "Ratio comparatur ad intellectum ut ad principium et ut ad terminum; ut ad principium quidem, quia non posset mens humana ex uno in aliud discurrere, nisi ejus discursus ab aliqua simplici acceptione veritatis inciperet, quae quidem acceptio est intellectus principiorum. Similiter nec rationis discursus ad aliquid certum perveniret, nisi fieret examinatio ejus quod per discursum invenitur, ad principia prima, in quae ratio resolvit. Ut sic intellectus invenitur rationis principium quantum ad viam inveniendi, terminus vero ad viam judicandi. Unde quamvis cognitio humanae animae propriae sit per viam rationis, est tamen in ea aliqua participatio illius simplicis cognitionis quae in substantiis superioribus invenitur, ex quo vim intellectivam habere dicuntur." *De Verit.*, q. 15, a. 1.

The entire operation of the intellect, from the simplest dictates of common sense up to the highest acts of wisdom, is a vision of evidence. The vision of first principles, the vision of inferences based on experiment, and the vision of "large situations" — that is, of wisdom — can be so spontaneous, so natural and quick that it may be likened to the spontaneity and quickness of instinct, and, on its perfection, may be called the power of intuition. The operation is strictly intellectual, and not, as Bergson would have us believe, a reaction of the organic sense, which means a purely organic, sensitive and non-intellectual activity. Not only is Aquinas' doctrine of intuition intellectual, but so spontaneous, quick and easy that, in the perfection of the operations of the intellect, it may be called intuition. Instead of sending off intellect and intuition toward opposite fields of activity and making them diverse faculties, the Thomistic concept of intuition requires the use of the intellect to its utmost capacity. The discursive reasoning of the human mind is, as it were, so oiled and its movements are so facilitated that it acquires the ease and grace of spontaneity and results in that ultimate judgment which comes as an intuition.[107]

107. "Ratio et intellectus in homine non possunt esse diversae potentiae. Quod manifeste cognoscitur, si utriusque actus consideretur. Intelligere enim est simpliciter veritatem intelligibilem apprehendere; ratiocinari autem est procedere de uno intellecto ad aliud, ad veritatem intelligibilem cognoscendam. Et ideo angeli qui perfecte possident, secundum modum suae naturae, cognitione intelligibilis veritatis, non habent necesse procedere de uno ad aliud; sed simpliciter et absque discursu veritatem rerum apprehendunt.... Homines autem ad intelligibilem veritatem cognoscendam perveniunt procedendo de uno ad aliud, ut ibidem dicitur: et ideo rationales dicuntur. Patet ergo quod ratiocinari comparatur ad intelligere sicut moveri ad quiescere, vel acquirere ad habere; quorum unum est perfecti, aliud autem imperfecti. Et quia motus semper ab immobili procedit, et ad aliquid quietum terminatur, inde est quod ratiocinatio humana secundum viam inquisitionis vel inventionis procedit a quibusdam simpliciter intellectis, quae sunt prima principia; et rursus in via judicii resolvendo redit ad prima principia, ad quae inventa examinat." *Sum. Th.*, I, q. 78, a. 8.

Also: "Certitudo rationis est ex intellectu; sed necessitas rationis est ex defectu intellectus. Illa enim in quibus vis intellectiva plenarie viget, ratione non indigent, sed suo simplici intuitu veritatem comprehendunt, sicut Deus et angeli." *Sum. Th.*, II-II, q. 49, a. 5 *ad* 2.

Whereas Bergson makes intuition a perfection of animal instinct, Saint Thomas makes it a perfection of the intellect, and found in its varying degrees of perfection only in those beings of the genus *intelligences*. Bergson aims at knowing life. Saint Thomas starts with the living *ego*. Bergson repudiates the only faculty capable of acquiring this knowledge; Saint Thomas postulates for this faculty the spontaneity of habit, and thus saves not only intellectualism but the primary notion of being and the self-evident principles spontaneously grasped by the mind in its understanding of being.

Saint Thomas does not repudiate the kinetic. Rather, he requires it. "Whoever is ignorant of movement is ignorant of nature," he declares. However, he is able to transcend mere empirical data and see the reason of the movement. Bergson declares that speculation enters into the domain of experiment as its own domain; Thomas begins with it to enable him to rise to the intelligible. It is the intellect which saves the situation, for Saint Thomas bases his thought on the principle: What is received, is received according to the mode of the receiver. Movement can be perceived by the mind according to the mode of receiving of the mind, that is, immaterially. The senses see the movement, for that is the mode of reception of the senses; the intellect sees the movement in a higher mode; it sees the essence of change and the sufficient reason of its being. There is required a constant kinetic process in the very understanding of the notion of movement, for the mind operates upon the material supplied it by the senses, and its first act is a de-materializing process, the abstraction of movement's essence. Thus the notion is attained. But the kinesis in the intellectual order goes on. Notions are worked up into principles; principles into knowledge; knowledge in wisdom. The composition and division of ideas goes on in a constant flow, for thought is as necessary to the mind as air to the lungs. There is no need to force the powers of the mind into opposing channels, the one toward the abstract flow of life and the other toward the realm of solids. The natural activity of the mind, drawing upon the senses for the matter, can attain even the heights of wisdom; yet never does it loose itself from the primary notion of being to which it first, spontaneously and irrevocably attaches itself. For the mind can never err when it asserts that that which is, is real, is existing, is being.

In summarizing, we note that an attempt has been made to point out the nature of Bergson's mistake. It would seem to lie in the fact that Bergson fails to understand "intellect." He fails to distinguish between intelligence, i. e., the apprehensive faculty, and reason, which is discursive. For Saint Thomas, man is king of earth's creatures because of his intellect; he is the infant in the genus of intelligences. *Intellectus animae humanae est infimus in ordine intellectum.*

Bergson would seem to want man in his understanding of reality to be completely intuitive, as angels are. But man's intellect is too imperfect for that. Man must reason, for discursive reasoning is characteristic of his intellectual activity, belonging as it does to a composite material and spiritual being. We have already shown how the acquisition of intellectual habits can cause spontaneity of judgments which, in their perfection, may be termed intuition. It is a perfection of the intellect, not its habitual condition. "The defect of the intellect is the reason why man reasons," Saint Thomas says.[108] We would never have to make a syllogism, never have to reason, if our intellect were more perfect. But imperfect as it is, it has by nature the power to reveal the real; and not only can it do this, but it can also know that it can do so.

With Bergson's mutilation of the intellectual faculty, we will have nothing to do. So, as it is preferable to hold ourselves steadfast in the conviction that that which our senses present to us as real, really *is,* we give to being the primacy over becoming and refuse to exchange our nature's most treasured faculty for a sublimated animal instinct. In other words, summing all this up, we prefer to retain our doctrine of abstractive intuition of being rather than discard it for an instinctive "feeling" of the flow of the "now."

There remains for us to offer criticism upon Bergson's notion of prime reality as change; his doctrine of a self-originating, self-perfecting, self-intensifying and self-bifurcating vital push whence all existence springs; and finally, his classification of nothing as a pseudo-idea, and the problem of the origin of existence as a pseudo-problem. Concerning the first, namely, that prime reality is change, we shall make no direct criticism in this place. Since that is the general char-

---

108. Cf. *Con. Gen.*, l. I, c. 57.

acteristic of all philosophies of becoming, we prefer to postpone our discussion of it to the general refutation in the following chapter of Hegelianism and Bergsonism. Of Bergson's notion of creation we have the following points to offer in criticism:

The notion of a self-creating principle which ever intensifies and perfects itself, is contrary to the laws of motion and of causality. "Whatever is moved, is moved by another," says Saint Thomas.[109] So, too, does Saint Thomas demand a cause for every effect. In establishing rational proofs for the existence of God, Saint Thomas tells us that motion is nothing other than the reduction of potentiality to actuality, which can be effected only by something in a state of actuality.[110] Further, the same thing cannot be at once in actuality and potentiality in the same respect. "It is therefore impossible that in the same respect and in the same way a thing should be both mover and moved; that is, that it should move itself." Hence his principle, that whatever is moved, is moved by another. But since this cannot go on indefinitely, he continues: "Therefore it is necessary to arrive at a first mover put in motion by no other, and this everyone understands to be God."[111] But this Bergson does not understand to be his "Principle of Creation" which is at the base of things. He says that even when one reaches back that far, one seeks to know the why of the existence of that very principle. If Bergson understands this to be God, his question is meaningless. He postulates a "finite" god since he equates God with duration, the impetus, the ascending spirit which is finite.[112]

Saint Thomas in the same article referred to above, *Utrum Deus sit*, says:

> There is no case known (neither is it indeed possible) in which a thing is found to be the efficient cause of itself; for so it would be prior to itself, which is impossible.[113]

---

109. *Sum. Th.*, I, q. 2, a. 3.
110. *Ibid.*
111. *Ibid.*
112. *Creative Evolution*, p. 254.
113. *Sum. Th.*, I, q. 2, a. 3.

He goes on to show the impossibility of an infinity of efficient causes (that is, of essentially subordinate, but not of accidentally subordinate causes): "Therefore it is necessary to admit a first efficient cause, to which everyone gives the name of God."[114]

The creative evolution, Bergson tells us, "takes directions without aiming at ends," and "is not the realization of a plan."[115] Saint Thomas, however, is a finalist. For him, activity involves an end to be sought which is the very reason of the activity and the reason why the means are pursued. Even nature (the vital impulse of Bergson) must seek an end.

> Since nature works for a determinate end under the direction of a higher agent, whatever is done by nature must needs be traced back to God, as to its first cause.... All things that are changeable and capable of defect must be traced back to an immovable and self-necessary first principle.[116]

Bergson postulates an evolutionary creative principle which can create both ideas and forms for its immediate ends;[117] it solves particular problems according as they are presented to it. But particular problems ought to be solved in view of a final problem to which they are related. There is a reason for a reason, and if we push back far enough we have ultimately the final purpose. How can Bergson's vital impulse direct immediate acts unless in view of an ultimate purpose?

> Every agent acts for an end (remarks Saint Thomas). Otherwise from any given action neither this particular thing nor that would happen, except by chance. But there are some agents which both act and are acted upon. These are imperfect agents, and whenever they act they must intend to acquire some new perfection.[118]

If direction is taken without reference to ends, how account for the remarkable development of instinct in bees and ants, but not in man?

114. *Ibid.*
115. *Op. cit.*, pp. 102, 3.
116. *Sum. Th.*, I, q. 2, a. 3, *ad* 2.
117. *Op. cit.*, p. 103.
118. *Sum. Th.*, I, q. 44, a. 4.

Some Non-Scholastic Interpretations of Reality   173

Or how account for the development of intellect in man and not in animals?

Bergson has separated himself from the common-sense dictate that every effect requires a cause. Since change is an effect, it must have a cause. How else could one rationally account for the potentialities and activities exhibited by the original impulse, except by a cause working toward a determinate effect — an agent working toward an end? But Bergson cannot cut himself off completely from this common-sense view. What he denies in one place he admits in another; or what he denies to the vital impulse as the creative principle, he postulates of mere creature activity: "We should not act if we did not set before ourselves an end, and we seek a thing only because we feel the lack of it."[119]

Bergson's identification of God with Time, Duration, Vital Push, makes of God a God of change, a God of time, a God of undirected activity, not the Immutable, Eternal, Intelligent Creator. His query, Why does this Principle of Creation exist rather than nothing?, is but the natural result of his repudiation of being and his substitution of becoming as the prime reality. He has not, as a result, a principle of identity of ontological validity at the basis of his system, and hence he cuts himself off from that being that is essentially being, the Being *a se* Who exists of Himself in one eternal, unchanging moment. Time is the measure of motion. It is an effect, not a cause. God, as Time, therefore, can never be the principle of things. Duration fares no better. That, too, is an effect, not a cause. It may reasonably be expected that a creative principle shall produce at least existence; but duration presupposes existence, and therefore God, as Duration, would be an effect causing its cause. God as Vital Push must also be rejected. As a movement requires a mover, so a push requires a pusher. Self-creation is as incoherent as the square circle of which Bergson himself spoke when he said that an idea which drove away its elements as fast as it collected them, was no idea at all.[120]

Creation postulates a creator. Bergson himself recognizes the postulate; witness his "Principle of Creation" referred to above. One of

---

119. *Op. cit.*, p. 297.
120. *Ibid.*, p. 280.

his errors lies in his failure to grasp the true nature of the principle of creation.

As Bergson implies a duration without a necessary pre-existence, he also postulates matter pre-existing its cause, the vital push. "It is the same inversion of the same movement that creates at once the intellectuality of mind and the materiality of things," he says.[121] The inversion of spirit creates matter. But we would ask: How can matter pre-exist its cause, as it must do if it is to provide that ascending current with obstacles and problems to overcome, which conquest is precisely the creative evolution? In order to ascend, the vital impulse must meet the descending obstacle, which is matter. Whence is the origin of this matter? Bergson says it is created by the movement of which it is itself the inversion; but that contradicts his doctrine that the ascent of spirit meets the descent of matter and thus, in overcoming the impediment, mounts higher.

Further, if matter is the inversion of the ascending spirit, how account for the fact that the impulse turns back upon itself? Whence comes the direction antagonistic to itself? How can ascent produce descent except by a contradictory force whose origin must be explained? These are the "torturing problems" which should "persist in haunting" Bergson,[122] not the notion of nothing, which can be explained rationally in a philosophy that builds itself solidly upon the concept of being as the fundamental notion of the mind and as the basis of the primary principles of thought and reality.

To designate the concept of nothing as a pseudo-idea and the problem of existence as a pseudo-problem may be a means of escape from a disagreeable situation, but it is no solution of the problem. Bergson finds himself in the difficult situation of trying to bolster up his philosophy of becoming by artificial means precisely because he has destroyed the foundation. Becoming has no sufficient reason, has no foundation, no validity except as an aspect of being. To being is opposed nothing, as existence is to non-existence, as reality to the unreal, as the possible to the impossible. To answer Bergson's question, How can the idea of the Nought be opposed to that of All?,

---

121. *Ibid.*, p. 206.
122. *Op. cit.*, p. 297.

the philosophy of being answers very simply: Not as you do, by the addition of a new note, namely, non-existence, to the accumulation of notes which characterize the existing thing; but rather we oppose the two terms as absolute contradictories, the one implying all that the other denies. Therefore in our philosophy there is *less*, infinitely less, in the notion of nothing than in that of existence, and not *more*, as you say. In fact, there is nothing at all in the notion of nothing, and its only possibility as an object of thought depends upon the intellect which can conceive it, not as being, but after the manner of being. The intellect conceives nothing merely as a notion that can be thought of. It is a being of the mind, a logical being, called in Scholastic philosophy an *ens rationis*. Saint Thomas says:

> Non-being has not that in itself whereby it may be recognized. Still it may be recognized insofar as the intellect renders it knowable. Hence, truth is only based on non-being insofar as non-being is a being of the reason, that is, insofar as it is apprehended by the reason.[123]

We offer a rational explanation. Our intellect seizes upon "being," and by considering it, reaches the distinction between "being" and "non-being," and so gives birth to that second concept which is recognized as being in opposition to being. The intellect naturally grasps primary notions, and so "the idea of nothing persists to haunt us" not at all. The intellect, says Bergson, is to blame. "Our life is spent in filling voids which our intellect conceives under the influence, by no means intellectual, of desire and of regret, under the pressure of vital necessities."[124] Speculation follows closely the lead of intellect, and the result is, claims the French philosopher, that we are doomed to illusion, and all this because of the "phantom of the nought."

Bergson has reversed the order of acquisition of concepts. We do not pass through the idea of nought in order to reach that of being,

---

123. "Non ens non habet in se unde cognoscatur, sed cognoscitur in quantum intellectus facit illud cognoscibile; unde verum fundatur in ente in quantum non ens est quoddam ens rationis, apprehensum scilicet a ratione." *Sum. Th.*, I, q. 16, a. 3, *ad* 2.

124. *Op. cit.*, p. 298.

but rather, as Saint Thomas tells us, the idea of being is the first notion conceived by the mind, and that of non-being second.[125] Nor does our intellect think the moving by means of the immovable, as is claimed.[126] Rather does the intellect pass from phenomena to the reality behind them, to the essence which constitutes the thing in its being. It grasps the essence in its static condition apart from the existence in which the essence is subject to conditions of time and space. Whatever is moved, is moved by another; and in his deduction of a proof for God's existence Saint Thomas concludes: "And this all men call God." His transition is from the moving to the Immobile Mover.

We must brand as false Bergson's conclusions:

> There is more in a movement than in the successive positions attributed to the moving object, more in the becoming than in the forms passed through in turn; more in the evolution of form than in the forms assumed one after another.[127]

This makes becoming more perfect than being; potentiality superior to actuality; mixed act and potency more perfect than pure act. That is to step on dangerous ground; on *terra firma* without the *firma*. Fundamental philosophical principles are involved; and since all philosophies of change are radically founded on the same contradictions, it is our purpose to offer in the following chapter a refutation of the basic fallacy of the philosophies of both Hegel and Bergson, in the light of the fundamental Thomistic principles derived from the intellect's notion of *ens*.

---

125. Cf. *IV Metaph., lect.* 3.
126. *Op. cit.*, p. 299.
127. *Ibid.*, pp. 316, 314.

CHAPTER VI

THE PHILOSOPHY OF FLUX AND THOMISTIC PRINCIPLES

BASIC PRINCIPLES OF THOMISTIC METAPHYSICS

Against the philosophy which gives primacy to becoming, it is necessary to begin by establishing the titles to the philosophy of being. Our aim in these closing pages of our work will be: 1. to establish the ontological validity of the primary notion of being; 2. to recall the intuitive apprehension of the primary principles in this first concept of being; 3. on the basis of the Thomistic philosophy, to indicate the self-evident principles which flow directly or indirectly from the principle of identity and which share its ontological validity; 4. to show the disastrous effects upon these principles of a philosophy which denies the dual character of reality or subordinates being to becoming; 5. to indicate our conclusions concerning the basic fallacy of a fluxian philosophy.

It is well known to the reader that for Saint Thomas the proper object of the human intellect is being. *Nam illud quod primo cadit in apprehensione, est ens.* Concerning the ontological validity of this primary notion of being, we hold it to be immediately evident, and must note at once that what is immediately evident cannot be demonstrated; it is intuitively grasped by the human mind. It is the *intus legere* from which the word intelligence has derived its meaning. Thus it is with the primary notion of being. We have already indicated earlier in this work in what way the mind apprehends being. We have said, with Saint Thomas, that it is the first notion the mind grasps;[1] that the first act of the mind is adherence to being; that all subsequent knowledge the mind attains can be resolved in terms of being, and all this is so because of the nature of man's intellect, which is in fact the faculty of being, as sight is of color and hearing is of sound. By the light of reason with which God endows man, he is able to plunge

---

1. *Sum. Th.*, I-II, q. 94, a. 2; — I, q. 5, a. 2.

into the heart of reality, to prescind from all passing enveloping phenomena and seize the static aspect underlying them. The human mind, in simple words, apprehends the being of all things.

Now ontological validity is nothing other than the aptitude to show forth the *esse* that lies beyond the phenomena. Sensible qualities must be disregarded and the intelligible must shine forth. Now this is precisely what occurs when the intellect is brought face to face with a sensible object. The intelligible being (*ens*) shines forth, making its presence known to the intellect with such cogency that the latter faculty immediately, spontaneously and naturally grasps the notion and knows it as being. Thus in the presence of sensible objects the mind is dominated and regulated by being; it discovers being because the latter so literally "shines forth" that the intellect must perforce judge it truly as being, and this vision of evidence is so cogent that the intellect consents without fear of error.[2] The intellect not only has an essential relation to being, but it knows it as such, and thus the very certitude of our primary affirmation of being is explained by the very objective evidence of being itself; for the intellect is to being as the eye to color and the touch to texture.[3] The veracity of the intellect in thus apprehending being is undemonstrable because it presupposes the natural aptitude of a faculty to attain its object.

The mind immediately perceives in this primary notion its identity with itself and so forms the first proposition: Being is being, or being is that which exists. Thus we derive the first principle of metaphysics, the principle of identity.[4] This, too, is a spontaneous and natural act

---

2. *Sum. Th.*, I, q. 84, a. 6, *ad* 1; — I, q. 17, a. 3 *corp. et ad* 2.

3. "Intellectus naturaliter cognoscit ens et ea quae sunt per se entis in quantum hujusmodi, in qua cognitione fundatur primorum principiorum notitia." *Con. Gen.*, l. II, q. 83. "Objectum formale intellectus est ens, sicut color est objectum formale visus." *Ibid*.

4. "Since being is the first principle of all human knowledge, it is *a fortiori* the first principle of metaphysics.... In the light of immediate evidence, the intellect sees that something is, or exists: that what exists is that which it is; that that which it is, or exists, cannot be and not at one and the same time; that a thing either is, or it is not, and no third supposition is conceivable.... Reason has not to prove any one of these principles, otherwise they would not be principles, but conclusions; but it is by them that reason proves all the rest." Gilson, *The Unity of Philosophical Experience*, p. 318.

of the intellect and the objectivity of this primary principle is as simply established as that of the primary notion upon which it is based. The mind refers this principle which it spontaneously perceives in being, to being itself, and thus perceives the truth of the proposition.[5] In the mere analysis of the terms of the proposition, the mind can defend the objective evidence of this principle.

The second notion attained by the mind is the negation of being, *non-ens,* and then, as a consequence, it grasps the concept of division.[6] These three notions are all that the intellect needs to formulate the principle of contradiction. Perceiving the distinction between being and the negation of being, the mind forms the proposition and sees its truth, that being cannot be that which is not. This is a very simple form of the principle, showing the incompatibility of being and non-being. Elsewhere in this thesis we dwelt more at length upon these primary principles. Our chief concern here is to indicate briefly the precise nature of the principles and to establish their validity in the light of their own self-evidence and that of being. The material element is provided by the senses:[7] the efficient cause lies in the intellect as a faculty of being whereby in the light of reason it seizes the intelligible behind the sensible; the formal reason of the mind's consent lies in the objective and immediate evidence presented. Thus the first principles are derived partly from within and partly from without.

5. "Veritas est in intellectu et in sensu, licet non eodem modo. In intellectu enim est sicut consequens actum intellectus, et sicut cognita per intellectum; consequitur namque intellectus operationem, secundum quod judicium intellectus est de re secundum quod est; cognoscitur autem ab intellectu secundum quod intellectus reflectitur supra actum suum, non solum secundum quod cognoscit actum suum, sed secundum quod cognoscit proportionem ejus ad rem, quod quidem cognosci non potest nisi cognita natura ipsius actus; quae cognosci non potest, nisi cognoscatur natura principii activi, quod est ipse intellectus, in cujus natura est ut rebus conformetur; unde secundum hoc cognoscit veritatem intellectus quod supra se ipsum reflectitur." *De Verit.,* q. 1, a. 9.

6. Cf. *De Pot.,* q. 9, a. 7, *ad* 15; *In X Metaph., lect.* 3; *Sum. Th.,* I, q. 11, a. 2, *ad* 4.

7. "Per verba illa Augustini datur intelligi veritas non sit totaliter a sensibus expectanda. Requiritur enim lumen intellectus agentis, per quod immutabiliter veritatem in rebus mutabilibus cognoscamus, et dicernamus ipsas res a similitudinibus rerum." *Sum. Th.,* I, q. 84, a. 6, *ad* 1.

They are known when their terms are understood.[8] We cannot escape the mind's instinctive act of affirming that something is; that something is itself; that something cannot be another at the same time and in the same respect that it is itself. It is well to note here that our certainty of the validity of our primary judgments is not wholly dependent upon the evidence obtained from sensation; rather, it is of the intellectual order and, as we have said, a vision of the intellect. This makes the certitude ontological in nature and signs our knowledge with the character of truth.[9]

These basic principles, a being is what it is, and it is not another at the same time and under the same aspect, provide the basis for all subsequent knowledge. In the genus of principles, the primary judgments have hierarchical order.[10] Whether the principle of identity or that of contradiction ranks first has been a question of dispute among Scholastics. Since all negation is founded upon affirmation, it seems logical to hold that the principle of identity holds the primacy, at least in order of intellectual apprehension, since the notion of being alone suffices for it. The mind perceives being and perceives its identity with itself and proposes: This is something. Something exists. However, in the order of reduction, tracing backward from proximate to ultimate principles, the principle of contradiction would seem to be the last stronghold of defense: This thing cannot be that thing at the same time and under the same aspect. This thing either is or it is not. Thus,

---

8. "Si igitur notum sit omnibus de praedicato et de subjecto quid sit, propositio illa erit omnibus per se nota; sicut patet in primis demonstrationum principiis, quorum termini sunt quaedam communia quae nullus ignorat, ut ens et non ens, totum et pars, et similia." *Sum. Th.*, I, q. 2, a. 1.

9. "Objectum autem proprium intellectus est quidditas rei; unde circa quidditatem rei, per se loquendo, intellectus non fallitur; sed circa ea quae circumstant rei essentiam vel quidditatem intellectus potest falli; dum unum ordinet ad aliud vel componendo vel dividendo vel etiam ratiocinando. Et propter hoc etiam circa illas propositiones errare non potest, quae statim cognoscuntur, cognita terminorum quidditate; sicut accidet circa prima principia, ex quibus etiam accidit infallibilitas veritatis secundum certitudinem scientiae circa conclusiones." *Sum. Th.*, I, q. 85, a. 6.

10. "In principiis per se notis, ordo quidam invenitur, ut quaedam in aliis simpliciter contineantur; sicut omnia principia reducuntur ad hoc, sicut ad primum: impossibile est simul affirmare et negare." *Sum. Th.*, II-II, q. 1, a. 7.

writes Thomas Aquinas, all principles are finally *reduced* to one; namely, that it is impossible for the same thing to be at the same time both affirmed and denied.[11]

Just what these principles are which are reducible to the two supreme principles of identity and contradiction, and so ultimately to the notion of being, it is our present purpose to show. Following here the method of eduction rather than of reduction, we progress from the notion of being to that of the judgment that being is identical with itself; in other words, to the principle of identity. Flowing from this, and consisting of merely a determination of it, we have the principle of substance, which enunciates that whatever is, is one and the same under its multiple and transitory modalities. From the multiple and transitory phenomena the intellect passes to this same thing which is permanent beneath the changes, that is, to being in its full sense as that which exists in itself. Every movement presupposes something immobile.[12] For while recognizing the changing element, reason recognizes the static as well. It knows that movement requires something permanent, a flow, something static. This is being in its static mode, as an object of abstract thought, that is, the being of the principle of identity; now it is in this same notion considered as existing in a certain way, namely, as requiring no subject in which to inhere, that we have the principle of substance.[13] Here we are touching upon that which distinguishes existence *per se* from existence *per accidens*. For the intelligible being which requires no subject in which to inhere differs radically from the being of the phenomena which reveal the subject's presence to the senses. The phenomena require a subject of inherence. The color of an object requires that object to give it being; the extension of an object as well as its location require the object to give to each their being. Now, ultimately, it is being in which all these sensible qualities of color, size and situation inhere; more determinately, it is substance, which is no other than an expression of that modality of

---

11. *Ibid.*
12. *Sum. Th.*, I, q. 84, a. 1, *ad* 3.
13. "Substantia est res, *cujus naturae debetur* esse non in alio; accidens vero est res, *cujus naturae debetur* esse in alio." *Quod. IX*, q. 5, a. 2. The explanation of the italicized words can be found in *Sum. Th.*, III, q. 77, a. 1, *ad* 2. "Substantia est rei, cui convenit esse non in subjecto." *Con. Gen.*, l. I, c. 25.

being whereby it subsists *per se* and *is* that very being and no other throughout any fleeting changes of accidental forms which take place. Substance is being properly so called precisely because it *is*,[14] and Saint Thomas tells us that being is predicated primarily and absolutely of substance.[15] The intellect therefore immediately perceives the principle of substance as a determination of the principle of identity, since it perceives behind the phenomena the being which remains one and the same, existing in itself and not as an attribute of another. To conceive being thus is to conceive it as substance. As is being, so is substance intelligible *per se* and not sensible except *per accidens*.[16]

The next principle derived from the notion of being through the principle of identity is that of sufficient reason. Expressed simply, it is this: Everything which exists has its sufficient reason. This principle is of universal application extending even to God, for nothing escapes the government exercised over all modes of being by the principles of identity and of sufficient reason. Under one aspect it is a determination of the principle of identity; under another aspect it is reducible to the principle of identity through that of contradiction. There are definite states in the understanding of this principle: 1. Everything which exists has its sufficient reason; 2. A thing may have its sufficient reason either in itself or in another; 3. A thing has its sufficient reason in itself if what belongs to it does so by reason of its own intrinsic constitution, that is, by its very nature. Thus, it belongs to God's nature to exist, and hence He is the sufficient reason of His own existence. Thus we say God's essence is His existence, meaning that in God essence and existence are identified. It is in this aspect, namely, that a thing may have its sufficient reason in itself, that the principle of sufficient reason is a determination of the principle of identity.

In its second aspect, the principle under discussion presents the alternative that a thing may have the reason of its being in another. Now as the Necessary Being is His own sufficient reason, so the beings

---

14. "Quod autem proprie dicitur esse, quod habet ipsum esse, quasi in suo esse subsistens. Unde solae substantiae proprie et vere dicuntur entia." *Sum. Th.*, I, q. 90, a. 2.
15. *De Ente et Essentia*, c. 2.
16. *Sum. Th.*, III, q. 76, a. 3.

which come to be and pass out of being (contingent beings) must have their sufficient reason in another; in such another, in fact, that it is outside the limitations of contingency. *Quod est non per se, est ab alio, quod est per se.* Whatever is not required by the nature of a subject comes to it through some external cause.[17] Man's essence does not require that he exist, and for this reason is man a contingent being. He is a being whose existence depends upon a cause other than his own nature. "Nothing can be the sufficient cause of its own existence if its existence is caused."[18]

This principle in its second understanding, namely, that of extrinsic sufficient reason, is reducible to the principle of identity by a *reductio ad impossibile.* A contingent being has not in itself the cause of its own being. Hence to deny that a contingent being must have its sufficient reason in another is to contradict the principle of contradiction. Its identity with itself would, for the contingent being, be destroyed, for one would be equivalently saying that a contingent being is not a contingent being, or that a thing is and is not at the same time and under the same aspects. The relation between the principles of contradiction and identity and the primary notion of being would be voided, and a being would at the same time and in the same respect be notbeing.

The principle of sufficient reason is fundamentally the principle of causality when applied to created realities.[19] Though the term *raison d'être* is broader than that of cause (as witness the distinction made in the case of God), nevertheless from a consideration of this principle there flows the principle of causality embracing the intrinsic causes of matter and form and the extrinsic causes, efficient and final. Our concern here will be with the efficient and final causes as flowing from the principle of extrinsic sufficient reason: that everything which does

---

17. "Omnes enim quod alicui convenit non secundum quod ipsum est, per aliquam causam ei convenit, nam quod causam non habet primum et immediatum est." *Con. Gen.,* l. II, c. 15.

18. "Nulla res sufficit quod sit sibi causa essendi, si habeat esse causatum." *Sum. Th.,* I, q. 3, a. 4.

19. This principle applies to God not as cause, but rather as a reason for His Being. Cf. *Con. Gen.,* l. II, c. 15.

not have its sufficient cause in its own intrinsic nature must have it in an extrinsic cause.

The notion of causality is intelligible *per se.* It is universal, deriving this character and its necessity from its connection with the principle of identity. We neither arrive at nor prove the principle of causality directly, but only indirectly, by showing that the denial of the principle is the denial of that of contradiction; for either the sufficient reason of a thing is in itself or in another; if in itself, it is its own nature, as in the case of God; if in another, it is caused, as in the case of contingent beings. But to deny causality is to affirm that a thing which has not its sufficient reason in itself has not its sufficient reason in another. Causality does not depend upon sensation, though sensation is a contributing factor in an accidental order, but the concept has an essential relation to being, since every being which is a contingent being requires an efficient cause. This principle, like the others, is an intuition of the human intellect.

Now the principle of efficient causality has objective validity. One thing actually and objectively influences another by its actions. We do not read this into the relations between things; we discover it. The very external sensation which is the beginning of our knowledge of the external world depends upon the real, objective influence of objects upon our senses; in other words, the only explanation of external sensation as distinct from internal is that there is efficient causality. The sensations in our mind are dependent upon experiences distinct from one another, and that is nothing more than objective reality of efficient causality.

Now whereas the efficient cause is the principle of actualization of a potency, the power that produces, there is another, the final cause which is the reason why a thing was produced. It is the sufficient reason of the means. Though last in execution, the final cause is first in intention; it is the reason why the efficient cause produces; the end of production or action draws out the efficient agent into action. The efficient cause alone cannot explain the determinateness of any action. Intelligence reveals that every action requires a final as well as an efficient cause. *Omnis agens agit propter finem.*

Every agent produces, moreover, a determinate effect to which it is naturally ordained, as sight is naturally ordained to vision and intellect to knowing and will to choosing. The agent's action is specified by its nature, and hence cannot be indifferent. Thus we might say that whereas efficient cause influences by its action, final cause influences by its attraction. The order of an action requires just as much explanation as the action itself.

The principle of finality is, as the principle of efficient cause, a derivative of that of sufficient reason, so that a denial of finality is a denial of the sufficient reason of a thing, which in its turn, as we noted previously, is a denial of the principle of contradiction. For if definite determinate effects were produced without ordination and intention, then there would be no sufficient reason for the determination of the effect. Then order would come from chaos, the greater from the lesser, perfection from imperfection. But such effects are impossible. A principle must actually be ordained to its act; an effect must virtually be precontained in its efficient cause, so that when determinate effects are produced, we say they pre-exist in the cause; thus, act is effected from potency and knowledge from the passivity of the intellect. This implies nothing other than a principle of finality in actions — a goal in a mind.

We have made the attempt in the pages just covered to show certain fundamental, necessary and universal principles which are derived from the principles of identity and contradiction. But these latter principles in turn are immediately perceived by the intellect in the notions of being and non-being. It has been our aim to stress being as the proper object of the intellect, as the basis of all apprehension of self-evident principles acquired by natural reason; as the ultimate basis of all secondary principles derived from the primary ones; as the ultimate foundation of all reality and all knowledge, all truth.

It remains for us now to show how philosophies of flux invalidate the above basic principles through the destruction of the foundation upon which they rest, and we judge Farges to have spoken justly when, in his *Philosophy of Bergson*, he says that the new metaphysics is the negation of being, of truth, of the principles of identity and contradiction, of sufficient reason and of causality, of the multiplicity of being, and finally, of reason itself.

PHILOSOPHIES OF FLUX AND PRIMARY PRINCIPLES

Beginning with the basic proposition of all philosophies of flux, we state their fundamental tenets as follows, together with the nature of their attack on fundamental principles:

1. *All is becoming. Nothing is static.* This denies the principle of identity. For if all is universal mobility, there is no longer foundation for that principle; a thing would never be itself since it would always be changing into something else. Being must have an essence, and an essence is unchangeable, so that if things were constantly in flux and all their reality consisted in the flux, they could never have determined essences. There could never be identity with oneself.

2. *There are appearances only; not things but only actions.* Thus the principle of substance vanishes, since there is only movement without anything which moves; only appearances without anything that appears; only flux but nothing that flows. We ask, does one ever find movement as such, or only moving things? It is the "things" which move that give us the concept of substance.

3. *Becoming is its own sufficient reason.* This proposition destroys the principle of sufficient reason, for becoming, being contingent, cannot be of itself. In the philosophies of becoming, that which *may be* is made absolute and there is assigned to it the same necessity for being which Thomistic metaphysics assigns only to the Necessary Being Whose essence is His existence. Despite fluxists, we must hold that becoming has no *raison d'être* apart from an extrinsic cause. Pure becoming can never be a first cause.

4. *The greater comes from the lesser; being comes from nothing through forces inherent in the flux itself.* Thus the principle of causality is violated. A potential and evolving principle cannot be the cause of its own actuation; self-creation is a contradiction in terms. *Nihil transit de potentia ad actum nisi per aliquod ens actu* is a frequently used Scholastic axiom. Hegel, for instance, seems to have no difficulty in admitting that the greater does come from the lesser, being from nothingness, mind from matter, because for him the principle of contradiction has no objective validity.

5. *All things are identified in becoming.* Hence no formal principle of anything exists whereby that thing is constituted in its own specific

nature and in no other. The principles of identity and contradiction both are violated, since truth and falsehood would be identified, as would be goodness and evil.

6. *The evolutionary principle is free and undetermined in its movement.* Thus finality is destroyed. Since nothing is fixed or determined, there can be no final end toward which things are directed. Everything is the result of chance.

7. *Becoming is an absolute without anything that changes; what is real is the continual change of form.* The principle of change is rejected, for there cannot be change without a potential subject that changes. To speak of becoming without a subject is to err. It is to make of potency a positive principle without its correlative act. "Hot" does not change to "cold" but rather a hot *something* becomes a cold *something*.

Let us note that with the resolution of the principles of identity and contradiction into universal mobility, the four causes of becoming itself disappear; for becoming is without a material principle, without a formal principle to specify it, without an agent to produce it, without an end toward which to tend. Thus good is evil, light is dark, flesh is spirit, unity is multiplicity, God is creature, creature is God — contradictories fuse, the basic principles are destroyed, knowledge is without certitude, reality without foundation, the intellect without absolute truth, the will without absolute good. This wholesale destruction is directly traceable to the repudiation of the concept of that ultimate apprehension of the human mind whereby it affirms without error that *something is.*

"All failures of metaphysics," remarks Gilson, "should be traced to the fact that the first principle of human knowledge (namely being) has either been overlooked or misused by the metaphysicians."[20] Saint Thomas is more severe in his condemnation of corrupters of being and the primary principles: "In speculative matters the most grievous and shameful error is that which is about things the knowledge of which is naturally bestowed on man."[21] And of what those things are the knowledge of which is naturally bestowed on man, Saint

---

20. Gilson, *The Unity of Philosophical Experience, loc. cit.*
21. *Sum. Th.,* II-II, q. 154, a. 12.

Thomas leaves us no doubt: "The first and indemonstrable principle is that the same thing cannot at the same time be affirmed and denied; and this is based on the notion of being and non-being, and on this principle all others are based."[22]

CONCLUSION

In conclusion and in accordance with Thomistic principles, we would indicate summarily certain basic propositions which traditional Scholasticism would apply as corrective measures to all evolutionary theories of philosophy of the Heraclitean, Hegelian, Bergsonian type:

1. Becoming of itself is unintelligible and can be rendered intelligible only in function of being, which alone is of and by itself intelligible. For becoming is a transitus, a movement, and motion cannot possibly be conceived apart from a subject; it is the subject which gives it its entity; motion is "this" motion only because it is the motion of "this" subject. Further, to become is to be in the state of becoming, as to act is to be in existence. Becoming is therefore a function of being.

2. Becoming can be rendered intelligible only in function of being provided being be conceived analogously. According as being is divided into actual being and potential being, it provides the necessary intelligibility of becoming. Becoming presupposes an intermediary state between being and nothing. It cannot be determined being, for that is already actually being; neither can it be nothing, for from nothing, nothing comes (*secundum naturam*). Hence becoming is undetermined being or being in potency. The only rational solution of the antinomy is in this Aristotelian-Thomistic doctrine of potency, which holds that becoming is the transition from potential being to actual being. But potency of itself is not act, and therefore it cannot of itself pass from undetermined being to determined being; hence there is required for becoming an extrinsic sufficient reason. Becoming cannot be its own sufficient reason.

3. Becoming presupposes the absence of identity, and its function is to effect a successive union of diverse elements. But a successive

22. *Sum. Th.*, I-II, q. 94, a. 2.

union of elements that of themselves are not one cannot be unconditioned, and to assert the contrary would mean a denial of the principle of identity. For elements of themselves diverse and not united would then be said to unite themselves and follow one another; but this cannot be unless the process were conditioned. And it *is* conditioned; it is conditioned by a determinate cause, an efficient agent called into activity by the final end which gives meaning to becoming and supplies the attractive power toward which the tendency tends. An evolutionary tendency which tends toward nothing is an absurdity. So too is a becoming which is said to be its own sufficient reason.

4. Since becoming presupposes a determinate cause, inasmuch as things in themselves different can unite not of themselves but only insofar as something causes them to unite, it is evident that we must go from *"fieri"* to *"esse"*; to the reality of that cause which is capable of exercising an efficient causal influence upon the movement, thereby giving to becoming the sufficient reason for its very becoming. Being is the efficient and final cause of becoming; the principle of actualization of the inherent potentialities in the diversity of elements.

5. If multiplicity and change be acknowledged, then substance must be acknowledged, for things of themselves diverse cannot of themselves be one. If nothing endures but everything becomes, then the primary principles of thought are meaningless. For a right understanding of these principles there must be substances which remain fixed throughout the flux. The transitory can be intelligible only in function of the permanent or identical. For unless change postulated something that remains, we should never know change, since there would be no distinction between the two termini and therefore no reason for movement at all.

6. Being is superior to that which as yet is not, just as a perfect state is superior to an imperfect state; as termination to transition; as rest to motion. Being is the cause of becoming; it is the termination of becoming; it remains after becoming has ceased.

Therefore it is our conclusion that to find an intelligible interpretation of reality, surrendering neither the rationally conceived static aspect nor the empirically perceived dynamic side, it is necessary to conceive being analogously and to make of becoming a function of that primary notion. To do this, it is required that the notion of potency be accepted as the indeterminate being whose passage to determinate being is known in Scholastic circles as the process of *fieri*. The establishment of the supremacy of being over becoming is not only a dictate of common sense, but it is intelligible to the intellect as the only solid foundation for the primary principles of both thought and reality, upon which rests all rational knowledge of contingent beings and of the Unique Necessary Being Who is the Eternal Cause of all things.

BIBLIOGRAPHY

Alamanno, Cosmo, S. J., *Summa Philosophiae*, Paris, 1895
Aquinas, St. Thomas, *Opera Omnia*, Vives ed., Paris, 1875:
  Summa Theologica
  Summa Contra Gentiles
  Comm. In IV Libros Sententiarum Magistri Petri Lombardi
  Quaestiones Disputatae De Potentia, De Veritate, De Malo
  Comm. In Aristotelis Libros:
    In Physicorum
    In Metaphysicorum
    In Post. Analyticorum
    In De Generatione et Corruptione
  Opuscula:
    De Aeternitate Mundi
    De Principiis Naturae
    De Natura Materiae
    De Mixtione Elementorum
    De Instantibus
    De Natura Accidentis
    De Principio Individuationis
    De Quatuor Oppositis
    De Pluralitate Formarum
    De Natura Generis
  In Librium De Trinitate Boetii
  De Substantia Separatis
  De Ente et Essentia
  Contra Gentiles, English trans. by the Dominican Fathers, London, 1924
  Summa Theologica, translation as above, London, 1920
Aristotle, *The Works of Aristotle*, trans. into English, Ross ed., Oxford, 1928:
  Physics
  Metaphysics
  On Generation and Corruption
  ———, *Aristotle's Works, Metaphysics*, trans. J. M. McMahon, London, 1910

Baille, J. B., *The Origin and Significance of Hegel's Logic*, London, 1910
Bakewell, C. M., *Source Book in Ancient Philosophy*, New York, 1907
Balmes, Rev. J., *Fundamental Philosophy*, trans. from the Spanish by H. F. Brownson; 2 vols., New York, 1856
Balsillie, D., *Professor Bergson's Philosophy*, London, 1912
Bandas, R. G., *Contemporary Philosophy and Thomistic Principles*, Milwaukee, 1932

Baschab, C. R., *A Manual of Neo-Scholastic Philosophy*, St. Louis, 1924
Bergson, Henri, *L'Évolution Créatrice*, Paris, 1907
──────, *Les Données Immédiates de la Conscience*, Paris, 1889
──────, *Matière et Mémoire*, Paris, 1896
──────, *An Introduction to Metaphysics*, trans. by T. E. Hulme, New York, 1912
──────, *Creative Evolution*, trans. by A. Mitchell, New York, 1911
──────, *Matter and Memory*, trans. by Nancy Margaret, Paul and W. Scott Palmer, London, 1911

Caird, Edw., *Hegel*, Edinburgh, 1899
Calkins, M. W., *The Persistent Problems of Philosophy*, New York, 1933
Carr, H. W., *The Philosophy of Change*, London, 1914
Coffey, P., *Ontology*, London, 1918
──────, *Epistemology*, 2 vols., London, 1917
Croce, B., *What Is Living and What Is Dead of the Philosophy of Hegel*, trans. by Douglas Ainslee, London, 1915
Cunningham, G. W., *A Study in the Philosophy of Bergson*, New York, 1916

D'Arcy, M. C., *Thomas Aquinas*, London, 1930
De Raeymaeker, L., *Metaphysica Generalis*, Louvain, 1931
De Regnon, T., *Metaphysique des causes d'àpres S. Thomas et Albert le Grand*, Paris, 1906
De Wulf, Maurice, *History of Medieval Philosophy*, London, 1909
──────, *Scholasticism — Old and New*, Dublin, 1907
Del Prado, N., *De Veritate Fundamentali Philosophiae Christianae*, Fribourg, 1911
Dodson, G. R., *Bergson and the Modern Spirit*, Boston, 1913
Dubray, Chas. A., *Introductory Philosophy*, New York, 1916

Eisler, Rudolph, *Worterbuch der philosophischen Begriffe*, Berlin, 1910
Elliot, H. S. R., *Modern Science and the Illusion of Professor Bergson*, London, 1912

Falckenberg, R., *History of Modern Philosophy*, New York, 1893
Farges, Albert, *La philosophie de M. Bergson*, Paris, 1914
Fischer, Kuno, *Geschichte der neuern Philosophie*, Heidelberg, 1889

Garrigou-Lagrange, R., *God, His Existence and His Nature*, trans. by Dom Bede Rose, St. Louis, 1936
──────, *Le Sens Commun, la Philosophie de l'être et les Formules dogmatiques*, Paris, 1909
Gerrard, T. J., *Bergson*, St. Louis, 1913

Gerrity, Bro. Benignus, *The Relations between the Theory of Matter and Form and the Theory of Knowledge in the Philosophy of St. Thomas*, Washington, 1936

Gilson, Etienne, *The Philosophy of St. Thomas Aquinas*, St. Louis, 1924

———, *The Unity of Philosophical Experience*, New York, 1937

Gomperz, Theodor, *Greek Thinkers*, 3 vols.

Gonzalez, Cardinal, *Histoire de la philosophie*, 4 vols., Paris, 1890

Goudin, Antonio, *Philosophia Thomistica d. Thomae Dogmata*, 4 vols., Paris, 1851

Grabmann, Martin, *Thomas Aquinas, His Personality and Thought*, trans. by Dom Virgil Michel, New York, 1928

Gredt, Jos., *Elementa Philosophiae Aristotelico-Thomisticae*, II, Fribourg, 1922

Gunn, J. A., *Bergson and His Philosophy*, London, 1920

Haldane, R. B., *The Pathway to Reality*, Vols. I and II, London, 1903-4

Hamilton, G. R., *Bergson and Future Philosophy*

Harper, Thomas, *The Metaphysics of the School*, 4 vols., London, 1879-84

Harris, Wm. T., *Hegel's Logic*, Chicago, 1890

Hawkins, D. J. B., *Causality and Implication*, London, 1937

Hegel, *Die Phänomenologie des Geistes*, Bamberg u. Würzburg, 1807

———, *Wissenschaft der Logik*, Nürnberg, 1841

———, *Encyclopadie der philosophischen Wissenschaften im Grundrisse*, Heidelberg, 1827

———, *Werke*, Berlin, 1832-1840

———, *The Phenomenology of Spirit*, trans. by J. B. Baille, London, 1910

———, *Lectures on the History of Philosophy*, trans. by E. S. Haldane, London, 1904

———, *Science of Logic*, trans. by W. H. Johnston and L. S. Struthers, New York, 1929

———, *Philosophy of Mind*, trans. by W. Wallace, Oxford, 1894

———, *The Logic of Hegel*, trans. by W. Wallace, 2d ed., Oxford, 1892

Hocking, W. E., *Types of Philosophy*, New York, 1929

Hoernlé, R. F. A., *Studies in Contemporary Metaphysics*, New York, 1920

Höffding, Harold, *A History of Modern Philosophy*, 2 vols., trans. by B. E. Meyer, London, 1900

Hugon, Edward, *Cursus Philosophiae Thomisticae*, 2 vols., 3d ed., Paris, 1922

Joannes a Sancto Thoma, *Cursus Philosophicus Thomisticus*, new ed., 3 vols., Turin, 1930-1933-1937

Jolivet, Regis, *Essai sur le Bergsonisme*, Paris, 1931

Kahl-Furthmann, Dr. G., *Das Problem des Nichts*, Berlin, 1934

Ladd, G. T., *Introduction to Philosophy*, New York, 1896

Leighton, J. A., *Man and the Cosmos: An Introduction to Metaphysics*, New York, 1922
Lepidi, Alberto, *Elementa Philosophiae Christianae*, 3 vols., Paris, 1877
Le Roy, E. L., *The New Philosophy of H. Bergson*, trans. by Vincent Benson, New York, 1913
Lindsay, A. D., *The Philosophy of Bergson*, London, 1911

MacWilliam, John, *Criticism of the Philosophy of Bergson*, Edinburgh, 1928
McDonald, Walter, *Motion: Its Origin and Conservation*, Dublin, 1898
McTaggart, J. McT. E., *Studies in Hegelian Cosmology*, Cambridge, 1910
Macran, H. S., *Hegel's Doctrine of Formal Logic*, Oxford, 1912
Mancini, H. M., *Elementa Philosophiae*, 3 vols., Rome, 1898
Maritain, Jacques, *The Degrees of Knowledge*, New York, 1938
—————, *An Introduction to Philosophy*, trans. by E. I. Watkins, New York, 1935
—————, *La philosophie bergsonienne, étude critique*, Paris, 1930
—————, *Sept Leçons sur l'Être*, Paris, 1935
Marling, J. M., *The Order of Nature in the Philosophy of St. Thomas Aquinas*, Washington, 1934
Mercier, Cardinal, *A Manual of Modern Scholastic Philosophy*, 2 vols., trans. by T. L. and S. A. Parker; St. Louis, 1921
Merz, J. T., *A History of European Thought in the Nineteenth Century*, 4 vols., London, 1912
Miltner, C. C., and O'Grady, D. C., *Introduction to Metaphysics*, New York, 1930
Mitchell, A., *Studies in Bergson's Philosophy*, University of Kansas, Lawrence, 1914
Morell, J. D., *An Historical and Critical View of the Speculative Philosophy of Europe in the 19th Century*, New York, 1847

Olgiati, Francesco, *Key to the Study of St. Thomas*, trans. by J. S. Zybura, St. Louis, 1929
O'Neill, John, *Cosmology: An Introduction to the Philosophy of Matter*, New York, 1923

Plato, *The Dialogues of Plato*, Jowett trans., New York, 1890
Phillips, R. P., *Modern Thomistic Philosophy*, 2 vols., London, 1934
Perry, R. B., *Philosophy of the Recent Past*, New York, 1926

Reginald, Anthony, *St. Thomas Tria Principia*, Paris, 1878
Rickaby, John, *General Metaphysics*, New York, 1890
Roland-Gosselin, M. O., *Le De Ente et Essentia de S. Thomas d'Aquin*, Kain, Belgium, 1926
Ross, W. D., *Aristotle*, 2d ed., London, 1930

Schütz, Dr. L., *Thomas Lexikon*, Paderborn, 1895
Sertillanges, A. D., *Les Principes de la Nature*, Paris, 1910
―――――, *Foundations of Thomistic Philosophy*, trans. by Godfrey Anstruther, St. Louis, 1931
Seth, A., *Hegelianism and Personality*, Edinburgh, 1893
Sheen, F. J., *Philosophy of Science*, Milwaukee, 1934
―――――, *God and Intelligence*, New York, 1925
Stace, W. T., *The Philosophy of Hegel: A Systematic Exposition*, London, 1924
Stallknecht, Newton P., *Bergson's Idea of Creation*, Princeton, 1934
Stewart, John M., *A Critical Study of Bergson's Philosophy*, London, 1911
Stirling, J. Hutchinson, *The Secret of Hegel*, 1st ed., London, 1865
Stöckl, Albert, *Geschichte der Philosophie des Mittelalters*, Mainz, 1864

Turner, Wm., *History of Philosophy*, New York, 1903

Uberweg, Friedrich, *History of Philosophy*, 3 vols., trans. by Geo. S. Morris, New York, 1903
University of California Publications in Philosophy, *The Problem of Substance*, Vol. IX, Berkeley, 1937
Urraburu, Joannes, *Institutiones Philosophicae*, Vol. I, Paris, 1891

Walker, Leslie, J., *Theories of Knowledge*, New York, 1910
Watkin, E. I., *The Philosophy of Form*, London, 1935
Weber, Alfred, *History of Philosophy*, trans. by Frank Thilly, New York, 1897
Whitehead, A. N., *Process and Reality*, New York, 1929
Wild, Miss K. W., *Intuition*, London, 1938

Zeller, Edward, *Outlines of the History of Greek Philosophy*, trans. by Alleyne and Abbott, New York, 1931
Zigliara, T. M., *Summa Philosophica*, Vol. 2, 16th ed., Paris, 1919

PERIODICALS

Bandas, R. G., "The Bergsonian Conception of Science and Philosophy," *The New Scholasticism*, Vol. 2, No. 3, 1928, pp. 215-235
Baudin, Abbé, "L'Acte et la Puissance dans Aristote," *Revue Thomiste*, Vol. 7, 1899, pp. 40-62; 153-172; 274-296; 584-608
Bittremieux, J., "Notes sur le principe de causalité," *Revue Néo-scolastique*, Vol. 22, 1920, pp. 310-330
Bouyssonie, A., "Les principes de la raison," *Revue Néo-scolastique*, Vol. 23, 1921, pp. 191-215; pp. 290-316

Copleston, F. C., "Bergson and Intuition," *The Modern Schoolman*, Vol. 11, No. 3, 1934, pp. 61-65

De Craene, G., "L'abstraction intellectuelle," *Revue Néo-scolastique*, Vol. 8, 1901, pp. 243-257

De Lantsheer, L., "Les caractères de la philosophie moderne," *Revue Néo-scolastique*, Vol. 20, 1913, pp. 39-51

De Munnynck, Marcus, "La Racine de principe de causalité," *Revue Néo-scolastique*, Vol. 21, 1914, pp. 193-211

————————, "Essai sur le principe de causalité," *The New Scholasticism*, Vol. III, No. 3, 1929, pp. 253-295

————————, "L'Idée de l'Être," *Revue Néo-scolastique*, Vol. 31, 1929, pp. 182-203; 257-279; 415-437

De Paulpiquet, A., "Le point central de la controverse sur la distinction de l'essence et de l'existence," *Revue Néo-scolastique*, Vol. 13, pp. 32-48

De Raeymaeker, L., "La structure metaphysique de l'être fini," *Revue Néo-scolastique*, Vol. 34, 1932, pp. 187-217

De Wulf, M., "La synthèse scolastique," *Revue Néo-scolastique*, Vol. 6, 1899, pp. 159-178

Dondeyne, A., "L'abstraction," *Revue Néo-scolastique*, Vol. 41, 1938, pp. 339-373

Dubray, C. S., "The Philosophy of Henri Bergson," *Catholic University Bulletin*, Vol. 20, No. 4, 1914, pp. 302-323

Ermoni, V., "Necessité de la metaphysique," *Revue Néo-scolastique*, Vol. 13, 1906, pp. 229-245

Farges, A., "L'erreur fondamentale de la philosophie nouvelle," *Revue Thomiste*, Vol. 17, No. 2, 1909, pp. 182-197; No. 3, pp. 299-312

————————, "La notion bergsonienne du temps," *Revue Néo-scolastique*, Vol. 19, 1912, pp. 337-378

————————, "Le sens commun," *Revue Néo-scolastique*, Vol. 21, 1914, pp. 441-479

Feldner, G., "Wesenheit und Existenz," *Divus Thomas*, Vol. 6, 1919, pp. 27-44

Forest, A., "La réalité concrète chez Bergson et chez Thomas," *Revue Thomiste*, Vol. 38, No. 3, 1933, pp. 368-398

Garrigou-Lagrange, R., "Le panthéisme de la philosophie nouvelle," *Revue Thomiste*, Vol. 15, No. 5, 1907, pp. 613-642

————————, "Comment le principe de la raison d'être se rattache au principe d'identité d'àpres Saint Thomas," *Revue Thomiste*, Vol. 16, No. 4, 1908, pp. 422-443

————————, "La valeur transcendante et analogique des notions premières," *Revue Thomiste*, Vol. 15, No. 5, pp. 628-648; Vol. 21, No. 1, 1913, pp. 17-48; No. 3, pp. 159-188

————————, "Le principe de finalité," *Revue Thomiste*, Vol. 26, No. 3, 1921, pp. 256-275

——————————, "Fundamentum distinctionis inter potentiam et actum ejusque praecipuae applicationes," *The Angelicum*, Vol. 2, No. 3, 1925, pp. 277-298

——————————, "Fondement de la Distinction de Puissance et Acte selon Saint Thomas," *The New Scholasticism*, Vol. 1, No. 4, 1927, pp. 320-325

Halpin, Anthony J., "The Location of Qualitative Essence: I. Aristotle and Aquinas," *The New Scholasticism*, Vol. 10, No. 2, 1936, pp. 145-166

Huys, J., "La notion de substance dans la philosophie contemporaire et dans la philosophie scolastique," *Revue Néo-scolastique*, Vol. 5, 1898, pp. 364-380

Jolivet, R., "L'intuition intellectuelle," *Revue Thomiste*, Vol. 39, No. 1, 1932, pp. 52-70

——————————, "De l'Evolution Créatrice aux Deux Sources," *Revue Thomiste*, Vol. 38, No. 3, 1933, pp. 347-367

La Guichaoua, P., "Conditions philosophiques de l'évolution," *Revue Néo-scolastique*, Vol. 18, 1911, pp. 197-211

Laminne, J., La permanence des éléments dans le composé chimique," *Revue Néo-scolastique*, Vol. 13, 1906, pp. 324-330

——————————, "Le principe de contradiction et le principe de causalité," *Revue Néo-scolastique*, Vol. 19, 1912, pp. 453-483

——————————, "La cause et l'effet," *Revue Néo-scolastique*, Vol. 21, 1914, pp. 34-70

——————————, "Les principes d'identité et de causalité," *Revue Néo-scolastique*, Vol. 21, 1914, pp. 357-364

Landry, B., "L'analogie de proportion chez Saint Thomas d'Aquin," *Revue Néo-scolastique*, Vol. 24, 1922, pp. 257-280

Lodge, Sir Oliver, "Balfour and Bergson," *The Hibbert Journal*, Vol. 10, 1911-1912, pp. 290-307

Manser, G. M., "Die Weltschöpfung bei Thomas von Aquin," *Divus Thomas*, Vol. 9, 1931, pp. 3-27; 320-336

Maritain, J., "Les deux bergsonismes," *Revue Thomiste*, Vol. 20, No. 4, 1912, pp. 433-450

McKenzie, J. L., "Mr. Demos on Non-being," *The Modern Schoolman*, Vol. 11, No. 2, 1934, pp. 39-41

McMahon, F. E., "Thomistic Metaphysics," *The New Scholasticism*, Vol. 8, No. 3, 1934, pp. 240-259

McWilliams, J. A., "Theories of Matter," *The New Scholasticism*, Vol. 1, No. 4, 1927, pp. 297-306

Nys, D., "Étude sur l'espace," *Revue Néo-scolastique*, Vol. 6, 1899, pp. 221-241

———, "La nature du composé chimique," *Revue Néo-scolastique*, Vol. 5, 1898, pp. 172-192; 388-404

———, "La notion de temps d'àpres Saint Thomas d'Aquin," *Revue Néo-scolastique*, Vol. 4, 1897, pp. 28-43; 225-246; 367-374.

———, "L'hylémorphisme dans le monde inorganique," *Revue Néo-scolastique*, Vol. 11, 1904, pp. 35-57

———, "Le temps a-t-il commencé et finira-t-il?" *Revue Néo-scolastique*, Vol. 20, 1913, pp. 409-430

O'Grady, D. C., "A Few Notes on the Metaphysics of Matter," *The New Scholasticism*, Vol. 4, No. 1, 1930, pp. 46-52

Osgniach, Augustine, "The Problem of Substance," *The New Scholasticism*, Vol. 2, No. 2, 1928, pp. 115-127; No. 3, pp. 236-249

Pégues, Th-M., "L'évolution créatrice," *Revue Thomiste*, Vol. 16, No. 1, 1908, pp. 137-163

Sauvage, G. M., "The New Philosophy in France — a Criticism," *Catholic University Bulletin*, Vol. 12, No. 4, 1906, pp. 147-159; Vol. 14, No. 3, 1908, pp. 268-286; Vol. 15, No. 6, 1909, pp. 521-536; No. 10, 1909, pp. 609-627; Vol. 16, No. 3, 1910, pp. 205-222

Scannell, R., "Being and Becoming," *The New Scholasticism*, Vol. 12, No. 3, 1938, pp. 254-283

Scott, J. W., "The Pessimism of Bergson," *The Hibbert Journal*, Vol. 11, No. 1, pp. 99-116

Sertillanges, D., "La création," *Revue Thomiste*, Vol. 33, No. 2, 1928, pp. 97-115

———, "La notion de création," *Revue Thomiste*, Vol. 35, No. 1, 1930, pp. 48-57

Simons, G., "Le principe de raison suffisante en logique et en métaphysique," *Revue Néo-scolastique*, Vol. 9, 1902, pp. 297-325

Thyrion, J., "La notion de création passive dans le thomisme," *Revue Thomiste*, Vol. 34, No. 4, 1929, pp. 303-319

Von Holtum, G., "Zur thomistischen Lehre von realen Unterschied zwischen Wesenheit und Dasein in den Geschöpfen," *Divus Thomas*, Vol. 3, 1916, pp. 291-306

Wesseling, Theodore H., "Being, Life and Matter," *The New Scholasticism*, Vol. 11, No. 3, 1937, pp. 220-236

Dictionnaire apologetique de la Foi Catholique, Paris, 1891:
Dieu
Substance
Création
Causalité, principe

Dictionary of Philosophy and Psychology, J. M. Baldwin, New York, 1901-1905:
Substance
Causality
Matter
Form
Subject
Generation
Creation
Cause
Principle

INDEX

Absolute Idea, The, 120-126; 132, 136, 137, 138
Accident, 37, 38, 84
Act and Potency, 19, 20, 21, 22, 23, 30, 45, 46, 67, 77, 78, 80, 93, 108, 116, 117, 118, 188
Actual and Possible Beings, 20, 21, 22, 23
Alteration, 59, 64, 79
——— and Change, 61, 62, 63, 105, 106
Aristotle, 2, 3, 8, 14, 16, 67, 76
———, on Change, 60 sqq., 69
———, on Causes and Principles of Things, 8, 9
———, on Act and Potency, 117
A-seity, 45, 46 n.

Becoming, 11, 15, 16, 46, 58, 59. See also *Fieri*, Change, Movement
———, Substantial, 43, 46
———, Accidental, 46
Heraclitus on, 116
Bergson on, 139, 140, 141
In Scholasticism *vs.* Fluxism, 187, 188, 189, 190
Being, 1, 2, 3, 4, 5, 8, 15, 16, 17, 18, 19, 20, 23, 32, 33, 37, 111, 157, 177, 189
———, of Parmenides, 112, 113, 114, 116
———, of Heraclitus, 115, 116
———, in Bergson, 141
———, in Hegel, 129, 130, 131, 132
———, in Parmenides *vs.* Hegel, 127, 132, 134, 136, 137, 138
Aristotle on, 117, 118
Absolute Being, 3, 4, 25, 122, 133, 134, 136

Being-in-general, 3, 5, 18, 20, 21, 137
Pure Being, 4, 13
Self-subsistent Being, 4, 5
Being *per se*, 5, 33, 45, 46
Being *per accidens*, 46
Determination of, in Thomas Aquinas, 135; in Hegel, 128 sqq., 133
Bergson, 11, 12, 119, 139 sqq.
———, and Becoming, 139, 140, 141

Causality, 34, 42, 43, 44, 45, 47, 173, 183, 184, 186
———, of God, 35, 37, 40, 41, 43, 45, 47, 48, 52, 55
———, in Generation, 104
Efficient, 34, 42, 43, 44, 45, 46, 48, 172, 184, 185, 189
Exemplary, 42, 47, 48, 49, 50, 55
Final, 47, 172, 184, 185, 187, 189
Cause, 43, 44, 46. See also Causality
———, *vs.* Principle, 43
Change, 12, 35, 58 sqq., 67, 69, 71, 74, 78, 79
———, Substantial *vs.* Accidental, 60, 63, 64, 65, 67
———, in Bergson, 141, 147, 148, 156
Extrinsic, 66
Instantaneous, 59, 106
Successive, 59
Aristotle on, 60 sqq., 74, 115
St. Thomas on, 12, 60, 63 sqq.
Parmenides on, 113, 114, 115, 117
Heraclitus on, 116
See also Movement, Substantial Change, *Fieri*
Contradiction, Doctrine of, in Hegel, 127 sqq.; in Thomas Aquinas, 9, 10, 15, 24, 25, 28, 35: See also Opposition

Index

Creation, 10, 28, 35 sqq., 55, 77
———, as a Relation, 37, 38, 39
———, *vs.* Generation, 38, 77
———, in Bergson, 147, 148, 151, 171, 173
Creative Evolution, 12, 146, 147, 172

Definition, 18
De Homine, Tractatus, in St. Thomas, 44
Development, Law of, in Hegel, 121, 123
Dialectic, in Hegel, 120, 121
Duration, 140, 141, 146, 147, 173

Ens Rationis, 6, 76, 88, 175. See also Logical Being
Essence, 19, 20, 30, 85
  Possible Essences, 6, 22, 30, 31, 34, 48, 50, 51, 52, 54
  Actual Essences, 31, 85
  Real Essences, 5, 85
Essence and Existence, 6, 19, 20, 21, 22, 30, 31, 100, 101
Existence, 19, 20, 22, 30, 31, 36, 37, 38, 40, 41, 42, 44, 95, 96
———, in Bergson, 146, 147

Fieri, 56, 57, 59, 64, 96 sqq. See also Becoming, Change, Movement
First Principles, 10, 15, 23, 24, 26, 27, 119, 166, 167, 168, 179, 180, 181, 182, 185, 188. See also Principle
————, of Contradiction, 15, 27, 119, 180
————, of Identity, 15, 42, 111, 115, 116, 117, 118, 178, 179, 180, 186, 187
————, of Excluded Middle, 15, 25, 26
Form, 80, 81, 82, 98, 99, 100, 101, 102, 105, 106, 107
  Substantial Forms, 96, 99, 100
  Eductio of, 103, 105, 106
  Inductio of, 103

Generation, 38, 56, 59, 64, 69, 75, 76, 79, 81, 89, 90, 97, 98
———, *vs.* Creation, 38, 77
———, and Form, 97, 98, 99, 100, 101
———, *per se,* 57
———, *per accidens,* 57
———, and Change, 61, 62, 63
God
  Divine Essence, 50, 51, 53, 54, 55
  Divine Knowledge, 51, 52, 55
  Divine Mind (Intellect) 50, 51, 52, 53, 54, 55
  Divine Power, 50. See also Omnipotence of God
  Divine Will, 50, 55

Hegel, 11, 12, 119, 120 sqq.
Heraclitus, 11, 13, 14, 15, 111, 115 sqq., 139

Impossibility, 27, 28, 29, 31, 32
Infinite Being, 8, 37, 39, 40, 45, 48, 50
Instinct, 144, 146 n., 162, 164, 165
Intellect (Intelligence), 143, 144, 145, 146, 148, 159, 167, 168
———, in Bergson, 160, 161, 162, 170
———, in Thomas Aquinas, 162, 163, 164, 165
Intuition, in Thomas Aquinas, 161, 162, 163, 164, 165, 166, 167, 169
———, in Bergson, 140, 141, 144, 145, 146, 161, 169

Life, in Bergson, 140, 141, 143, 144, 145, 146, 148, 149, 151
Logical Being, 6, 21. See also *Ens Rationis*
Logical Idea. See Absolute Idea

Matter. See Prime Matter
———, in Bergson, 149

Matter and Form, 82, 83, 84, 85, 86, 96, 98, 99
Motus, 59 sqq.
Movement, 41, 42, 150, 156, 160, 169, 181. See also Change, Becoming, *Fieri, Motus, Mutatio*
Mutatio, 59 sqq.

Non-being (*non-ens*) 1, 3, 8, 9, 15, 16, 17, 18, 23, 24, 25, 33, 57, 58, 175, 179. See also Nothing
absolute, 24, 25, 27, 57
relative, 3, 77
Nothing, 2, 24, 40, 135
———, in Hegel, 129, 130, 131
———, in Bergson, 152, 153 sqq.
absolute, 10, 24, 28, 31, 32, 71
Nothingness, See Nothing, Non-being

Omnipotence of God, 29, 32, 33, 47, 48, 50. See also God, Power of
Opposition, 10, 24, 25, 57, 67, 74
——— of Contradiction, 9, 10, 15, 24, 25, 28, 35, 46, 68, 69, 70, 71, 72, 73, 74, 75, 76. See also Contradiction
——— of Privation, 10, 68, 69, 70, 71, 72, 73, 74, 75, 76
——— of Contrariety, 10, 46, 69, 70, 71, 72, 73, 74, 75, 76
——— and Change, 61, 62

Parmenides, 11, 13, 15, 111 sqq., 134
Per-seity, 45, 46 n.
Plato, 2, 3
Possible Beings, 6, 22, 23, 27, 31, 33. See also Possible Essences
Possibility, 27-36, 42, 48, 49, 50, 55, 56, 108, 109
Intrinsic (absolute), 29, 31, 32, 36, 47, 48, 49, 50, 51, 52, 54, 55, 56, 110
Extrinsic (relative), 31, 47, 50, 56
Potency, 2, 3, 67, 76, 77, 81 sqq., 91-95. See also Potentiality
Active, 91-95

Passive, 41, 57, 92, 93, 94, 95, 96, 108, 109
Active *vs.* Passive, 92, 93, 94
Objective, 108, 109
Subjective, 20, 95, 96, 108
Potential Beings, 6, 57, 81, 88, 89
Potentiality, 45, 57, 60, 91, 92, 94, 95, 96. See also Potency
Absolute, 7
Relative, 6, 7
Passive, 41, 57, 95, 96, 108, 109
Prime Matter, 7, 36, 40, 60, 64, 65, 67, 79, 80, 81, 82 sqq., 89, 95, 96
——————— *vs.* Privation, 88, 89
——————— in Bergson, 174
Principle, 43
——— *vs.* Cause, 43
Principles of Nature, 8, 9, 90, 111
Principle of Sufficient Reason, 26, 27, 42, 48, 82, 183, 184, 186
Privation, 6, 43, 57, 79, 80, 81, 88 sqq.
——— *vs.* Matter, 88, 89
Process, The. See Absolute Idea
Real Being, 21, 22, 23, 27
Reality, in Bergson, 119, 120, 140, 141, 142, 146, 147, 150, 151
———, in Hegel, 119, 120
———, in Thomas Aquinas, 156, 157. See also Being
Reason, Reasoning, Ratiocination. See Intellect

Sense Knowledge, 160, 161, 164
Space, 142, 158, 159, 160
Substance, 11, 12, 38, 84, 88, 182, 186, 189
Substantial Change, 78, 79, 106, 107. See also Change, Movement, *Fieri*
——————— *vs.* Accidental Change, 78, 79
Thomas Aquinas, Saint, 16
Time, 158, 173
Zeno, 15

www.ingramcontent.com/pod-product-compliance
Lightning Source LLC
Chambersburg PA
CBHW071441150426
43191CB00008B/1199

9 781498 294867